The Illustrated Buyer's Guide to Used Airplanes

3rd Edition

The Illustrated Buyer's Guide to Used Airplanes

3rd Edition

Bill Clarke

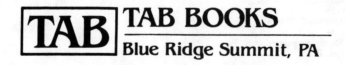

TAB BOOKS

Blue Ridge Summit, PA

THIRD EDITION
SECOND PRINTING

© 1992 by **TAB Books**.
TAB Books is a division of McGraw-Hill, Inc.

Library of Congress Cataloging-in-Publication Data

Clarke, Bill (Charles W.)
    The illustrated buyer's guide to used airplanes / by Bill Clarke.
    —3rd ed.
        p.   cm.
    Includes index.
    ISBN 0-8306-2571-2 (hard)   ISBN 0-8306-2570-4 (paper)
    1. Used aircraft—Purchasing. I. Title.
TL685.1.C54   1992
629.133'34'0297—dc20   91-45357
                                             CIP

TAB Books offers software for sale. For information and a catalog, please contact TAB Software Department, Blue Ridge Summit, PA 17294-0850.

Acquisitions Editor: Jeff Worsinger
Editor: Christopher Cortright
Director of Production: Katherine G. Brown
Book Design: Jaclyn J. Boone
Cover Photo: Brent Blair Photography, Harrisburg, Pa.
Cover: Holberg Design, York, Pa.   AV1

This book is dedicated to my wife,
for keeping me on course.

Contents

Part II   Used airplane fleet

Introduction

ARE YOU GIVING THOUGHT to airplane ownership? At one time or another, nearly every pilot will consider owning his or her own airplane. Airplane ownership is not difficult, although, like everything else, certain complexities must be known and understood. Since most of these complexities involve dollars, a thorough understanding of the subject is necessary.

In 1980, a new Cessna 172 sold for about $39,000. By 1986 the same model of airplane carried a price tag of nearly $75,000 and quickly marched off into history as production stopped. The world's most popular four-place airplane was priced out of existence. At the time of the 172's death, top-of-the-line planes such as the Beechcraft Bonanza A36 were sporting prices of nearly $250,000 and by 1990 the sticker had risen to over $350,000.

Although high prices are a way of life in our society, it seems aviation costs have soared more than the average. Many factors contribute to the phenomenon, including the high cost of labor, ever-increasing premiums paid for product liability insurance, increased charges for materials, and so on. Regardless of the reason, most pilots are financially excluded from the new airplane market. However, a viable alternative to an expensive new airplane exists: a good used airplane.

The Illustrated Buyer's Guide to Used Airplanes—3rd Edition is written to help you, the prospective used airplane buyer, in the successful search for a suitable and cost-effective airplane (and not get burned in the process). Part I of the book discusses the pro's and con's of airplane ownership, and explains how to determine the size and type of aircraft most suitable for your flying needs. The chapter then explains how to locate and evaluate a used airplane and how to read those cryptic used-airplane advertisements.

You will gain an understanding of the mountains of paperwork required for airplane ownership, learn how to select a home base, save money by doing your own preventive maintenance, and how to care for and protect your investment.

Although you may have a basic idea of what a particular used airplane looks like, or what some of the specifications are, you must have a ready source of additional and specific information. Part II of this book is such a source, containing historical information, photographs, and specifications for most airplanes that can be found on today's used market.

The book's third part provides stories and other tidbits of information heard around the hangar. Alternative aircraft are investigated, including float planes, personalized homebuilts, serene gliders, and the fast powerful war birds.

Appendices list many of the airworthiness directives that apply to airplanes described in this book. Check the NTSB aircraft accident chart and see where your dream plane rates. The Appendices also list addresses for FAA offices, state aviation agencies, manufacturers, and airplane clubs.

Last in the book is the all-important used airplane price guide, an up-to-date listing of typical used airplane selling prices.

In summary, *The Illustrated Buyer's Guide to Used Airplanes—3rd Edition* was written to help you in economical decision making and to guide you around many pitfalls encountered when buying and owning a used airplane.

Part I

Practical used airplane buying

1

To own or
not to own

SO, YOU WANT your own airplane do you? Well, sooner or later nearly everyone who earns a pilot's license has the desire to own an airplane. The fact that you're reading this book means you at least dream of having your own plane (Figs. 1-1 and 1-2).

Although new airplane prices have gone straight through the roof, the prudent purchase of a used airplane can actually reduce the cost of flying. The portion of ownership examined in this chapter is financial justification. In other words, is owning your own airplane worth what it will cost?

Owning an airplane brings the pride and responsibility of ownership, the freedom to fly anytime and anywhere you choose, and the opportunity to modify and equip your airplane as you wish. Like a marriage, you protect, you care for, you cherish, and you love your airplane; but, most of all you pay for it.

THE EXPENSE OF OWNERSHIP

Ask yourself this question: Can I *really* afford to own an airplane? Before you answer, consider the following:

- Do I fully understand the total costs of airplane ownership?
- Will I use the airplane often enough to justify ownership?
- Have I thoroughly considered the alternatives to ownership?

Let's examine the real costs of ownership, costs that are not included in the price of purchase. Assume that cash will be paid for the example airplanes used, with the understanding that funds from a loan will only serve to make the total expenses even higher.

Fig. 1-1. Airplane ownership can be as serious as family and business traveling, requiring speed, equipment, and considerable expense.

Fig. 1-2. Airplane ownership can also represent loads of economical fun.

Vocabulary

The language of airplane ownership and operation abounds with a vocabulary of new words and phrases:

Fixed costs are the expenses of ownership regardless of the amount of use the airplane gets. These costs will be incurred even if the airplane sees no use at all. Included in fixed costs are hangar or tiedown fees, state or local property taxes on the aircraft, insurance premiums, and the cost of the annual inspection (difficult to estimate due to the mechanical variables of each individual aircraft).

Operating costs include the price of fuel used per hour, an engine reserve, and a general maintenance fund.

Hourly cost is a calculated figure based upon the annual total of fixed and operating costs, divided by the total hours of operation. Hourly cost is the all-important number that shows whether owning your own airplane is worth what it will cost.

Engine reserve is a monetary fund, built up on an hourly basis, to pay for the eventual engine overhaul or rebuild. Figure this hourly rate as the estimated cost of an engine overhaul or rebuild divided by the recommended overhaul time limit (generally called TBO, or time between overhaul).

General maintenance fund is a cumulative savings used to pay for minor repairs and service (normally, $3 to $10 per hour of operation, depending upon aircraft complexity) to those small items often needing a mechanic's or technician's attention, including: oil changes, periodic Airworthiness Directives (ADs), minor mechanical defects, avionics problems, and so on.

Worksheets

A worksheet (Fig. 1-3) will aid you in figuring the costs of ownership. The sheet asks for considerable specific information, so you may find it helpful to call

---

OWNERSHIP WORKSHEET

Fixed Costs

1. Twelve months of storage . . . . _____
2. Annual taxes . . . . _____
3. Annual state license . . . . _____
4. Insurance premium (12 months) . . . . _____
5. Annual inspection (estimate) . . . . _____
6. Total fixed costs (add lines 1–5) . . . . _____

Operating Costs

7. Fuel cost per gallon X GPH . . . . _____
8. Engine reserve per hour . . . . _____
9. General maintenance per hour . . . . _____
10. Total operating costs (add lines 7–9) . . . . _____

Hourly Cost

11. Total fixed costs (from line 6) . . . . _____
12. Total operations (line 10 X hours) . . . . _____
13. Total costs (add lines 11 and 12) . . . . _____

14. Total hourly cost (line 13 ÷ by hours) . . . . _____

Practicality of ownership

15. Rental price for comparable airplane . . . . _____
16. Total hourly cost (from line 14) . . . . _____

Fig. 1-3. This worksheet can be used for figuring if airplane ownership is economically practical.

your local airport to obtain some of that data. After filling in the blanks, follow the instructions for computations.

Examples

Let's examine a hypothetical case of ownership. The airplane is a 1975 Cessna 150 valued at $12,000 to be flown 100 hours annually. This example is based upon $35 per month for outside tiedown (very modest), a 1 percent local tax applied to the value of the airplane, and a state aircraft registration costing $9. The insurance cost is an estimate based on the value of the airplane and the pilot's experience. The annual inspection cost is based on the average of estimates made by several FBOs (assuming no serious problems are found).

The five GPH is an estimate for fuel usage at a cost of $2.20 per gallon and the engine reserve of $3 per hour should be adequate for overhaul/rebuild. The general maintenance rate of $3 per flying hour will allow a reserve to build up for the repair of routine mechanical difficulties (brakes, tires, nosewheel shimmy, flap actuator jack problems, radio failure, and so on).

Fixed costs

12 months of storage	$ 420.00
Annual taxes	$ 120.00
Annual state registration	$ 9.00
Insurance premium (12 months)	$ 840.00
Annual inspection (est.)	$ 400.00
Total fixed costs	$ 1,789.00

Operating costs

Fuel Cost per gallon × GPH	$ 11.00
Engine reserve per hour	$ 3.00
General maintenance per hour	$ 3.00
Total operating costs	$ 17.00

Hourly cost

Fixed costs	$ 1,789.00
Operating costs × hours flown	$ 1,700.00
Total costs	$ 3,489.00
Total hourly cost	$ 34.89 per hour

Practicality of ownership

Rental price for comparable airplane	$ 42.00
Total hourly cost	$ 34.89

The preceding example was for an airplane operated (flown) 100 hours during the year. Notice that the total hourly cost was less than the cost of renting a similar airplane. Now let's try other operating times and see how usage, or the lack of it, affects the total hourly cost.

One hour. A worst-case scenario of only one flying hour for the entire year is used in this example to drive the point home that usage is necessary to make ownership practical.

Fixed costs

12 months of storage	$	420.00
Annual taxes	$	120.00
Annual state registration	$	9.00
Insurance premium (12 months)	$	840.00
Annual inspection (est.)	$	400.00
Total fixed costs	$	1,789.00

Operating costs

Fuel cost per gallon × GPH	$	11.00
Engine reserve per hour	$	3.00
General maintenance per hour	$	3.00
Total operating costs	$	17.00

Hourly cost

Fixed costs	$	1,789.00
Operating costs × hours flown (assume 100)	$	17.00
Total costs	$	1,806.00
Total hourly cost	$	1,806.00 per hour

Practicality of ownership

Rental price for comparable airplane	$	42.00
Total hourly cost	$	1,806.00

Notice how those fixed costs never changed to reflect the lack of usage. They are fixed for the year, even if you never touch that plane!

50 hours. Many privately owned airplanes see only 50 hours of operation a year. Unfortunately, this is a reasonably accurate average. The sad part is the number of planes not used at all, as witnessed by the grass growing around their wheels.

Fixed costs	$	1,789.00
Operating costs × hours flown	$	850.00
Total costs	$	2,639.00
Total costs/hours flown	$	52.78 per hour

In this example of only 50-hour annual usage, the practicality of ownership has disappeared.

200 Hours. The fortunate owner who flies his plane 200 hours a year gets the most return from his investment of any examples cited thus far. It is very simple: the more use the airplane gets, the lower the total hourly cost.

Fixed costs	$	1,789.00
Operating costs × hours flown	$	3,400.00
Total costs	$	5,189.00
Total costs/hours flown	$	25.95 per hour

More examples

Let's see what a four-place airplane with a 255-hp engine and retractable landing gear will cost. The example airplane is based near a large metropolitan area.

The charge for outside tiedown is $100 per month, which is relatively typical near major cities. Indoor storage could be as high as $400 per month. A 4-percent local tax applies to the $65,000 value of the airplane. A state registration, based upon the plane's weight, costs $60. The insurance cost is an estimate based on the value of the airplane and the pilot's experience (or lack of experience) in a retractable aircraft. The annual inspection reflects the increased cost of a more complex airplane over that of the original example (Cessna 150). Fuel usage is calculated at 16 gallons per hour at $2.35 per gallon. The engine reserve is $7 per hour, based on the current overhaul costs for a 225-hp engine. The general maintenance rate of $8 per flying hour allows for a repair reserve.

Fixed costs	
12 months of storage	$ 1,200.00
Annual taxes	$ 2,600.00
Annual state registration	$ 60.00
Insurance premium (12 months)	$ 3,200.00
Annual inspection (est.)	$ 1,050.00
Total fixed costs	$ 8,110.00

Operating costs	
Fuel cost per gallon × GPH	$ 37.60
Engine reserve per hour	$ 7.00
General maintenance per hour	$ 8.00
Total operating costs	$ 52.60

Hourly cost	
Fixed costs	$ 8,110.00
Operating costs × hours flown (assume 100)	$ 5,260.00
Total costs	$13,370.00
Total costs/hours flown	$ 133.70 per hour

What now?

Compare these figures, or figures based upon the airplane you wish to own, with the straight hourly rental charged for a similar airplane at the local FBO. Keep in mind that you can sometimes purchase blocks of time at a reduced rate, often as much as 20 percent below the posted rate.

AGAINST OWNERSHIP

As the owner of the airplane, all maintenance will be your responsibility. You won't have a squawk book to write pilot/renter complaints into and expect the

FBO to address them before the next flight. You will have to either fix your problems yourself or pay out of your own pocket to have them repaired.

Do you like the clean airplane rented from the FBO? If you own an airplane, you will have to keep it clean yourself. Consider the size of an airplane. The top surface of the wings can exceed 200 square feet, and that is a lot of area when you are the one doing the washing and polishing. I haven't even mentioned the windshields, upholstery, carpets, or oil-stained belly.

But don't get all glum yet. Many families enjoy flying as a group activity. Maintenance and cleaning of the airplane is just part of the fun. Often, small airports operate in a country club fashion with cookouts and other get-togethers.

A PRIMER ON AIRCRAFT FINANCING

Financing any big ticket item costs money. The exact cost is usually well hidden within the fine print of a loan contract; however, most purchasers only concern themselves with the monthly payment (a fact well known by profit-making bankers). Monthly payments amortize (pay back) a loan and include a portion of the principal and a portion of the interest of the entire loan. How much of each is determined by the type of loan.

The principal is the amount borrowed and the interest is the price paid for use of another person's money. This applies whether you borrow from a bank, loan company, or individual. Generally, two forms of interest are available: fixed and variable rate. Fixed rate means a single interest rate is fixed by the loan contract and remains unchanged for the life of that contract. Variable rate interest can go up or down during the life of the loan contract, normally tracking the prime lending rate.

When purchasing an airplane, or any other expensive item, always plan for the worst if the loan is based upon a variable interest rate. A variable rate loan could produce higher monthly payments, because of a rise in the prime interest rate, than was originally anticipated (or budgeted for). A fixed rate loan is best because you know from month to month what the payment is going to be.

A mixture of fixed and variable interest rates is the variable term loan that sets a never changing monthly payment for the life of the contract; however, the length of the contract can vary depending on the prime interest rate. Should the interest rate rise, the total of your loan will increase (principal + interest). You will owe more money, hence your loan payment plan will be extended, at the set monthly payment, for the number of months necessary to pay all the additional accrued interest.

Some loan contracts have a balloon payment tacked onto the end (last payment) to keep monthly payments artificially low. For example, a $20,000 loan which, during the life of the contract the sum total of the payment, less the interest, will only amortize $5,000 of the principal. The remaining $15,000 of the principal becomes the last payment, thus the term balloon payment.

A rather nasty surprise often found in loan contracts is the prepayment penalty clause, which means that you will have to pay an additional premium (penalty) to complete the loan contract at a date earlier than agreed. Prepayment clauses often demand such a stiff penalty for early payment that there will be no savings realized by early payoff. A prepayment penalty clause can be very expensive if you must satisfy a loan contract before completing the payment schedule, as would be the case when selling or trading an airplane.

2

Making decisions

BEFORE PURCHASING, the prospective airplane owner needs to give serious thought to how the plane will be used. Being completely objective and honest in your thinking is necessary. Remember, you plan to have this airplane for a long time and you want to be very satisfied with it.

QUESTIONS AND ANSWERS

To aid you in determining what airplane is best suited to your particular needs, you need to answer some questions about your flying. A good method of answering these questions is in the form of discussions with other pilots or owners.

Planned use

Why do you fly? Is your flying for sport and relaxation, for business or family transportation, or for hauling cargo?

Sport pilots fly for recreational purposes—generally in the evenings and on weekends. Sometimes forays will be made to other airports, to fly-ins or other social gatherings, or just over the local area.

The pilot using his airplane for serious business or family transportation wants reliable speedy transportation with good load-carrying characteristics. His reason for flying is to get from point A to point B.

The small cargo pilot, usually associated with bush flying in Alaska, Canada, or on large ranches, will generally be interested in airplanes capable of operation from unimproved areas and having large carrying abilities.

Flying skills

What are your real flying skills? Are you most comfortable with a low-performance tricycle gear airplane or are you well qualified in a high performance retractable or small twin?

Review your current piloting skills and the types of airplanes you most often fly. Your proficiency and flying comfort level (where you are most secure) are good indicators for selecting an airplane. Skills you plan to acquire should also be given weight.

Passengers

How many people fly with you? Is most of your flying solo or perhaps with your wife or a flying buddy? Do you only occasionally take the entire family for a day of adventure?

You buy an airplane to do a job. There is no real reason to select an airplane with capabilities far exceeding the requirements of that job. If you usually rent a two-place plane, and it suits your needs, then stay in the two-place category. There is no financial justification for owning something larger. When the infrequent need for a larger airplane does arise, you can always rent one.

Distance traveled and speed

How far do you generally fly? Are most of flights fewer than 100 miles or are they frequently hundreds of miles? Closely related to the issue of distance traveled is the question of speed. How quickly do you really need to get there? Be tough with the answers. Remember, be objective.

Where you are planning to fly to and how quickly you must get there are valid points for consideration. The pilot flying from point A to point B for a business meeting is interested in speed. A three or four hundred mile morning trip could take as little as two hours or as long as four hours. Hurry-up-want-to-get-there and get-it-done—type attitudes require fast airplanes.

For the family on vacation, seeing the countryside is important and speed will not be as important. High speed could even be a detractor. Slow down and enjoy the ride. An important point to remember is that speed equates to larger engines, more complex airplanes, and the resulting higher costs of ownership. Speed is expensive.

VFR/IFR

Related to speed and distance are the problems associated with all-weather flying. The airplane used for business transportation from point A to point B probably should be IFR equipped. This allows for travel during poor weather conditions and eliminates most weather-caused delays. Do you need to go at anytime? Can you afford to wait for good weather?

Avionics adds to the value of a used airplane; it also adds to maintenance expenses. Radio navigation equipment is expensive to purchase, install, and maintain. If the need exists for IFR, then be equipped for it; however, if you are not instrument rated or don't fly in bad weather, save your money. Buy only what you need.

Airports

The airports that you will regularly fly in and out of will influence your choice of airplanes. If all your flying will be from paved runways, the choice of airplanes is wide open. However, if you find yourself flying from rough grass strips or unimproved areas, you must select an airplane that will stand up to the use and abuse that it will receive.

Put it together

After studying and answering these questions and discussions—objectively of course—you have determined your level of piloting skills and identified your hardware requirements. You are well on your way to selecting an airplane appropriate for *you*.

Of course, merely having a basic airplane in mind will not do for very long. Many more factors must be considered before a final choice can be made.

MAINTENANCE

Maintenance is one of aviation's biggest expenses. All airplanes require upkeep, it's just that some require more than others and the more required the more expenses incurred.

Basic automobile maintenance usually equates to fill it up, check the oil and water, then drive away. Airplanes are quite different: annual inspections (required by regulation), minor repairs, major repairs, and equipment installations are all part of the airplane maintenance picture. Maintenance, when selecting a used airplane, should weigh heavily in the decision making process. The more complex an airplane, the more maintenance dollars you will spend. Consider the following different maintenance requirements:

- Airframe coverings may be metal or fabric. Fabric will need periodic replacement. Metal is for life.
- Landing gear can be fixed or retractable. Retractable gear has many moving parts. These parts wear and will eventually need repair or replacement.
- Propellers are fixed-pitch or constant-speed (variable pitch). The latter may have as many as 200 moving parts.
- Engines are often modified for performance reasons, for example, adding a turbocharger. Such modifications are expensive in themselves and often lead to further maintenance expenses and, in some instances, to shorter engine life.
- Aircraft age is a prime aspect of maintenance. Older airplanes require far more maintenance, because of the ravages of time, than do newer planes. This makes the purchase of an older, inexpensive airplane less attractive than a newer, yet higher priced, plane.

These five comparative examples illustrate that simple means less expensive. I'll not use the word cheap because there is nothing cheap about airplane maintenance. All airplane maintenance is, in varying degrees, expensive.

When it comes to airplane equipment: If you don't have it, it can't break, and therefore it will cost nothing to maintain.

Expensive forced maintenance

Along with routine maintenance, you will find the AD (Airworthiness Directive) and General Aviation Airworthiness Alerts of prime concern, as they can mandate immediate maintenance expense.

Airworthiness Directives

Unfortunately, airplanes are not perfect in design or manufacture. They will, from time to time, require inspection, repairs, or service as a result of unforeseen manufacturing problems or defects. These faults might not be identified until years after the actual date of manufacture; however, the faults often affect a large number of a particular make/model airplane. The required procedures are set forth in the ADs, as described in FAR Part 39, and must be complied with.

An AD might require only a simple one-time inspection to assure that the defect does not exist, a periodic inspection (every 50 hours of operation) to watch for an impending problem, or a major airframe or engine modification to remedy a current difficulty. Compliance with some ADs can be relatively inexpensive, particularly those involving only minor inspections. However, complying with an AD requiring extensive engine or airframe modifications or repairs can devastate a bank account.

Although ADs correct deficient design or poor quality control of parts and/ or workmanship, manufacturers are not normally considered responsible for the costs incurred in AD compliance. Unlike automobile recalls, the financial burden of meeting AD requirements is routinely met by the owner. Unfortunately, the manufacturer may even profit from selling the parts necessary to comply with the AD. There is no large consumer voice involving aircraft manufacturer responsibility.

Mechanics, inspectors, and the FAA maintain AD files. An AD compliance check is part of the annual inspection, thereby assuring continued compliance. Records of AD compliance become a part of the aircraft logbooks. When looking at an airplane with purchase in mind, always check for AD compliance. (A brief list of ADs appears in Appendix A of this book.)

General Aviation Airworthiness Alerts

On a monthly basis, the FAA compiles the Malfunction or Defect Reports (MDRs), as submitted by owners, pilots, and mechanics from all over the nation, into a single listing. Called General Aviation Airworthiness Alerts, the list is published and sent to interested parties, including manufacturers, mechanics, inspectors, and the like. Alerts are not the word of law that ADs are, but they should be referenced when considering a specific make/model of airplane.

Some aircraft are so laden with ADs and reported mechanical difficulties that they scream out, "Spend money on me!" Check your proposed airplane selection carefully against AD and alert lists. It is better to be discouraged now, at decision making time, than discouraged later when it's time to spend your hard earned dollars for all the required service work.

AD and General Aviation Airworthiness Alert information specific to a particular make/model/serial number aircraft is available through the Aircraft Owners and Pilots Association. (See AOPA information in Chapter 5.)

Warning, don't buy more airplane than you can afford to properly maintain. Good maintenance not only promotes flying safety, it protects your investment.

Insurability

Insurance companies are in business to make money by providing a service called *coverage*. The insurance *premium*, the amount charged for this coverage, is based upon two main factors: the pilot and the airplane (sometimes called risk factors).

The pilot factor

The *pilot factor* is determined by the total number of hours flown, types of airplanes flown, ratings, and violation/accident history. In other words: What are the chances of the pilot causing a financial loss to the insurance company?

The airplane factor

Examination of the loss ratio history for that particular make and model of airplane and what the current availability of replacement parts is, in the event of a loss, determine the *airplane factor*. Parts availability is directly related to the total number of the make/model manufactured. Orphan airplanes, those long out of production, are expensive to insure and maintain because of parts problems.

RESALE

What is the possibility of quick resale at a sum near the purchase price? If you are concerned about resale of the airplane, it is very important to consider current values and, in the event you need money in a hurry, how quickly the airplane would sell.

An orphan airplane can be a very economical buy, but is usually not a hot seller. If you purchase one, understand that when the time comes to sell it, you might have to sell cheap, or wait a long time to find a buyer. This is not to condemn orphans for they can represent some very affordable flying, rather to have you realize what you are getting into.

If resale is a prime concern, then buy a Cessna or Piper basic four-place fixed-gear airplane. There is always a market for them.

WATCH OUT FOR BARGAINS

There are few bargains in the world and the field of used airplanes is no exception to the rule. Any plane selling for a price that is seemingly lower than it should be, probably has a serious flaw. Even if you know of the flaw and feel it is not as bad as it sounds, get some professional advice before buying a bargain airplane. It may be worse than you can imagine.

Repairing even simple things on an airplane generally calls for the prime ingredient called money, lots of it. For example, replacement of a typical four-place airplane's interior can cost more than $3,000. Of course you could get the materials and do the work yourself for about $1,000. This looks like a good savings, until you find it takes the better part of the summer to get the job done. The part of summer during which you expected to take a flying vacation.

Don't even consider one of those back-of-the-hanger planes. You know, the one that doesn't have an engine on it. Planes long in disuse and in pieces are not even wanted by mechanics, except for parts. They don't represent an economical entry into airplane ownership for the average person.

When it comes to spending money, it might be good to consider the purchase of an airplane as the tip of the iceberg. You can either pay a higher price for a plane in good shape, or pay less for a plane requiring work and additional money for maintenance. In the end, the total spent will be nearly equal.

ARE WE HAVING FUN YET?

If you are still being objective and honest with yourself, you are now ready to look at the specific makes and models of aircraft currently available on the used market and evaluate them with respect to your individual needs. Remember, the final objective in the purchase of a used airplane is to fulfill personal desires with an airplane that is affordable to own and operate and does not overtax your flying skills.

A short hangar story

Some years back a friend of mine earned his private pilot's license, then bought an airplane. He learned to fly in a Cessna 150 but he bought a Cessna 180, a taildragger with a big engine that can be a fire-breathing dragon in inexperienced hands. After the airplane dealer checked him out in the 180 and, after paying high insurance rates based upon his lack of proficiency in that type of airplane, he went out to play bush pilot.

It only took a couple of flights for his inexperience to catch up with him, and the plane took him for an unforgettable ride across the infield during a landing. The plane was undamaged, but the experience scared him so badly that the airplane sat unused for months, costing tiedown fees, insurance premiums, and all the other things known as fixed costs.

Finally, I flew it a few times, then demonstrated and sold it for him. He later bought a Cessna 172 and I guess lived happily ever after.

The point is: Don't buy more airplane than you can handle, because if you can't handle it, you won't enjoy it, and you won't fly it.

3

Valuations

PLACING A CASH VALUE on a used airplane is not as simple as with a used automobile. Certain high-dollar items must be judged very carefully to place an accurate value on an airplane:

Airframe, subject to fatigue, damage, or corrosion
Engine(s), the engine's life expectancy is limited
Modifications, for better performance or particular use
Avionics, become outdated as electronic technology improves

Each of these areas must be examined very carefully, for it is the total valuation of these items that gives an airplane's worth.

THE AIRPLANE MARKET

The airplane market has experienced a general rise in prices over the past years and a sharp rise in the most recent five years. The recent rise is steep enough that an airplane can often be purchased, operated, and properly maintained for several years—and later sold at a profit.

In simple terms, supply and demand determines the high prices. No manufacturer of small airplanes is producing an appreciable number of aircraft on a yearly basis while only a few are building less than one per month and some none at all. During the mid-1970s, annual American production levels averaged about 13,000 single engine general aviation airplanes. Records for the most recent two years show current production levels down to only 600 to 800 airplanes yearly.

What caused this situation? It is hard to say, and the fingers of blame don't all point in the same direction. There is little doubt that product liability on the part of the manufacturers has been a major contributor, although the lack of an economical means of certifying new models of airplanes (limited by outdated FAA Regulations), and the increased costs of labor and materials have all contributed to the general rise in new airplane prices.

The reason behind the price rise, however, is not the real problem confronting the prospective used airplane purchaser. It is the effect the current new airplane prices—combined with the small numbers in production—has on used airplane values that is of immediate concern. An additional aspect in the airplane market is the sale of new airplanes directly to overseas purchasers. Selling *new* airplanes overseas, however, does not have the direct effect on the used airplane market that selling *used* airplanes in overseas markets does.

According to information from the United States Department of Commerce, during the most recent years of record (1989 and 1990) an average of 70 general aviation piston-powered airplanes of gross weight under 10,000 pounds (the type of planes that this book is about) were exported worldwide monthly. That is over 800 yearly!

What small airplanes do you think they are exporting? I can guarantee that the Department of Commerce figures do not include Ercoupes, old rag wings, or even many of those planes built in the 1960s or 1970s. It is only the best airplanes that are shipped overseas. Of course, this export market keeps the prices inflated and reduces the total airplane selection pool. However, before you get completely discouraged, there are still over 170,000 airplanes in the civilian single-engine fleet of the U.S. to select from.

Fact: The average age of two-place small airplanes is nearly 30 years and four-seat planes about 25 years.

AIRFRAMES

Airplanes, for most purposes, consist of two types of airframes: all-metal or tube-and-fabric. Most modern airplanes are of all-metal construction. The several notable exceptions to this rule are Aviat, Maule, and Taylorcraft.

The advantages of all-metal construction are easier outdoor storage and the fact that fabric recovering is never necessary. The disadvantages are expensive repairs and outrageous painting costs. Painting a typical four-place airplane is likely to cost between $3,000 and $5,000. Tube and fabric airplanes are very expensive to re-cover and do not weather well outside. Exceptions are airplanes covered with synthetic coverings, which may last for many years, and those covered with fiberglass, which is considered permanent.

If an airframe has a history of severe damage, the airplane's value will be reduced. The method used for repairing damage is the determining factor of the amount of value reduction. Was the airplane repaired to be like new or was it just a "make do job"? Proper reconstruction of a severely damaged airplane requires considerable time, skill, and expense. The work must be done in a properly equipped shop using jigs to ensure the alignment of all parts.

Consider the airplane's past usage. Was it a trainer, crop duster, patrol, or rental airplane? If so, the hours are likely high and the usage rough. Yet, commercial use can also denote very good maintenance. After all, maintaining what you have is cheaper than running it into the ground and replacing it.

Consider the airplane's past usage. Was it a trainer, crop duster, patrol, or rental airplane? If so, the hours are likely high and the usage rough. Yet, commercial use can also denote very good maintenance. After all, maintaining what you have is cheaper than running it into the ground and replacing it.

Recognize that there is no such thing in aviation as a "little fixing up" to remedy small problems. Upgrading a complete interior, repainting the plane's outside, replacement of windows, and the like, is very expensive. Therefore, a plane that needs a little fix up is worth less money than a plane needing no fix up.

ENGINES

Engines are the most costly single item, maintenance wise, attached to an airplane. An engine failure involving internal breakage can cost thousands of dollars to repair. Therefore, condition and history of the engine becomes an important part of the overall airplane's value.

Engine buzzwords

The following phrases and words are part of the airplane vocabulary you must learn when searching for, owning, and selling an airplane:

TBO (time between overhaul). Engine manufacturer's recommended maximum engine life and has no legal bearing for airplanes not used in commercial service; however, is certainly an indicator of engine life expectancy. Many well-cared-for engines last hundreds of hours beyond TBO, but not all.

Rebuild. Disassembly, repair, alteration, inspection, cleaning and reassembly of an engine, including bringing all specifications back to factory-new limits. Only the engine's manufacturer can rebuild an engine which comes with a new logbook and zero time.

Overhaul. Disassembly, repair, inspection, cleaning, and reassembly of an engine. The work may be done to new limits or to service limits. Some engine repair centers refer to engines overhauled to new limits as *remanufactured*, a term having no official validity.

Top overhaul. Rebuilding the head assemblies but not the entire engine. The case of the engine is not opened; only the cylinder and head assemblies are serviced. A top overhaul is a means for stretching the life of an otherwise sound engine that burns oil, has valve problems, or has low compression. Unfortunately, a top overhaul can also be a cheap/quick fix that will not make the engine last longer, just make it run better.

New limits. Dimensions and specifications used when constructing a new engine. Parts meeting these specifications will normally reach TBO with no further attention, except for routine maintenance.

Service limits. Dimensions and specifications below which use is forbidden. Many used parts fit into this category, making their use legal; however, it is unlikely such parts will last the full TBO as they are already partially worn.

Nitriding. Method of hardening cylinder barrels and crankshafts to reduce wear, thereby extending the useful life of the part.

Chrome plating. Process that brings the internal dimensions of a cylinder back to specifications by producing a hard, machinable, and long-lasting surface. Due to the hardness of chrome, break-in time for chromed cylinders is longer than for normal cylinders. An advantage of chrome plating is resistance to destructive oxidation (rust) within combustion chambers.

Magnaflux/magnaglow. Used in examinations to detect invisible defects in ferrous metals (cracks). Engine parts normally examined by these means are crankshafts, camshafts, piston pins, rocker arms, and cases.

Cylinder codes. Modified cylinders are coded with paint or banding. The color of that paint or band indicates the cylinder's physical properties:

Orange, chrome-plated cylinder barrel
Blue, nitrided cylinder barrel
Green, cylinder barrel .010 inches oversize
Yellow, cylinder barrel .020 inches oversize.

Used engines

Many airplane ads proudly state the hours on the engine, for instance: 745 SMOH, which equates to 745 hours of use since the engine was overhauled. Not stated is type of usage or thoroughness of overhaul. Few standards exist and SMOH, a popular abbreviation form of Since Major Overhaul, has little real meaning except to suggest that something was done with the engine.

Time and value

The time (hours) since new or overhaul/rebuild is an important factor in placing overall value on an airplane. The recommended TBO, less the hours now on the engine, is the remaining time. There are three basic terms usually used for referring to time on an airplane engine:

Low time, first third of TBO
Mid time, second third of TBO
High time, last third of TBO.

Other variables also come into play when referring to TBO (see also Table 3-1 and Fig. 3-1):

- Are the hours on the engine since new, rebuilt, or overhauled?
- When (the date) was the engine new, rebuilt, or overhauled?
- What type of flying was the engine used for?
- Was it used on a regular basis?
- What kind of maintenance did the engine get?

Table 3-1. Value of the engine.

Value	Time	Status	Flying Type	TBO
Poor	1800	New	Training	2000
Good	1000	New	X-country	1800
Fair	800	New	Training	2000
Excell	500	New	X-country	2000
Vy Poor	1800	SMOH	Any type	2000
Fair	1000	SMOH	X-country	1800
Poor	1000	SMOH	Training	2000
Good	500	SMOH	X-country	2000

Fig. 3-1. The very expensive heart of a power airplane.

Avco-Lycoming, Inc.

Airplanes that have not been flown on a regular basis, nor maintained in a like fashion, have engines that will never reach full TBO. Manufacturers refer to regular usage as 20 to 40 hours monthly. That equates to 240 to 480 hours yearly and means a lot of flying. Few privately owned airplanes meet the upper limits of this requirement. Let's face it, most of us don't have the time or money required for such constant use. The average flying time annually accumulated in the American general aviation fleet for a single engine is about 130 hours. Some planes in commercial service run an engine to TBO in one year, while some privately owned planes bake in the sun and are never flown.

When an engine isn't run, acids and moisture in the oil will oxidize (rust) engine components. In addition, the lack of lubricant movement will cause the seals to dry out. Left long enough, the engine will seize and no longer be operable.

Abuse is just as hard on engines as no use. Hard climbs and fast descents cause abnormal heating and cooling conditions and are extremely destructive to air-cooled engines. Training aircraft often exhibit this trait because of intensive takeoff and landing practice.

It goes without saying that preventive maintenance, such as changing spark plugs and oil, should have been done, and logged, throughout the engine's life. Tracking preventive maintenance should be easy, as all maintenance must be logged, so say the FARs (*Federal Aviation Regulations*).

Beware the engine that has only a few hours use since overhaul! Perhaps something is not right with the overhaul, or it was a very cheap job, just to make the plane more salable. When it comes to overhauls, seek out the large shops that specialize in aircraft engine rebuilding. I'm not saying that the local FBO can't do a good job; I just feel that the large organizations specializing in this work have more experience and equipment to work with. In addition, they have reputations to maintain and most will back you in the event of difficulties.

Typical costs for a complete engine overhaul to new limits (based on current average pricing):

- O-200 $7,000
- O-300 $8,000
- O-320 $8,000
- O-360 $8,000
- O-470 $9,000
- IO-520 $10,000
- TIO-540 $15,000

It is possible to spend less when overhauling an engine if some parts of the engine are still serviceable. It is also possible to spend about 30 percent more and get a factory rebuilt engine.

MODIFICATIONS

Many airplanes found on today's market have been modified to update or otherwise improve them. Modifications can take many forms, but are normally to improve performance, attain greater economy of operation, or modernize the appearance of the plane. Most modifications require an STC (Supplemental Type Certificate) and cost hundreds or thousands of dollars. They do not, however, necessarily add a similar amount to the airplane's value.

Short takeoff and landing

Short takeoff and landing (STOL) conversions are perhaps king of all the modifications available to the airplane owner. The typical STOL modification changes the wing's shape (usually by the addition of a leading edge cuff), adds stall fences (to prevent air flow disruption from proceeding along the length of the wing), gap seals, and wing tips. A larger engine is often installed. The results of a STOL modification can be spectacular; they are also quite expensive.

Power

Power-increase modifications are the second most popular improvement made to airplanes and are often done, as previously mentioned, in conjunction with STOL modifications. Engine replacement increases the useful load and flight performance figures of the aircraft. A power modification appears very costly, yet is often no more expensive than a quality engine overhaul.

Wing tips

Wing tips are changed to increase flight performance. Dr. Sighard Hoerner, Ph.D., designed a high-performance wing tip for the U.S. Navy that led to the development of improved general aviation wing tips. A properly designed wing tip can provide an increase of 3 to 5 mph in cruise speed and a small increase in climb performance, but most important are the improved low-speed handling characteristics:

- 10 to 20 percent reduction in takeoff roll
- 3 to 5 mph lower stall speed
- Improved slow-flight handling

Wing tip installation time can be as low as two to three hours, making this an usually inexpensive modification (Fig. 3-2).

Fig. 3-2. Modified wing tips can improve slow flight, landing, and take-off characteristics.

Landing gear

Taildragger conversions have become popular among owners of Cessna 150, 152, and 172 aircraft. The conversion requires the permanent removal of the nose wheel, moving the main gear forward, and adding a tailwheel. Performance benefits of 8 to 10 mph increase in cruise, shorter takeoff distances, and better rough-field handling are claimed.

Gap seals

Gap seals are extensions of the lower wing surface from the rear spar to the leading edge of the flaps and ailerons. They cover several square feet of open space, causing a smoother flow of air around the wing. This smoother flow, or reduction of drag, causes the aircraft to cruise from 1 to 3 mph faster and stall from 5 to 8 mph slower. Gap seals are often part of a STOL installation.

Fuel tanks

Larger or auxiliary fuel tanks are sometimes installed to increase operational range. A drawback of carrying more fuel is that you will carry less load (passengers).

Auto fuels

Considerable controversy surrounds the use of auto fuels (sometimes called mogas) in certified aircraft engines. There are pro's and con's for both sides; however, I feel that it is up to the individual aircraft owner to make the choices about the use of non-aviation fuels. Among the arguments are:

- Many FBOs (Fixed Base Operators) are reluctant to make auto fuel available for reasons of product liability and less profit. This is slowly changing, as more mogas become available at airports.
- Economy is the center of mogas usage. Unleaded auto fuel is certainly less expensive than 100LL (LL=low lead) and it does appear to operate well in the older engines that requires 80 octane fuel. This gives two-fold savings: once at the pump and again for reduced maintenance.
- Engine manufacturers claim the use of auto fuel will void warranty service. Realistically, this threat is limited in scope as few airplanes using mogas have new engines that would be eligible for warranty coverage anyway.
- If you have a storage tank and pump, it might be advantageous to use auto fuel. It will be easier to locate a jobber, willing to keep an auto fuel storage tank filled than it will be to find an *avgas* (aviation gasoline) supplier willing to make small deliveries. This is particularly true for private airstrips.
- Before purchasing an airplane with an auto fuel STC (Supplementary-Type Certificate) or acquiring an auto fuel STC for a plane, check with your insurance carrier and get their approval in writing.

For further information about the legal use of auto fuels in an airplane contact:

Petersen Aviation, Inc.   Experimental Aircraft Association
Rt. 1 Box 18   Wittman Airfield
Minden, NE 68959   Oshkosh, WI 54903

Value of modifications

Expensive modifications do not always increase a plane's value in proportion with the cost of said modification. Many modifications are only of value in the eye of the current owner. Before extensively modifying an airplane to do some new form of service it was not originally designed for, I recommend changing airplanes. As an example: If rough-field operations are necessary, you may find it more cost-effective to purchase a Cessna 180 or Maule, versus modifying your Cessna 172. Without doubt, the 180 or Maule would be easier to sell than a highly modified 172.

AVIONICS

New airplanes have instrument panels that reflect our move into the space age, often displaying more than necessary for simple flying. However, what appears complex is usually straightforward in operation and is designed to make flying and navigation easier and safer.

Avionics today are filled with capabilities: digital displays, computerized functions, small size. They are about as similar to past equipment as a portable computer is to a pad and pencil. As far as prices, the new equipment represents bargains never before seen.

A good NAV/COM cost roughly $1,800 15 years ago, and provided 200 navigation channels and 360 communication channels. It was panel-mounted and the VOR display (CDI) was mounted separately. Considering that, as a rule of thumb, most consumer goods today cost three times what they did 15 years ago; that NAV/COM should cost $5,400 today, but it won't. Electronics have changed in the past few years. Today the radio for $1,800 (sometimes a good deal less) is a NAV/COM with the same 200 navigation channels, plus the necessary increase to 760 communication channels, digital display, user-programmable memory channels, and a built-in CDI.

It seems that everything about aviation is identified by abbreviations or buzzwords. Avionics are no different, with the following abbreviations commonly used:

A-Panel, audio panel
ADF, automatic direction finder
CDI, course deviation indicator
COMM or COM, a VHF transceiver for voice radio communications
DME, distance measuring equipment

ELT, emergency locator transmitter
HT, hand-held transceiver
LOC/GS, localizer/glide slope
LORAN-C, a computer/receiver navigation system
MBR, marker beacon receiver
NAV, a VHF navigation receiver
NAV/COM, a combination of a COM and NAV in one unit
RNAV, random area navigation
XPNDR, transponder

VFR flying

Equipping a plane for VFR flying is based upon where you intend to fly. Are you going to large airports or small uncontrolled fields? Your equipment could limit you, particularly with today's TCA and ARSA requirements. At the barest minimum, VFR operation requires a NAV/COM, transponder, and ELT.

Not too many years ago, most cross-country flying involved pilotage using charts and looking out the windows for checkpoints. Today's aviator has become accustomed to the advantages of modern navigation and communication systems. Take advantage of the modern systems, and the safety they can provide, with a VFR installation that includes a 760-channel NAV/COM, an altitude reporting transponder, ELT, and Loran-C. With this installation you can be comfortable and go pretty much wherever you desire.

IFR flying

Flying IFR (Instrument Flight Rules) requires considerably more equipment, representing a much higher cash investment. IFR operations require the following minimum equipment:

Dual NAV/COM (760 channel)	Loran-C
Clock	Transponder
MBR	Audio Panel
ADF	ELT
LOC/GS	DME

New avionics

New equipment is state-of-the-art, offering the newest innovations, best reliability, and a warranty. An additional benefit of new equipment is that solid-state electronics units are physically smaller and allow a fuller panel in a small plane, draw considerably less electric power than their tube-type predecessors, and are much more reliable in operation.

Used avionics

Used avionics can be purchased from dealers or individuals. *Trade-A-Plane* is a good source of used equipment. However, regardless of where you buy used avionics, don't purchase anything with tubes in it, more than six years of age, or built by a manufacturer now out of business. In any of these cases, parts and service could be a real problem.

Additionally, don't purchase anything that is out of date technically, for example a COMM with less than 720 channels (preferred is 760 channels). Such out-of-date equipment could present lack of capability problems at a later date.

Reconditioned avionics

Several companies advertise reconditioned avionics at bargain, or at least low, prices. The equipment was removed from service and completely checked out by an avionics shop. Parts that have failed, are near failure, or are likely to fail have been replaced. Albeit reconditioned, it is not new, it is used. Everything in the unit has been used, but not everything will be replaced during reconditioning. You will have some new parts and some old parts.

Reconditioned equipment purchases can make sense for the budget-minded owner by offering a fair-priced buy that usually comes with a limited warranty. Few pieces of reconditioned equipment will exceed six or seven years in age.

Computerized navigation

Long-range navigation, called Loran, has been around for many years. It is based upon low-frequency radio signals, rather than the VHF (very high frequency) signals normally associated with FAA navigational aids. Although not originally intended for general aviation, its use has become common place because of computer-based Loran-C.

Propagation properties of radio waves at the frequencies used by Loran are not limited to line-of-sight range. This gives distinct advantages over normal VHF navaids (radio navigational aids) such as VORs. Unlike a VOR's limited range of 50 to 100 miles, Loran is usable hundreds of miles from the actual transmitting station. This can be very practical for many general aviation operations. A Loran-C receiver can cost from less than $1,000 to more than $4,000. Installation can cost several hundred additional dollars.

Some airplane owners view the instrument panel as a functional device while others see it as a statement to be made. In either case, care must be taken when filling up the panel. Don't install instrumentation merely for the sake of filling holes. Plan it well and make it functional and easy to use. Above all else, do it economically.

FINAL VALUATION

When you have looked at the engine, airframe, any modifications, and the avionics of an airplane, you should have a good feel for the overall worth of the airplane. Compare the airplane with other similar available airplanes realizing that small items such as new brakes, intercoms, tires, plastic or vinyl parts, and most modifications add little to the total dollar value of the airplane.

Valuable possessions and boxes of rocks

There is a rule of thumb about the selling price of used airplanes which says: The selling price of an airplane is set when the dollar value the seller places upon his valued possession is equaled by the top amount offered by the prospective purchaser for the same box of rocks.

4

Before you purchase

SEARCHING FOR A GOOD USED AIRPLANE that suits your needs can be a frustrating experience. While it is possible to contract with an airplane broker and let him do all the leg work, most individuals elect to do the searching themselves. After all, frustrating or not, it is a part of airplane ownership.

THE SEARCH

Used airplanes of many makes/models and prices are available. For this reason it is important to begin the search by having an idea of what airplane you want to purchase and setting a range of expectations for that airplane including the acceptable overall condition, extra equipment desired, and the spending dollar limit you are comfortable with.

Usually, the search for a used airplane starts at the home airport. The FBO (Fixed Base Operator) may be helpful; discuss your search with him. Normally an FBO will know of any airplanes for sale, advertised and unadvertised, at his airport and, being an insider to the business, probably knows about the condition and history of those planes.

If there is nothing acceptable at your airport, then broaden the search. Visit other nearby airports, check the bulletin boards and ask around. While you're there, walk around and look for airplanes with *For Sale* signs in the windows (Figs. 4-1 and 4-2). If you find nothing, you may want to put an "Airplane Wanted" ad on the bulletin board.

Used airplane ads are sometimes seen in local newspapers and always in the various flight-oriented magazines (*AOPA Pilot*, *Flying*, *Private Pilot*, and so on). Unfortunately, the magazine ads are usually stale because of the 60 to 90 days lag time between ad placement and printing. There are, however, other recommended sources of timely advertising: *Trade-A-Plane* and *The General Aviation News and Flyer*.

Trade-A-Plane has been in business for over 50 years and publishes their yellow-colored paper three times monthly. Within its pages you will find nearly everything you would ever need in the airplane business including airplanes,

Fig. 4-1. Could be you'll see something like this while walking around a small airport.

Fig. 4-2. No! No! No! This is not what you are looking for! This airplane needs a complete rebuild (loads of money and time). Remember, there is no such thing in aviation as a little fixing for a few dollars.

parts, service, insurance, avionics, and much more. If you don't see it in *Trade-A-Plane*, I doubt if you will ever see it (Fig. 4-3). Contact:

Trade-A-Plane
P.O. Box 509
Crossville, TN 38555
(615) 484-5137

Fig. 4-3. Symbol of *Trade-A-Plane*, those yellow sheets with all the airplanes listed for sale. Trade-A-Plane

For those really in a hurry to see the *Trade-A-Plane* before anyone else, I recommend a First Class U.S. Mail subscription, or better yet, a Federal Express 2nd Day Air Priority subscription. Expensive? Yes, but if you are looking for bargains you have to be at the head of the line.

General Aviation News and Flyer is a twice-monthly newspaper carrying loads of up-to-the-minute news affecting general aviation. "You read it here months before the magazines print it," is a phrase I have heard more than one pilot say. Their classifieds are printed on pink paper and carried as an insert to the newspaper. Typically the pink pages number more than 20. Contact:

General Aviation News and Flyer
P.O. Box 98786
Tacoma, WA 98498-0786
(206) 588-1743

The following states have the largest population of general aviation aircraft based in them (in descending order):

1. California
2. Texas
3. Florida
4. Ohio
5. Michigan

6. Illinois
7. New York
8. Washington
9. Pennsylvania

Of course, there are small airplanes in every state.

Alternate sources

Three additional sources of used airplanes exist, however, that are not usually mentioned because they all-too-often include airplanes that are not desirable for the individual purchaser to consider for ownership. These sources include repossessions, law enforcement seizure auctions, and government surplus sales. All three sources have a common thread; you can normally make only a quick cursory inspection (and sometimes not even that) and a test flight of the airplane is totally out of the question.

Of the three, repossession is the safest bet. Repossessed airplanes were legally flying in the civilian fleet and should represent no difficulty in titling or registration. When considering the purchase of a repossessed airplane, remember: If an owner can't make his payments, he probably didn't spend money on maintenance either. However scanty the maintenance was, it should be recorded in the log books. Banks are often a good starting point for looking for repossessed airplanes.

The remaining sources are more complicated to use and the aircraft involved often have serious mechanical defects which can preclude legal flight.

Aircraft sold at a government auction may have very limited records (log books) placing airworthiness of the entire aircraft, or any part thereof, in question. This is particularly true when purchasing a surplus military airplane. The military often uses replacement parts that are not certified. This is not to say the parts are defective, only that they are not certified for use. The lack of parts certification can cause nightmares when attempting to register the airplane in the civil fleet. In all cases it is the responsibility of the owner (you) to prove airworthiness.

Obtaining a clear title is not a problem because the selling agency will provide it. Cash payment is expected at auctions (unless advanced arrangements are made) and the purchaser is required to remove the airplane immediately or within a few days. For more information contact:

Defense Surplus Sales Office
Dept. RK-24
P.O. Box 1370
Battle Creek, MI 49016

Or contact the local office for the following agencies:

United States Marshals Service
United States Customs Service
Drug Enforcement Agency

Purchasing an airplane at auction is not for everyone; however, if you are working with a good mechanic and have the extra finances available to correct all mechanical deficiencies, it may save you money in the long run.

READING THE ADS

Most airplane ads use various cryptic abbreviations to describe the airplane, suggest the use it has had, and tell how it is equipped. Ads normally include a telephone number.

Sample ad:

68 Cessna 182, 2243TT, 763 SMOH,
Oct ANN, FGP, Dual NAV/COM,
GS, MB, ELT, Mode C XPNDR, NDH.
$28,750 firm. (607) 555-1234.

Translated: For sale, a 1968 Cessna 182 airplane with 2,243 total hours on the airframe and an engine with 763 hours since a major overhaul. The next annual inspection is due in October. It is equipped with a full gyro instrument panel, has two navigation and communication radios, a glideslope receiver and indicator, a marker beacon receiver, an emergency locator transmitter, Mode-C transponder. The airplane has no damage history. The price is $28,750, and the seller claims he will not bargain (most do, however). A telephone number is given for contacting the seller.

A lot of information is packed inside those four little lines by using abbreviations. The following is a list of the more commonly used advertising abbreviations:

AD	airworthiness directive
ADF	automatic direction finder
AF	airframe
AF&E	airframe and engine
ALT	altimeter
ANN	annual inspection
ANNUAL	annual inspection
AP	autopilot
ASI	airspeed indicator
A&E	airframe and engine
A/P	autopilot
BAT	battery
B&W	black and white
CAT	carburetor air temperature
CHT	cylinder-head temperature
COM	communications radio
CS	constant-speed propeller

C/S	constant-speed propeller
C/W	complied with
DBL	double
DG	directional gyro
DME	distance measuring equipment
FAC	factory
FBO	fixed-base operator
FGP	full gyro panel
FWF	fire wall forward
GAL	gallons
GPH	gallons per hour
GS	glideslope
HD	heavy-duty
HP	horsepower
HSI	horizontal situation indicator
HVY	heavy
IFR	instrument flight rules
ILS	instrument landing system
INSP	inspection
INST	instrument
KTS	knots
L	left
LDG	landing
LE	left engine
LED	light-emitting diode
LH	left-hand
LIC	license
LOC	localizer
LTS	lights
L&R	left and right
MB	marker beacon
MBR	marker beacon receiver
MP	manifold pressure
MPH	miles per hour
MOD	modification
NAV	navigation
NAVCOM	navigation/communication radio
NDH	no damage history
OAT	outside air temperature
OX	oxygen
O2	oxygen

PMA	parts manufacture approval
PROP	propeller
PSI	pounds per square inch
R	right
RC	rate of climb
REMAN	remanufactured
REPALT	reporting altimeter
RH	right-hand
RMFD	remanufactured
RMFG	remanufactured
RNAV	area navigation
ROC	rate of climb
SAFOH	since airframe overhaul
SCMOH	since (chrome/complete) major overhaul
SEL	single-engine land
SFACNEW	since factory new
SFN	since factory new
SFNE	since factory new engine
SFREM	since factory remanufacture
SFREMAN	since factory remanufacture
SFRMFG	since factory remanufacture
SMOH	since major overhaul
SNEW	since new
SPOH	since propeller overhaul
STC	supplemental type certificate
STOH	since top overhaul
STOL	shore takeoff and landing
TAS	true airspeed
TBO	time between overhaul
TC	turbocharged
TLX	telex
TNSP	transponder
TNSPNDR	transponder
TSN	time since new
TSO	technical service order
TT	total time
TTAF	total time airframe
TTA&E	total time airframe and engine
TTE	total time engine
TTSN	total time since new
TXP	transponder
T&B	turn and bank
VAC	vacuum
VFR	visual flight rules

VHF	very high frequency
VOR	visual omni range

XC	cross-country
XLNT	excellent
XMTR	transmitter
XPDR	transponder
XPNDR	transponder

3LMB	three-light marker beacon

United States telephone area codes

Don't forget the value of the area code in the telephone number; it usually tells the location of the plane, which for two reasons is very important. Airplane location can dictate whether you would be interested in seeing it, as you may not want to travel a couple of thousand miles to look at one airplane. The other aspect of location is the effect that climatic conditions have on the airplane:

1. Salt-laden air along a sea coast can cause serious corrosion problems.
2. Abrasive sands of the Southwest take their toll on the gyros, moving parts, and paint.
3. Cold winters of the North can cause excessive engine wear during engine starts and cracking of plastic materials.
4. Acid rain found around manufacturing centers can increase corrosion and paint failure.

Generally, these problems can be avoided if the airplane is well cared for and treated properly.

Area Code List

201	NJ north (Newark)
202	DC (Washington)
203	CT
204	Manitoba, Canada
205	AL
206	WA west (Seattle)
207	ME
208	ID
209	CA central (Fresno)
212	NY southeast (New York City)
213	CA southwest (Los Angeles)
214	TX northeast (Dallas)
215	PA southeast (Philadelphia)
216	OH northeast (Cleveland)
217	IL central (Springfield)

218 MN north (Duluth)
219 IN north (South Bend)

301 MD
302 DE
303 CO
304 WV
305 FL southeast (Miami)
306 Saskatchewan, Canada
307 WY
308 NE west (North Platte)
309 IL northwest (Peoria)
312 IL northeast (Chicago)
313 MI southeast (Detroit)
314 MO east (St. Louis)
315 NY north central (Syracuse)
316 KS south (Wichita)
317 IN central (Indianapolis)
318 LA northwest (Shreveport)
319 IA east (Dubuque)

401 RI
402 NE east (Omaha)
403 Alberta, Canada
404 GA north (Atlanta)
405 OK west (Oklahoma City)
406 MT
407 FL east (Melbourne)
408 CA northwest (San Jose)
409 TX southeast (Galveston)
410 MD (Baltimore)
412 PA southwest (Pittsburgh)
413 MA west (Springfield)
414 WI southeast (Milwaukee)
415 CA central (San Francisco)
416 Ontario, Canada
417 MO southwest (Springfield)
418 Quebec, Canada
419 OH northwest (Toledo)

501 AR
502 KY west (Louisville)
503 OR
504 LA southeast (New Orleans)
505 NM
506 New Brunswick, Canada

507 MN south (Rochester)
508 MA east (except Boston)
509 WA east (Spokane)
512 TX south (San Antonio)
513 OH southwest (Cincinnati)
514 Quebec, Canada
515 IA central (Des Moines)
516 NY southeast (Long Island)
517 MI central (Lansing)
518 NY northeast (Albany)
519 Ontario, Canada

601 MS
602 AZ
603 NH
604 British Columbia, Canada
605 SD
606 KY east (Lexington)
607 NY south central (Binghamton)
608 WI southwest (Madison)
609 NJ south (Trenton)
612 MN central (Minneapolis)
613 Ontario, Canada
614 OH southeast (Columbus)
615 TN east (Nashville)
616 MI west (Grand Rapids)
617 MA east (Boston)
618 IL south (Centralia)
619 CA south (San Diego)

701 ND
702 NV
703 VA north & west (Arlington)
704 NC west (Charlotte)
705 Ontario, Canada
707 CA northwest (Santa Rosa)
708 IL north (Chicago)
709 Newfoundland, Canada
712 IA west (Council Bluffs)
713 TX southeast (Houston)
714 CA southwest (Anaheim)
715 WI north (Eau Claire)
716 NY west (Buffalo)
717 PA central (Harrisburg)
718 NY southeast (Brooklyn)
719 CO south (Pueblo)

801 UT
802 VT
803 SC
804 VA southeast (Richmond)
805 CA west central (Bakersfield)
806 TX northwest (Amarillo)
807 Ontario, Canada
808 HI
812 IN south (Evansville)
813 FL southwest (Tampa)
814 PA northwest (Altoona)
815 IL northwest (Rockford)
816 MO northwest (Kansas City)
817 TX north central (Fort Worth)
818 CA southwest (Glendale)
819 Quebec, Canada

901 TN west (Memphis)
902 Nova Scotia, Canada
903 Mexico
904 FL north (Jacksonville)
906 MI northwest (Escanaba)
907 AK
912 GA south (Savannah)
913 KS north (Topeka)
914 NY southeast (White Plains)
915 TX southwest (San Angelo)
916 CA northwest (Sacramento)
918 OK northeast (Tulsa)
919 NC east (Raleigh)

THE TELEPHONE INQUIRY

When you see an interesting airplane listed in printed advertising, or on a bulletin board, you will need to make contact with the owner. Generally, a telephone call will suffice. Sounds simple enough, but first consider what you are going to ask. Don't pretend to be an expert, but, don't be a tire kicker either. The owner wants to sell his airplane, not relive past experiences. Use the telephone and ask questions, making notes as you get answers.

Is he the owner of the airplane? If not, ask for the owner's name, address, and telephone number. *Owner* means the individual owner or dealer owner (as recorded by FAA records). If he is not the owner, but is selling the airplane for another party, he is most likely an airplane broker. Ask the year, make, and model of the plane. You would be surprised at the number of mistakes I see in airplane ads that appear in the trade magazines and papers. This way you are sure you are both talking about the same airplane. Sometimes an owner will have more than one airplane for sale. Inquire about:

- General appearance and condition of the plane?
- Total hours on the airframe?
- Make and model of engine?
- Hours on the engine since new?
- Hours since the last overhaul?
- What type of overhaul?
- Damage history?
- Asking price?
- Where can it be seen?
- What color is it?
- What is the N-number?

The last three questions will sometimes elicit evasive answers when a freelance airplane broker is involved. Often these brokers are reluctant to give out particulars about a specific airplane, as they have no real control over the plane. The plane's owner has not listed it exclusively with the freelance broker for sale, therefore the broker is afraid of losing his commission if you deal directly with the owner (which you are free to do). Airplane brokers attempt to match callers with known planes for sale and can be very useful when looking for a used airplane. Let them do the leg work and ad reading for which they receive a sales commission; sometimes from the seller, other times from the buyer, and often from both.

A broker differs from a dealer. The dealer owns the aircraft he sells and the broker does not.

Sometimes an owner who is hot to sell will fly the airplane to you for inspection. Don't ask someone to do this unless you are serious and have the money to make the purchase.

Pre-purchase inspection

The object of the pre-purchase inspection of a used airplane is to preclude the purchase of a less-than-worthy airplane. No one wants to buy someone else's troubles. The pre-purchase inspection must be completed in an orderly, well-planned manner. Take your time during this inspection, for these few minutes could well save you thousands of dollars later.

The very first item of inspection is the most-asked question of anyone selling anything: Why are you selling it? Fortunately, most people answer honestly. Often the owner is moving up to a larger airplane, and if so, he will start to tell you all about his new prospective purchase. Listen to him, you can learn a lot about the owner from what he says; gaining insight into his flying habits and how he treated the plane you are considering purchasing. Perhaps he has other commitments: spouse says, "Me or the plane," or maybe he can no longer afford the plane. Both of these reasons are common and can be to your advantage, as they create a motivated seller.

Warning: If the seller is having financial difficulties, consider the quality of maintenance done on the airplane.

Ask the seller if he knows of any problems or defects with the airplane. Again, he will probably be honest, but there could be things he doesn't know about.

Remember: Buyer beware! It's your money and your safety.

Definitions

Airworthy. The airplane must conform to the original type certificate, or those STCs (Supplemental Type Certificates) issued for this particular airplane (by serial number). In addition, the airplane must be in safe operating condition relative to wear and deterioration.

Annual Inspection. All small airplanes must be inspected annually by an FAA-certified airframe and power plant (A&P) mechanic who holds an IA (Inspection Authorization), by an FAA-certified repair station, or by the airplane's manufacturer. This is a complete inspection of the airframe, power plant, and all sub-assemblies.

100-Hour Inspection. An inspection made every 100 hours of the same scope as an annual inspection. It is required on all commercially operated small airplanes (rental, training, air taxi, and so forth). This inspection may be done by an A&P without an IA rating. An annual inspection will fulfill the 100-hour inspection requirement, but the reverse is not true.

Preflight Inspection. A thorough inspection, by the pilot, of an aircraft before flight. The purpose is to spot obvious discrepancies by inspection of the exterior, interior, and engine of the airplane.

Preventive Maintenance. FAR Part 43 lists a number of airplane maintenance operations that are preventive in nature and may be done by a certificated pilot, provided the airplane is not flown in commercial service. (These operations are described in Chapter 6.)

Repairs and Alterations. The two types of repairs and alterations are major and minor. Major repairs and alterations must be approved for return to service by an A&P mechanic holding an IA authorization, a repair station, or by the FAA. Minor repairs and alterations may be returned to service by an A&P mechanic.

PERFORMING THE INSPECTION

The pre-purchase inspection consists of a walk-around inspection, test flight, and mechanic's inspection. The purpose of the inspection is to determine what is deteriorating on the airplane from the effects of weather, stress, heat, vibration, friction, and age:

- *Weather* can affect the airplane with an arsenal of weapons including: heat, sunlight, rain, snow, wind, temperature, humidity, and ultraviolet light.
- *Stress* includes overloading of the structure causing deformation or outright structural failure from excessive landing weights, high speed maneuvers, turbulence, and hard landings.
- *Heat*, other than heat caused by weather, is engine-associated and usually causes degrading of rubber parts such as hoses and plastic fittings. It can also be associated with heat from a defective exhaust system.
- *Vibration* is caused by the engine or by fluttering of control surfaces. Damage from vibration is in the form of cracks in the aircraft structure or skin.
- *Friction* can affect any moving part of the airplane. Frictional damage can be reduced by the use of lubricants and fixed only by complete repair.
- *Age* is by years and the number of hours the plane has accumulated.

It is common for a prospective purchaser to desire a "low-time" airplane and engine, but there are times when this is detrimental. For example: the 20-year-old airplane with a mere 800 hours on the engine and airframe. This airplane could harbor considerable deterioration due to lack of use. Like human bodies, an airplane requires exercise to stay healthy. Engines and airframes, as well as most moving parts, suffer when not used on a regular basis. The low-time example used here could require an engine overhaul, considerable airframe parts replacement and lubrication, and cosmetic work.

The pre-purchase inspection is very similar to a pre-flight inspection, only more thorough. It's divided into four parts, exploring each section of the airplane: cabin, airframe, engine, and logbook.

Cabin

1. Starting in the cabin, ensure that all required paperwork is with the airplane:
   ~ Airworthiness Certificate
   ~ Aircraft Registration Certificate
   ~ FCC radio station license
   ~ Flight manual or operating limitations
   ~ Logbooks (airframe, engine(s), and propeller(s))
   ~ Equipment list and weight and balance chart
2. While inside the airplane looking for the paperwork, notice the general condition of the interior. Does it appear clean, or has it recently been scrubbed after a long period of inattention? Look in the corners, just like you would when buying a used car. Care given the interior is a good indication of what care was given to the remainder of the airplane. By the way, the interior of the typical four-place airplane can cost upwards of $3,000 to replace, some even more than that.

3. Look at the instrument panel; does it have what you want and need? Are the instruments in good condition? Any knobs missing and glass faces broken? Is the equipment all original or updated? If updates were made, are they neat in appearance and workable? Avionics updating is often done haphazardly with results that are neither pleasing to the eye nor workable for the pilot (Figs. 4-4 through 4-6).

Fig. 4-4. You won't go far with this panel, unless you are only interested in simple sport flying. And there is nothing wrong with that. Just be sure you get enough panel to do what you want.

4. Look out the windows; are they clear, unyellowed, and uncrazed? Side windows are not expensive to replace and you can usually do the job yourself. Windshields, however, are another story and another price (typically several hundred dollars—and you cannot do the work yourself).
5. Check the operation of the doors. They should close and lock with little effort and the door seals should be tight, allowing no outside light to be visible around door edges.
6. Check the seats for freedom of movement and adjustability. Check the seat tracks and the adjustment locks for damage.
7. Check the carpet for wetness or moldy condition suggesting long-term exposure to water, possibly inducing corrosion.
8. Open the rear fuselage compartment behind the seats and use a flashlight to look back towards the tail. You are looking for corrosion, dirt, debris, damage or frayed cables, loose fittings, and previously repaired areas.
9. Be on the lookout for mouse houses, usually fluffy piles of insulation, fabric, or paper materials. The biggest problem with mouse houses is that

Fig. 4-5. Although not state-of-the-art, this is a good panel with everything you would normally need.

mice have bad bathroom manners; they urinate in their beds. Mouse urine is one of the most caustic liquids known to aircraft mechanics because it eats through aluminum like battery acid. Watch for signs of it.

10. Finally, write down times shown on the tachometer and Hobbs meters, then reference them when checking the logbooks.

Airframe

1. Stand behind the airplane and look at all surfaces comparing one to another. Are they positioned as they should be or does one look out of place compared with the others? This could mean past damage and/or a

Fig. 4-6. State-of-the-art panel found in a light twin.

rigging problem. Repeat this procedure from each side and from the front of the airplane.

2. Sight along each flying and control surface looking for dents, bends, or other signs of damage. Dents, wrinkles, or tears of the metal skin might indicate prior damage, or just careless handling. An additional indicator of past damage is the cherry rivet.

3. The cherry rivet is commonly used during repairs, particularly in locations where bucking from the back would be impossible (inside wings and control surfaces). The cherry rivet is recognized by a small hole in its center, where it is pulled into itself during tightening, that does not appear on regular rivets. Note that not all cherry rivets indicate damage, as some are used during manufacture.

4. Each discrepancy found must be examined very carefully and a total of all dings and dents will reveal if the airplane has had an easy life or a rough life. Wrinkles in the skin are usually caused by hidden structural damage and should be checked by a mechanic (Figs. 4-7 and 4-8). Damaged belly skins on retractables usually mean a wheels-up landing.

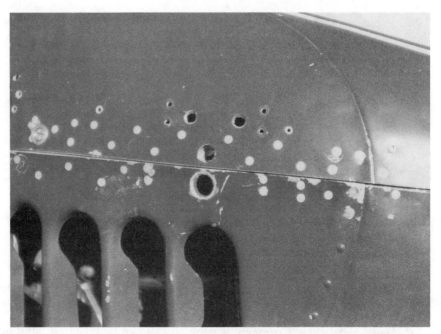

Fig. 4-7. Planes with metal parts in poor condition, such as this cowl, should be avoided.

Fig. 4-8. Repaired minor damage such as this split wheel pant will be added together in the total valuation.

5. Is the paint in good condition, or is some of it flaking onto the ground underneath the airplane (Fig. 4-9)? Paint jobs are expensive, yet necessary for the protection of metal surfaces from corrosive elements and are also pleasing to the eye of the beholder.

6. Corrosion or rust on surfaces or control systems is cause for alarm. Corrosion is to aluminum what rust is to iron. It's a form of oxidation and is

Fig. 4-9. Peeling paint can break the bank.

very destructive. Corrosion is generally shown by blistered paint (similar to a rusted car) and/or a white powdery coating of bare metal. Any signs of corrosion or rust must be brought to the attention of a mechanic for judgment.

7. Check landing gear for evidence of being sprung. Check the tires for signs of unusual wear that might indicate structural damage. Look at the oleo strut(s) for signs of fluid leakage and proper extension.

8. Move all control surfaces and check each for damage. They should be free and smooth in movement, not be loose, subject to rattle, or exhibit sideward movement (they should only move in their designed plane). When the controls are centered, the surfaces should also be centered. If they are not centered, a rigging problem exists.

9. Remove the wing root fairings and check the condition of the wiring and hoses inside. Look for mouse houses and check the wing attachment bolts.

10. Check the antennas for proper mounting and any obvious damage.

Engine

1. Look for signs of oil leakage when checking the engine. Do this by looking at the engine, inside the cowl, and on the fire wall. Oil will be dripping to the ground or onto the nose wheel, if the leaks are bad enough. Assume that the seller has cleaned all the old drips away and remember that oil leaves stains; look for these stains (Fig. 4-10).

2. Check all hoses and lines for signs of deterioration or chafing and assure that all the connections are tight and that there are no indications of leak-

Fig. 4-10. Removing the engine cowling makes inspection easy.

age. Examine the baffles for proper shape, alignment, and tightness. Baffles control the airflow for engine cooling and if they are improperly positioned the engine will not be properly cooled. The long-term result of poor baffling is damage to the engine.

3. Check control linkages and cables for obvious damage and easy movement and the battery box and battery for corrosion.

4. Examine the exhaust pipes for rigidity, then reach inside and rub your finger along the inside wall. If your finger comes back perfectly clean, you can assume that someone washed the inside of the pipe(s) to remove any telltale deposits that had accumulated there (Fig. 4-11). Oily or sooty deposits can be caused by a carburetor in need of adjustment or a large amount of oil blow-by. The latter shows an engine in need of major expenditures for overhaul. A light gray dusty coating means proper engine operation.

5. Check for exhaust stains on the belly of the plane to the rear of the stacks. This area has probably been washed, but look anyway. If you find black oily goo, then, as above, see a mechanic (Fig. 4-12).

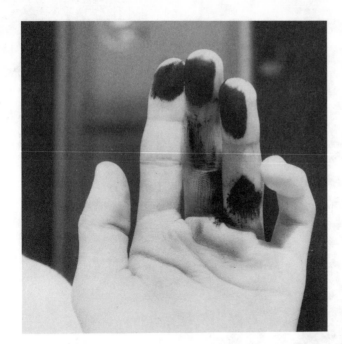

Fig. 4-11. Goo on the fingers like this means a mechanic should check the engine.

Fig. 4-12. A dark trail from the exhaust stack calls for a mechanic to check the engine.

6. Inspect the propeller for damage such as nicks, cracks, or gouges. These (often small) defects cause stress areas on the propeller and require checking by a mechanic. Also, observe any movement that could suggest propeller looseness at the hub.
7. Look for oil change or other maintenance stickers. Compare the times written on these stickers with those you wrote down from the tachometer and Hobbs meter. Copy the additional sticker information for later referral to logbooks.

Logbooks

1. If you are satisfied with what you've seen up to this point, then go back to the cabin and have a seat. Pull out the logbooks and start reading them. Be sure that you're looking at the proper logs for this particular aircraft, determine that they are the original logs, and verify serial numbers of the airframe, engine, and equipment listed for the airplane.
2. Sometimes logbooks get lost and must be replaced by new ones because of carelessness or theft. The latter is the reason that many owners keep photocopies of their logs in the aircraft and the originals in a safe place. Replacement logs often lack very important information or could be outright frauds. Fraud is always a distinct possibility, so be on guard if the original logs are not available. In the event of missing original logbooks, a complete check of the airplane's FAA records will provide most of the missing information.
3. Look in the back of the airframe logbook for AD compliance. Check that it's up-to-date and that any required periodic inspections have been done. Then return to the most recent entry, generally an annual or 100-hour inspection. The annual inspection will be a statement that reads:

March 27, 1991   Total Time: 2,815 hrs.

I certify that this aircraft has been inspected in accordance with an annual inspection and was determined to be in airworthy condition.

[signed]

[IA # 0000000]

4. From this point, back to the first entry in the logbook you'll be looking for similar entries, always keeping track of the total time for continuity purposes and to show the regularity of usage (number of hours flown between inspections). Also, you will be looking for statements about major repairs and modifications. The latter will be flagged by the phrase, Form 337 filed. A copy of Form 337 should be with the logs and will explain what work was completed; the work may be described in the log-

book also. Form 337 is filed with the FAA and copies become a part of the official record of each airplane which are retrievable from the FAA.

5. Review the current weight and balance sheet with the logbook and with equipment you see (radios, etc.). The engine logbook will be similar to the airframe logbook and will contain information from the annual or 100-hour inspections. Total time will be noted and possibly an indication of time since any overhaul work, although you may have to do some math here. It's quite possible that this log and this engine are not the originals for the aircraft. As long as the facts are well-documented in the logs, there is no cause for alarm. After all, this would be the case if the original engine was replaced with a rebuilt engine.

6. Check the engine's ADs for compliance and the appropriate entires in the log.

7. Pay particular attention to the numbers that show the results of a differential compression check. These numbers can say a lot about the overall health of the engine. Each cylinder checked is represented by a fraction, with the bottom number always 80. The 80 is the air pressure (pounds per square inch) utilized for the check, which is the industry standard. The top number is the air pressure that the combustion chamber maintained while tested; 80 would be perfect, but is unattainable and therefore the top figure will always be less.

   The lesser number is caused by air pressure loss resulting from loose, worn, or broken rings, scored or cracked cylinder walls, or burned, stuck, or poorly seated valves. A mechanic can determine which is the cause of the lack of compression and, of course, repair the damage.

   Normal readings are in the 70s, with a minimum of 70/80, and should be uniform (within two or three pounds) for all cylinders. A discrepancy between cylinders could indicate the need for a top overhaul of one or more cylinders. The FAA says that a loss in excess of 25 percent is cause for further investigation. That would be a reading of 60/80, from a very tired engine in need of much work and much money.

   If the engine had a top or major overhaul (or any repairs), there will be a description of the work done, a date, and the total time on the engine when the work was completed.

8. Read the information from the last oil change, which might contain a statement about debris found on the oil screen or in the oil filter. Oil changes, however, are often done by owners, and may or may not be recorded in the log (all preventive maintenance is required to be logged). How often was the oil changed? Every 25 hours shows excellent care, but every 50 hours is acceptable. Oil is cheap insurance for a long engine life. If there is a record of oil analysis, ask for it. Oil analysis can indicate internal engine wear problems.

9. Get your notebook out and cross-check those meter readings and the information from the engine maintenance stickers.

Test flight

The test flight is a short flight to determine if the airplane feels right to you. It is not meant to be a "rip-snort'n—slam-bang—shake-down-ride." I suggest that either the owner or a competent flight instructor accompany you on the test flight to eliminate problems of currency and ratings with the FAA and the owner's insurance company (the plane *is* insured isn't it?). It will also foster better relations with the owner.

Start the engine and pay particular attention to the gauges. Do they jump to life or are they sluggish? Watch the oil pressure gauge in particular. Did the pressure rise within a few seconds of start? Scrutinize the other gauges. Is everything "green"? Watch them during the ground runup, then again during the takeoff and climb out. Do the numbers match those specified in the operational manual?

Operate all avionics. This might require flight to an airport that is equipped for IFR operations. A short cross-country jaunt would be an excellent chance to get familiar with the plane. Observe the gyro instruments for stability. Study the ventilation and heating system for proper operation. Make a few turns, some stalls, and fly level. Does the airplane perform as expected? Can it be trimmed for hands-off flight?

Return to the airport for a couple of landings. Watch for improper brake operation and nosewheel shimmy.

Park the plane, shut the engine down, and open the engine compartment to again look for oil leaks. Look along the belly for signs of oil leakage and blow-by. A short flight should be enough to dirty things up again.

Mechanic's inspection

If you are still satisfied with the airplane and want to pursue the matter further, have it inspected by an A&P or IA. The inspection will not be free, but it could save thousands of your dollars. The average for a pre-purchase inspection is three to four hours labor at shop rates.

The mechanic will do a search of ADs, a full review of the logs, and an overall analysis of the airplane. An engine compression check and a borescope examination must be done. A borescope is the best means of determining the real condition of the engine combustion chambers. It is an optical device used for looking into each cylinder and viewing the top of the piston, the valves, and the cylinder walls.

POINTS OF ADVICE

Always use your personal mechanic for the pre-purchase inspection; someone *you* are paying to watch out for *your* interests, not someone who might have an interest in the sale of the plane, such as an employee of the seller. Get the plane checked even if the annual was just done, unless you know and trust the mechanic who did the annual inspection. You might be able to make a deal with the owner regarding the cost of the mechanic's inspection, particularly if an annual is due.

It is not uncommon to see airplanes listed for sale with the phrase "annual on date of sale." I'm always leery of this because who knows how complete this annual will be? I know that the FARs are very explicit in their inspection requirements, but I am not sure that all mechanics do equal work. To make matters worse, this annual is part of the airplane deal—done by the seller as part of the sale. Who is looking out for your interests?

Thanks but no thanks

If an airplane seller refuses anything that has been mentioned in this chapter, then thank him for his time, walk away, and look elsewhere. Never let a seller control the situation. Your money, your safety, and possibly your very life are at stake. Airplanes are not hot sellers, and there is rarely a line forming to make a purchase. You are the buyer and have the final word.

5

As you purchase

IF YOU HAVE COMPLETELY INSPECTED the prospective purchase and found the airplane acceptable at an agreeable price, you're ready to sit down and complete the paperwork that will lead to airplane ownership.

THE TITLE SEARCH

The first step in the paperwork of purchasing an airplane is to ensure that the airplane has a clear title. This can only be done by a title search, performed by checking the plane's individual records at the Mike Monroney Aeronautical Center in Oklahoma City, Oklahoma. These records include title information, chain of ownership, major repair and alteration (Form 337) information, and other data pertinent to a particular airplane. The FAA files this information by N-number in individual folders for each airplane. It is not an automated system at this time; however, in the future the FAA will move into the modern computer era with the rest of the world.

The object of a title search is to make sure that there are no liens or other hidden encumbrances against clear ownership of the airplane. The search may be conducted by you, your attorney, or other personal representative. Most prospective airplane purchasers find it inconvenient to travel to Oklahoma City to research the FAA's files themselves; instead, they contract with a third party specializing in title search service. As well as doing aircraft title searches, title clearing, 337s, registered owners, and so forth, these service providers usually offer inexpensive title insurance that will protect the purchaser against unrecorded liens, FAA recording mistakes, or other "clouds" on the title. Contact:

AOPA
Aircraft and Airmen Records Dept.
P.O. Box 19244
Southwest Station
Oklahoma City, OK 73144
(800) 654-4700

King Aircraft Title, Inc.
1411 Classen Blvd. Suite 114
Oklahoma City, OK 73106
(800) 688-1832

LAST LOOK

Before taking possession of the airplane, make one last inspection before signing *any* documents. This will confirm that no new damage has occurred and that any items questioned during the pre-purchase inspection have been repaired.

Documents

The following documents must be presented with the airplane at the time of sale:

☐ Airworthiness certificate
☐ Airframe logbook
☐ Engine logbook(s)
☐ Propeller logbook(s)
☐ Equipment list (including weight and balance data)
☐ Flight manual

Assistance

Many forms must be completed and, although they are not complicated, you may desire assistance in completing them; check with your FBO or call another party:

- *AC Form 8050–2, Bill of Sale*, is the standard means of recording the transfer of ownership (Figs. 5-1 and 5-2).

FORM APPROVED
OMB NO. 2120-0042

UNITED STATES OF AMERICA
DEPARTMENT OF TRANSPORTATION — FEDERAL AVIATION ADMINISTRATION

AIRCRAFT BILL OF SALE INFORMATION

PREPARATION: Prepare this form in duplicate. Except for signatures, all data should be typewritten or printed. *Signatures must be in ink.* The name of the purchaser must be identical to the name of the applicant shown on the application for aircraft registration

When a trade name is shown as the purchaser or seller, the name of the individual owner or co-owners must be shown along with the trade name.

If the aircraft was not purchased from the last registered owner, conveyances must be submitted completing the chain of ownership from the last registered owner, through all intervening owners, to the applicant.

REGISTRATION AND RECORDING FEES: The fee for issuing a certificate of aircraft registration is $5.00. An additional fee of $5.00 is required when a conditional sales contract is submitted in lieu of bill of sale as evidence of ownership along with the application for aircraft registration ($5.00 for the issuance of the certificate, and $5.00 for recording the lien evidenced by the contract). The fee for recording a conveyance is $5.00 for each aircraft listed thereon. (There is no fee for issuing a certificate of aircraft registration to a governmental unit or for recording a bill of sale that accompanies an application for aircraft registration and the proper registration fee.)

MAILING INSTRUCTIONS:

If this form is used, please mail the original or copy which has been signed in ink to the FAA Aircraft Registry, P.O. Box 25504, Oklahoma City, Oklahoma 73125.

AC Form 8050-2 (8-85) (0052-00-629-0002)

Fig. 5-1. AC Form 8050-2 Bill of Sale instructions.

UNITED STATES OF AMERICA
DEPARTMENT OF TRANSPORTATION FEDERAL AVIATION ADMINISTRATION

FORM APPROVED
OMB NO. 2120-0042

AIRCRAFT BILL OF SALE

FOR AND IN CONSIDERATION OF $ THE
UNDERSIGNED OWNER(S) OF THE FULL LEGAL
AND BENEFICIAL TITLE OF THE AIRCRAFT DES-
CRIBED AS FOLLOWS:

UNITED STATES
REGISTRATION NUMBER N

AIRCRAFT MANUFACTURER & MODEL

AIRCRAFT SERIAL No.

DOES THIS   DAY OF   19
HEREBY SELL, GRANT, TRANSFER AND
DELIVER ALL RIGHTS, TITLE, AND INTERESTS
IN AND TO SUCH AIRCRAFT UNTO:

Do Not Write In This Block
FOR FAA USE ONLY

PURCHASER

NAME AND ADDRESS
(IF INDIVIDUAL(S), GIVE LAST NAME, FIRST NAME, AND MIDDLE INITIAL.)

DEALER CERTIFICATE NUMBER

AND TO   EXECUTORS, ADMINISTRATORS, AND ASSIGNS TO HAVE AND TO HOLD
SINGULARLY THE SAID AIRCRAFT FOREVER, AND WARRANTS THE TITLE THEREOF.

IN TESTIMONY WHEREOF   HAVE SET   HAND AND SEAL THIS   DAY OF   19

NAME (S) OF SELLER (TYPED OR PRINTED)	SIGNATURE (S) (IN INK) (IF EXECUTED FOR CO-OWNERSHIP, ALL MUST SIGN.)	TITLE (TYPED OR PRINTED)

SELLER

ACKNOWLEDGMENT   (NOT REQUIRED FOR PURPOSES OF FAA RECORDING: HOWEVER, MAY BE REQUIRED
BY LOCAL LAW FOR VALIDITY OF THE INSTRUMENT.)

ORIGINAL: TO FAA

AC FORM 8050-2 (8-85) (0052-00-629-0002)

Fig. 5-2. AC Form 8050-2 Bill of Sale.

- *Form 8050–1, Aircraft Registration*, is filled with the Bill of Sale. If you are
  purchasing the airplane under a contract of conditional sale, then that contract must accompany the registration application in lieu of the AC Form
  8050–2. The pink copy of the registration is retained by you and will

remain in the airplane until the new registration is issued by the FAA (Figs. 5-3 and 5-4).

- *AC 8050—41, Release of Lien,* must be filed by the seller if he still owes money on the airplane.

FORM APPROVED
OMB No. 2120-0042

UNITED STATES OF AMERICA-DEPARTMENT OF TRANSPORTATION
FEDERAL AVIATION ADMINISTRATION-MIKE MONRONEY AERONAUTICAL CENTER
AIRCRAFT REGISTRATION INFORMATION

PREPARATION: Prepare this form in triplicate. Except for signatures, all data should be typewritten or printed. Signatures must be in ink. The name of the applicant should be identical to the name of the purchaser shown on the applicant's evidence of ownership.

EVIDENCE OF OWNERSHIP: The applicant for registration of an aircraft must submit evidence of ownership that meets the requirements prescribed in Part 47 of the Federal Aviation Regulations. AC Form 8050-2, Aircraft Bill of Sale, or its equivalent may be used as evidence of ownership. If the applicant did not purchase the aircraft from the last registered owner, the applicant must submit conveyances completing the chain of ownership from the registered owner to the applicant.

The purchaser under a CONTRACT OF CONDITIONAL SALE is considered the owner for the purpose of registration and the contract of conditional sale must be submitted as evidence of ownership.

A corporation which does not meet citizenship requirements must submit a certified copy of its certificate of incorporation.

REGISTRATION AND RECORDING FEES: The fee for issuing a certificate of aircraft registration is $5; therefore, a $5 fee should accompany this application. An additional $5 recording fee is required when a conditional sales contract is submitted as evidence of ownership. There is no recording fee for a bill of sale submitted with the application.

MAILING INSTRUCTIONS: Please send the WHITE original and GREEN copy of this application to the Federal Aviation Administration Aircraft Registry, Mike Monroney Aeronautical Center, P.O. Box 25504, Oklahoma City, Oklahoma 73125. Retain the pink copy after the original application, fee, and evidence of ownership have been mailed or delivered to the Registry. When carried in the aircraft with an appropriate current airworthiness certificate or a special flight permit, this pink copy is temporary authority to operate the aircraft.

CHANGE OF ADDRESS: An aircraft owner must notify the FAA Aircraft Registry of any change in permanent address. This form may be used to submit a new address.

AC Form 8050-1 (3/90) (0052-00-628-9006) Supersedes Previous Edition

---

Fig. 5-3. AC Form 8050-1 Aircraft Registration instructions.

FORM APPROVED
OMB No. 2120-0042

UNITED STATES OF AMERICA DEPARTMENT OF TRANSPORTATION
FEDERAL AVIATION ADMINISTRATION-MIKE MONRONEY AERONAUTICAL CENTER
AIRCRAFT REGISTRATION APPLICATION

CERT. ISSUE DATE

UNITED STATES REGISTRATION NUMBER **N**	
AIRCRAFT MANUFACTURER & MODEL	
AIRCRAFT SERIAL No.	

FOR FAA USE ONLY

TYPE OF REGISTRATION (Check one box)

☐ 1. Individual ☐ 2. Partnership ☐ 3. Corporation ☐ 4. Co-owner ☐ 5. Gov't. ☐ 8. Non-Citizen Corporation

NAME OF APPLICANT (Person(s) shown on evidence of ownership. If individual, give last name, first name, and middle initial.)

TELEPHONE NUMBER: (   )

ADDRESS (Permanent mailing address for first applicant listed.)

Number and street: _____

Rural Route:		P.O. Box:	
CITY	STATE		ZIP CODE

☐ **CHECK HERE IF YOU ARE ONLY REPORTING A CHANGE OF ADDRESS**
    ATTENTION! Read the following statement before signing this application.
    This portion MUST be completed.

A false or dishonest answer to any question in this application may be grounds for punishment by fine and / or imprisonment (U.S. Code, Title 18, Sec. 1001).

CERTIFICATION

I/WE CERTIFY:

(1) That the above aircraft is owned by the undersigned applicant, who is a citizen (including corporations) of the United States.

(For voting trust, give name of trustee: _____), or:

CHECK ONE AS APPROPRIATE:

a. ☐ A resident alien, with alien registration (Form 1-151 or Form 1-551) No. _____

b. ☐ A non-citizen corporation organized and doing business under the laws of (state) _____ and said aircraft is based and primarily used in the United States. Records or flight hours are available for inspection at _____

(2) That the aircraft is not registered under the laws of any foreign country; and

(3) That legal evidence of ownership is attached or has been filed with the Federal Aviation Administration.

NOTE: If executed for co-ownership all applicants must sign. Use reverse side if necessary.

TYPE OR PRINT NAME BELOW SIGNATURE

EACH PART OF THIS APPLICATION MUST BE SIGNED IN INK.	SIGNATURE	TITLE	DATE
	SIGNATURE	TITLE	DATE
	SIGNATURE	TITLE	DATE

NOTE   Pending receipt of the Certificate of Aircraft Registration, the aircraft may be operated for a period not in excess of 90 days, during which time the PINK copy of this application must be carried in the aircraft.

AC Form 8050-1 (3/90) (0052-00-628-9006) Supersedes Previous Edition

Fig. 5-4. AC Form 8050-1 (keep the pink copy in the plane).

- *AC 8050 – 64, Assignment of Special Registration Number*, will be issued upon written request. All N-numbers consist of the prefix N, followed by one to five numbers, one to four numbers and a single letter suffix, or one to three numbers and a two-letter suffix. A special registration number is similar to a personalized license plate for an automobile, sometimes called a vanity plate (Fig. 5-5).

	ASSIGNMENT OF SPECIAL REGISTRATION NUMBERS	Special Registration Number N
US Department of Transportation	Aircraft Make and Model	Present Registration Number
Federal Aviation Administration	Serial Number	N

Issue Date

This is your authority to change the United States registration number on the above described aircraft to the special registration number shown.

Carry a duplicate of this form on the aircraft together with the old registration certificate as interim authority to operate the aircraft pending receipt of revised certificate of registration. Obtain a revised certificate of airworthiness from your nearest Flight Standards field office.

The latest FAA Form 8130-6, Application For Airworthiness on file is dated

The airworthiness classification and category

SAMPLE

SIGN AND RETURN THE ORIGINAL of this form to the FAA Aircraft Registry, within 5 days after placing the special registration number on the aircraft. A revised certificate will then be issued. Unless this authority is used and this office so notified, the authority for use of the special number will expire on

CERTIFICATION: I certify that the special registration number was placed on the aircraft described above.

Sign . of Owner:	RETURN FORM TO:
Title of Owner:	FAA Aircraft Registry
Date Placed on Aircraft	P.O. Box 25504 Oklahoma City, Oklahoma 73125 -4939

BELOW THIS POINT FOR FAA USE ONLY

1. ☐ FP NAME
2. ☐ NF
ADDRESS

CITY   FC   ZIP   EMP CODE   DATE

AC Form 8050-64 (12/87)

- *FCC (Federal Communications Commission) Form 404, Application for Aircraft Radio Station License*, must be completed if radio transmitting (COM or NAV/COM) equipment is on board. The tear-off section will remain in the airplane as a temporary authorization until the new license arrives (Figs. 5-6 and 5-7).

It is also good practice to have a sales contract signed by all parties stating prices, terms of sale, and any warranties provided.

The AOPA, for a small fee, will provide closing services via telephone, then prepare and file the necessary forms to complete the transaction. This is particu-

---
Federal Communications Commission
Gettysburg, PA 17326

APPLICATION FOR AIRCRAFT RADIO STATION LICENSE

Approved by OMB
3060-0040
Expires 4/30/92

- Read instructions above before completing application.   • Use typewriter or print clearly in ink.
- Sign and date application.   • Place First Class Postage on the reverse side of the card and mail.

| 1. FAA Registration or FCC Control Number.
(If FAA Registration is not required
for your aircraft, explain in item 8.)   **N** | 2. Is application for a fleet license? ☐ No   ☐ Yes
If yes, give the number of aircraft in fleet,
including planned expansion......................... |

3. Type of applicant (check one)

☐ I—Individual   ☐ C—Corporation

☐ P—Partnership   ☐ D—Individual with
                          Business Name

☐ A—Association   ☐ G—Governmental entity

4. Applicant/Licensee Name (See Instructions)

5. Mailing Address (Number and Street, P.O. Box or Route No., City, State, ZIP Code)

6. Frequencies Requested (check appropriate box(es) in 6A and/or 6B.)

6A. DO **NOT** CHECK BOTH BOXES

☐ A—Private Aircraft   ☐ C—Air Carrier

6B. ADDITIONAL INFORMATION IS REQUIRED IF YOU CHECK HERE (See Instructions)

☐ T—Flight Test HF   ☐ V—Flight Test VHF   ☐ P—Portable   ☐ O—Other (Specify)

7. Application is for:

☐ New Station   ☐ Renewal
☐ Modification

8. Answer space for any required statements

9. READ CAREFULLY BEFORE SIGNING: 1. Applicant waives any claim to the use of any particular frequency regardless of prior use by license or otherwise. 2. Applicant will have unlimited access to the radio equipment and will control access to exclude unauthorized persons. 3. Neither applicant nor any member thereof is a foreign government or representative thereof. 4. Applicant certifies that all statements made in this application and attachments are true, complete, correct and made in good faith. 5. Applicant certifies that the signature is that of the individual, or partner, or officer or duly authorized employee of a corporation, or officer who is a member of an unincorporated association, or appropriate elected or appointed official on behalf of a governmental entity.

| WILLFUL FALSE STATEMENTS MADE ON THIS FORM
ARE PUNISHABLE BY FINE AND/OR IMPRISONMENT
U.S. CODE TITLE 18, SECTION 1001 | 10. Signature | Date |

FCC 404
September 1989

Fig. 5-6. FCC Form 404 Application for Aircraft Radio Station License (send this to the FCC).

Federal Communications Commission
Gettysburg, PA 17326

TEMPORARY AIRCRAFT RADIO STATION
OPERATING AUTHORITY

Approved by OMB
3060-0040
Expires 4/30/92

Use this form if you want a temporary operating authority while your regular application, FCC Form 404, is being processed by the FCC. This authority authorizes the use of transmitters operating on the appropriate frequencies listed in Part 87 of the Commission's Rules.

- DO NOT use this form if you already have a valid aircraft station license.
- DO NOT use this form when renewing your aircraft license.
- DO NOT use this form if you are applying for a fleet license.
- DO NOT use this form if you do not have an FAA Registration Number.

ALL APPLICANTS MUST CERTIFY:

1. I am not a representative of a foreign government.
2. I have applied for an Aircraft Radio Station License by mailing a completed FCC Form 404 to the Federal Communications Commission, P.O. Box 1040, Gettysburg, PA 17326.
3. I have not been denied a license or had my license revoked by the FCC.

4. I am not the subject of any adverse legal action concerning the operation of a radio station.
5. I will ensure that the Aircraft Radio Station will be operated by an individual holding the proper class of license or permit required by the Commission's Rules.

WILLFUL FALSE STATEMENTS VOID THIS PERMIT AND ARE PUNISHABLE BY FINE AND/OR IMPRISONMENT.

| Name of Applicant (Print or Type) | Signature of Applicant |
| FAA Registration Number (Use as Temporary Call Sign) | Date FCC Form 404 Mailed |

Your authority to operate your Aircraft Radio Station is subject to all applicable laws, treaties and regulations and is subject to the right of control of the Government of the United States. This authority is valid for 90 days from the date the FCC Form 404 is mailed.

YOU MUST POST THIS TEMPORARY OPERATING AUTHORITY ON BOARD YOUR AIRCRAFT

NOTICE TO INDIVIDUALS REQUIRED BY PRIVACY ACT OF 1974 AND THE PAPERWORK REDUCTION ACT OF 1980
Sections 301, 303 and 308 of the Communications Act of 1934, as amended, (licensing powers) authorize the FCC to request the information on this application. The purpose of the information is to determine your eligibility for a license. The information will be used by FCC staff to evaluate the application, to determine station location, to provide information for enforcement and rulemaking proceedings and to maintain a current inventory of licensees. No license can be granted unless all information requested is provided. Your response is required to obtain this authorization.

Fig. 5-7. FCC Form 404 Temporary Aircraft Radio Station Operating Authority (retain this in your plane).

larly convenient if the parties involved in the transaction are spread all over the country, which would be the case when purchasing an airplane long distance.

Another source of help in completing the necessary paperwork is a bank, particularly if that bank has a vested interest in your airplane (they hold the lien)! Many banks will not accept a title search unless they requested it. The search may well be completed by the same organization you contracted with, but don't worry, you'll get to pay for this one, too. One way or another, banks charge the customer for everything.

Who really owns the airplane

Fraudulent airplane ownership is a rising problem. Although not as widespread a blight as auto theft, each instance can result in aggravation, embarrassment, and expense.

An old tale. An example of the simplest form of title fraud is when you pay for an airplane and another person's name appears on the title, unbeknownst to you. The story goes like this:

> A student pilot finds an airplane he wants and makes a deal with the owner. Funds change hands and a local flight instructor is asked to complete the paperwork. Fraud enters the picture when the instructor places his name on the FAA forms as the owner, takes the airplane, and is never seen again.

This old story has been flying around the hangar circuit for years, but it is something to think about. Other methods of fraud exist, both by omission and commission.

Links of ownership. The chain of ownership follows the paperwork filed with the FAA; no other paperwork is acknowledged as proof of ownership. This means that if ownership was not changed with the FAA, then technically, ownership never changed. For example:

> Mr. Smith sells his Piper Cub to Mr. Adams in 1983. Mr. Adams dies in 1988 leaving the airplane as part of his estate. The airplane is subsequently advertised for sale, and Mr. Kent decides to purchase it. Mr. Kent runs a title check on the Cub and finds that the airplane is owned by Mr. Smith, not the estate of Mr. Adams.

How could this happen? Simple! Mr. Adams never completed or filed the paperwork necessary to make the change with the FAA. Ownership will have to be cleared before Mr. Kent can purchase the airplane. Most likely he will need legal assistance.

Fixing responsibility. A new specter in ownership fraud is fixing financial responsibility in the event of injury. The latter in the form of property damage or personal injury. An example:

> You are upgrading to a larger airplane. You sell your trusty Ercoupe to Mr. Benson. The necessary papers are completed and presented with the air-

plane at the time of sale. The next time you hear about the Ercoupe is when you are served papers in a lawsuit. It seems the airplane crashed and several people were injured on the ground. Mr. Benson never filed the paperwork with the FAA and you are still listed as the legal owner. The injured parties are seeking redress for their losses.

Make copies of all papers related to the sale (and purchase) of an aircraft and save them for future reference. With proper copies as proof of sale, and an attorney's help, you should survive this type of legal action.

Outright theft. The registration numbers and general appearance of stolen aircraft are often altered, making simple detection difficult. The stolen airplane is then listed for sale through a broker with a place of business and good reputation. The broker, through no fault of his own, is ignorant of the theft and sells the airplane to an unsuspecting buyer. As follows:

Mr. Cody selects Piper N1234A from an airplane broker's inventory. He gets a title check and finds there are no "clouds" on the title. All appears in order and Mr. Cody makes the purchase. Four months later the FBI shows up and interviews Mr. Cody. They explain that he is the victim of fraud; the real N1234A is in the Midwest. The airplane Mr. Cody purchased was stolen from Southern California, renumbered, and sold.

The Piper will be returned to its rightful owner; Mr. Cody will have no airplane, and will be out a considerable sum of money. He may have recourse against the broker; however, it will be a costly battle.

Too good. Some things are just too good to be true, and, as mortal humans we sometimes cannot see this and will jump at such offers. So goes this story:

You are seated in the airport lounge one afternoon when a sharp-looking Cessna 210 lands. The pilot enters and asks if anyone is interested in purchasing his airplane. The price is unusually low and the plane looks good. You check the plane, fly it, and wind up purchasing it. The pilot represents himself as the owner listed on the aircraft's papers. However, the real owner is in Florida for the winter and the airplane was stolen by the pilot from a small airport in the Northwest.

It is likely that the fraud won't be exposed until the airplane is reported stolen in the spring when the owner returns from Florida. The FBI will visit and take the airplane, leaving you with memories and an empty wallet.

All those little pieces

Some used airplanes are rebuilds constructed from many parts around an aircraft data plate (the metal information plate containing the make/model and serial number). This happens when an unscrupulous person purchases, or otherwise obtains, the logbooks and data plate for a plane that has been wrecked or scrapped. A plane to match the data plate is constructed from assorted parts, possibly from other wrecks.

Often, the logbooks will not reflect the full extent of the repairs made. Unfortunately, some planes reconstructed in this fashion will never fly properly, while others are downright dangerous to take into the air. The average purchaser can easily be fooled by a reconstruction job, this is why he should have a mechanic inspect any airplane being considered for purchase.

Self defense

How do you protect yourself? Where can you turn for assistance in making sure everything is as represented? Actually there is no single easy answer. These suggestions may, however, help avoid a problematic situation:

1. Purchase from a known individual or dealer. Ask for positive ID.
2. Check serial numbers of the airframe, engine, propeller, and avionics against the logs, paperwork, and title search information.
3. If you are not dealing directly with the owner, contact him/her on the telephone or in person and ask him if it is indeed his airplane at which you are looking.
4. Do a title check and purchase title insurance.
5. If the deal appears too good to be true, it probably is!
6. When selling an airplane, do a title check 90 days after the sale to assure title transference to the new owner.

If anyone gets upset, so what! *You* are protecting *your* interests. If something is wrong, back out of the deal. Take care of number one! You might even wish to call the authorities and report any suspicious activity.

INSURANCE

Insure your airplane from the moment you sign on the dotted line. No one can afford to take risks. For the purposes of airplane ownership you will be concerned with two types of insurance, liability and hull.

Liability insurance protects you, or your heirs, in instances of claims against you resulting from your operation of an airplane for bodily injury or property damage. It is generally true that if someone is injured or killed as a result of your flying you will be sued, even if you are not at fault.

Hull insurance protects your investment from loss caused by nature, by fire, by theft, by vandalism, or while being operated. Lending institutions require hull insurance for their protection.

A couple of insurance pits to avoid

Beware of the policies with exclusions. Some policies use exclusions to avoid payoff in the event of a loss, for instance by a requirement that all installed equipment be functioning properly during operation. For example:

A survivable accident occurs after an engine malfunction. During the post-crash investigation the insurance company discovers the ADF wasn't working properly. They refuse to pay for the loss because they require all installed equipment to be functioning properly during flight operations. The fact that the nonworking ADF had nothing to do with the cause of the accident is, in their eyes, irrelevant. Another exclusion example—and all too often seen—says no payment will be made if any FARs have been violated.

Avoid policies that have parts replacement limitations or exclusions, or other specific rules, setting maximum predetermined values for replacement airframe parts. Sometimes called a *component parts schedule*, such policies limit the amount paid for replacement parts and can leave you holding the bag for the difference of the sum paid by the insurance company and the actual cost of repair parts.

Limits

Beware of the policy that states: $1 million total coverage with per-seat limits of $100,000. If you own a two-place airplane your $1 million passenger liability limits are effectively reduced to only $100,000. After all, you only carry one other person in a two-placer. Combined single limit is the recommended coverage, then you don't have to deal with per-seat limits and know your total coverage from the very start.

Always read the policy carefully and understand the exclusions. Ask questions about the policy, demand changes, even refuse the policy. Do whatever is necessary to get the coverage you desire. Careful selection of insurance coverage can save money; however, the savings must be based on solidly informed decisions. Discuss your specific needs with an experienced aviation insurance agent. During your discussion about coverage include questions about in motion, not in motion, in flight, not in flight, and ground risk only losses. Understand your coverage completely.

Check various aviation publications for telephone numbers of aviation underwriters; many list toll-free telephone numbers. Consult with more than one company because services, coverage, and rates do differ. Ask other pilot/owners about their insurance and how well they have been served by the agents/companies they purchase coverage from. If your bank has an aviation department, check with them about the reputations of insurance companies.

Other insurance

Examine your personal health and life insurance policies. Be sure you are covered while flying a small airplane. It is not uncommon to find exclusions in personal policies that will leave you completely uncovered in the event of injury or death while flying a small airplane.

GETTING THE AIRPLANE HOME

In most cases you, the new owner, will fly the airplane home to where it will be based. However, in some instances the plane will be flown by the past owner or a dealer. Whatever the case may be, be sure the pilot is qualified to handle the airplane, legally and technically.

- *Legally* means rated and current for the particular airplane, possessing a current medical, and covered by insurance.
- *Technically* means that an individual can actually handle the airplane in a safe and proper manner.

In some instances the purchased aircraft might not be legal to fly because of damage or an outdated annual inspection. If that is the case, contact the FAA office nearest where the aircraft is located. They can arrange a Special Flight Permit, generally called a *ferry permit*, which allows an otherwise airworthy aircraft to be flown to a specified destination one time, one way. Before flying an aircraft on a ferry permit, check with your insurance company to ensure that you and your investment will be covered if there is a loss.

Local regulations

Many states and local jurisdictions register and tax aircraft. Remember, ignorance of the law does not excuse you from compliance. Appendix D contains a list of various state aviation agencies. Contact your respective state agency for information regarding additional rules and regulations.

6

After you purchase

AN AIRPLANE OWNER MUST RECOGNIZE that proper care of his airplane directly influences the well-being of the financial investment and the safety aspects of flight. Care includes: proper maintenance, storage, and cleaning. Fortunately, most steps taken for financial reasons also aid the safety aspect; the opposite is also true.

MAINTENANCE

All airplanes need maintenance, repairs, and inspections. In general, service work is expensive; however, there are ways to save money and learn about your airplane in the process.

FINDING A GOOD FBO

When considering an FBO, check with other airplane owners and see what they think and who they like (Fig. 6-1). In selecting an FBO ask these questions:

- ☐ How long has he been in business?
- ☐ What is the quality of his work?
- ☐ Are his prices reasonable?
- ☐ Does he provide quick service?
- ☐ Can you discuss problems with him?
- ☐ Is he an authorized dealer for your make of airplane?
- ☐ Is flight instruction available?
- ☐ Can he service avionics?

These are important points to consider; however, the easiest and quickest means of sizing up an FBO is to examine the facility. Do the buildings look clean and well-kept and does the area offer proper physical security for an airplane?

Fig. 6-1. This nice general aviation airport is located in Frederick, Md. and offers all services including a place to eat.

Servicing your own plane

In accordance with regulations, preventive maintenance is simple or minor preservation operations and the replacement of small standard parts not involving complex assembly operations.

FARs (Federal Aviation Regulations) specify that preventive maintenance may be done by the pilot of an airplane not used in commercial service. All preventive maintenance work must be done in such a manner, and by use of materials of such quality, that the airframe, engine, propeller, or assembly worked on, will be at least equal to its original condition according to regulations.

I strongly advise that before you undertake any of the allowable preventive maintenance procedures, discuss your planned work with a licensed mechanic. The advice you receive will help you avoid costly mistakes. You may have to pay a consultation fee, but it will be money well spent. Besides, the mechanic's time is his money and you should not expect him to be very free with it.

FAR Part 43, Appendix A lists the allowable preventive maintenance items. *Only* those operations listed are considered preventive maintenance. Those applicable to powered airplanes are:

- ☐ Removal, installation, and repair of landing gear tires.
- ☐ Replacing elastic shock absorber cords (bungees) on landing gear.
- ☐ Servicing landing gear struts by adding oil, air, or both.
- ☐ Servicing landing gear wheel bearings, such as cleaning and greasing.
- ☐ Replacing defective safety wiring or cotter pins.
- ☐ Lubrication not requiring disassembly other than removal of non-structural items such as cover plates, cowlings, and fairings.
- ☐ Making simple fabric patches not requiring rib-stitching or the removal of structural parts or control surfaces.
- ☐ Replenishing hydraulic fluid in the hydraulic reservoir.
- ☐ Refinishing decorative coatings of the fuselage, wing, and tail-group surfaces (excluding balanced control surfaces), fairings, cowlings, landing gear, cabin, or cockpit interior when removal or disassembly of any primary structure or operating system is not required.
- ☐ Applying preservative or protective material to components when no disassembly of any primary structure or operating system is involved and when such coating is not prohibited or is not contrary to good practices.
- ☐ Repairing upholstery and decorative furnishings of the cabin or cockpit when it does not require disassembly of any primary structure or operating system, does not interfere with an operating system, or affect the primary structure of the aircraft.
- ☐ Making small, simple repairs to fairings, non-structural cover plates, cowlings, and small patches, and reinforcements not changing the contour so as to interfere with the proper airflow.
- ☐ Replacing side windows where that work does not interfere with the structure or any operating system, such as controls, electrical equipment, and so forth.
- ☐ Replacing safety belts.
- ☐ Replacing seats or seat parts with replacement parts approved for the aircraft, not involving disassembly of any primary structure or operating system.
- ☐ Troubleshooting and repairing broken landing light wiring circuits.
- ☐ Replacing bulbs, reflectors, and lenses of position and landing lights.
- ☐ Replacing wheels and skis where no weight and balance computation is required.
- ☐ Replacing any cowling not requiring removal of the propeller or disconnection of flight controls.
- ☐ Replacing or cleaning spark plugs and setting of spark plug gap clearance.
- ☐ Replacing any hose connection except hydraulic connections.
- ☐ Replacing prefabricated fuel lines.
- ☐ Cleaning fuel and oil strainers.

☐ Replacing batteries and checking fluid level and specific gravity.

☐ Replacement of nonstructural standard fasteners incidental to operations.

Required logbook entries

Entries must be made in the appropriate logbook whenever preventive maintenance is done. The aircraft cannot *legally fly* without the logbook entry, which must include a description of work, the date completed, the name of the person doing the work, and approval for return to service (signature and certificate number) by the pilot approving the work.

Tools

A minimum number of quality tools should allow the owner to do preventive maintenance operations on his airplane:

- Multipurpose Swiss Army knife
- 3/8" ratchet drive with a flex head as an option
- 2, 4, or 6" drive extensions
- Sockets from 3/8" to 3/4" in 1/16" increments
- 6" crescent wrench
- 10" monkey wrench
- 6- or 12-point closed (box) wrenches from 3/8" to 3/4"
- Set of open-end wrenches from 3/8" to 3/4"
- Pair of channel lock pliers (medium size)
- Phillips screwdriver set in the three common sizes
- Flathead screwdriver set short (2") to long (8") sizes
- Plastic electrician's tape
- Container of assorted approved nuts and bolts
- Spare set of spark plugs
- A bag or box is handy to keep tools in order and protected

The FAA encourages pilots and owners to carefully maintain their airplanes and recognizes that properly done preventive maintenance provides the pilot or owner a better understanding of the airplane, saves money, and offers a great sense of accomplishment. If an FBO voices concerns about your doing preventive maintenance (on your own airplane), Advisory Circular 150/5190-2A states, in part:

"Restrictions on Self-Service: Any unreasonable restriction imposed on the owners and operators of aircraft regarding the servicing of their own aircraft and equipment may be considered a violation of agency policy. The owner of an aircraft should be permitted to fuel, wash, repair, paint, and otherwise take care of his own aircraft, provided there is no attempt to perform such services for others. Restrictions which have the effect of diverting activity of this type to a commercial enterprise amount to an exclusive right contrary to law."

With these words the FAA has allowed the owner of an aircraft to save his hard-earned dollars, and to become very familiar with his airplane, which no doubt contributes to safety.

One last point of information many pilots and owners fail to understand is the maintenance statement found in FAR 91.163(a): "The owner or operator of an aircraft is primarily responsible for maintaining that aircraft in an airworthy condition . . . ." Put very simply, your mechanic is not primarily responsible for the mechanical condition of your airplane, you, as the pilot/owner, are responsible.

STORAGE

Proper aircraft storage is more than mere parking in a hangar or at a tiedown. Unfortunately, too many pilots pay little heed to the requirements of proper storage of their airplanes during periods of nonuse. Sad but true, the majority of small airplanes are stored outdoors because hangar space is limited at most airports. When found, hangar space is very expensive. It is not uncommon to find a two-to-five-year waiting list for hangar space.

Tiedown

Basic airplane storage is a tiedown. I don't think there is a pilot anywhere not familiar with the basics of proper tiedown. After all, most trainer airplanes are tied down and the pre-flight and post-flight parts of each lesson include untying and tying the plane down (Fig. 6-2).

Fig. 6-2. If you don't tie your airplane down this can happen.

An airplane should be parked facing into the wind, if possible. This is not always feasible because many airports have engineered tiedown systems with predetermined aircraft placement. A proper tiedown must include secure anchors such as concrete piers with metal loops on their top surface. Each anchor must provide a minimum of 3,000 pounds (4,000 pounds for light twins) holding power. Three anchors are used for each airplane.

Some airports use an anchor and cable system for tiedowns. This consists of stout steel cables connecting properly installed anchors in two long parallel lines. The lines are approximately one airplane length apart. Airplanes are parked perpendicular to the cables, allowing the wings to be tied to one cable and the tail to the other cable. All planes are parked side-by-side, oftentimes facing in alternate directions (Fig. 6-3).

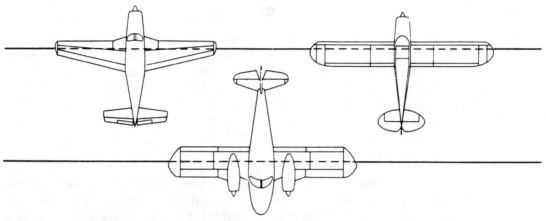

Fig. 6-3. Typical airport anchor and cable system (from FAA AC20-35C).

Tiedown ropes must have a minimum 3,000 pounds tensile strength (4,000 pounds for twins). The use of nylon or Dacron ropes is recommended over natural fiber ropes such as manila, which tends to shrink when wet and is prone to rot and mildew. Chains or steel rope can be used if care is taken to prevent damage at the tiedown points on the airplane. Fasten tiedowns only to those points on the aircraft designed for the purpose. This mean use the tiedown rings, not just any handy surface (Fig. 6-4).

Fig. 6-4. Use the proper tie points (from FAA AC20-35C).

Cover the pitot tube and fuel vents to keep insects and debris out, plug or cover nacelles or the cowling to discourage birds from building nests in the engine compartment, and lock control surfaces with an internal control lock or fasten gust locks on the control surfaces to prevent movement during windy conditions. Mark all external control surface locks with colorful ribbons as a reminder to remove them before flight.

A few don'ts

- Don't depend upon wooden stakes driven into the ground for tiedown anchors.
- Don't use the wing struts for tiedown points.
- Don't use cheap or lightweight rope for tiedowns.
- Don't leave an airplane parked and not tied down.
- Don't forget to lock the controls.

Heat and sunlight protection

Research shows us that the interior temperature of a parked aircraft can reach as much as 185°F. This heat buildup will not only affect avionics, but it will cause problems with instrument panels, upholstery, and a variety of other plastic items. It is for this reason that many aircraft tied down outside have a cover over the windshield, either inside or outside.

An inside cover's metallic-like reflective surface protects the plane's interior and reduces heat by reflecting the sun's rays. The shields (covers) attach to the interior of the aircraft with Velcro fasteners (Fig. 6-5).

Fig. 6-5. Interior window covers reflect the sunlight and help to reduce interior temperatures.

Exterior covers will provide similar protection for the cabin interior, and provide additional exterior protection for refueling caps and fresh-air vents. They also protect expensive window surfaces from blowing debris (Fig. 6-6).

Fig. 6-6. An exterior aircraft cover keeps out sunlight and protects window surfaces from airborne debris.

Hangars

The two types of indoor storage are the large hangar and the individual hangar. The individual hangar is generally called a *Tee-hangar* because of its shape. Many owners prefer Tee-hangars because they offer more security for the airplane. Security means one airplane stored in the hangar, therefore no one has access to the airplane without your knowledge. Also, there is less exposure to airplane thieves and vandals. The dreaded disease *hangar rash* is generally averted with private hangar storage.

Hangar rash is associated with large hangars and occurs when planes are carelessly handled by non-caring ground personnel. In short, they get banged into one another, into walls, and equipment. The result is numerous small dings, dents, and scratches (Fig. 6-7).

An often forgotten point of indoor storage is the hours of airplane accessibility. The hangar will be locked when the FBO is closed, requiring prior arrangements for access during unusual hours. Of course the plane stored in an individual hangar is accessible at anytime.

Fig. 6-7. Hangar rash comes from careless moving in tight quarters.

NONUSE OF THE AIRPLANE

Nothing is worse for an airplane than sitting on the ground unused. Of course this is true of all mechanical things, but particularly so for airplanes.

All too often I see airplanes parked for months on end without ever moving. Then one day the terror-of-the-air arrives at the airport, sticks his finger into the wind and says, "Let's go flying." He does a quick swing around the plane assuring that both wings are still attached, unties it, jumps in and starts it up, and madly rushes off into the wild blue yonder, all without a care about what has been happening to the airplane while it sat unattended.

Engines in aircraft that are flown only occasionally tend to exhibit more cylinder wall corrosion than engines in aircraft that are flown on a regular basis. The recommended method of preventing cylinder wall corrosion and other corrosion is to fly the aircraft at least weekly. While flying, the engine warms to operating temperature, which vaporizes moisture and other by-products of combustion that can cause engine damage.

Proper storage and preservation techniques are a must, but are not done by many owners. As you shall see, these procedures take time and effort. Some people don't, for one reason or another, wish to extend themselves. Yet, without proper care, the airplane value will be reduced and flying safety impaired. Aircraft storage recommendations are broken down into three categories:

- Flyable storage, used infrequently
- Temporary storage, up to 90 days of nonuse
- Indefinite storage, over 90 days of nonuse

Flyable storage

Most modern aircraft are built of corrosion-resistant Alclad aluminum that will last indefinitely under normal conditions, if kept clean. However, Alclad aluminum is subject to oxidation (corrosion); the first indication of which is the formation of white deposits or spots on metal surfaces. The corrosion can resemble white dust or take on a linty look on bare metal and cause discoloration or blistering of painted surfaces. Storage in a dry hangar is essential for good preservation and should be procured if possible.

Minimum care of the engine calls for a weekly propeller pull-through and, at a minimum, a flight once every 30 days. The propeller should be rotated by hand without starting the engine. For four-and six-cylinder non-geared engines, rotate the propeller six revolutions, then stop the propeller 45 degrees to 90 degrees from the original position. For six-cylinder geared engines, rotate the propeller four revolutions and stop the propeller 30 degree to 60 degrees from the original position.

The monthly flight must have a minimum 30-minute duration to assure that the engine has reached normal oil and cylinder temperatures. Ground run-up is not an acceptable substitute for flight.

Temporary storage

When an airplane will remain inoperative for a period not exceeding 90 days, it becomes necessary to take specific measures to protect it from the elements.

☐ Fill the fuel tanks with the correct grade of fuel.

☐ Clean and wax the aircraft.

☐ Clean any grease and oil from the tires and coat them with a tire preservative.

☐ Cover the nosewheel to protect it from oil drips.

☐ Block up the fuselage to remove the weight from the tires.

☐ Cover all airframe openings to keep vermin, insects, and birds out.

☐ Remove the top spark plug and spray preservative oil at room temperature through the upper spark plug hole of each cylinder with the piston roughly in bottom dead center position. Rotate the crankshaft as each pair of opposite cylinders is sprayed. Stop the crankshaft with no piston at top dead center. Re-install spark plugs.

☐ Apply preservative to the engine interior by spraying approximately two ounces of preservative oil through the oil filler tube.

☐ Seal all engine openings exposed to the atmosphere using suitable plugs or moisture-resistant tape. Attach red streamers at each sealed location.

Indefinite storage

An aircraft unused in excess of 90 days must be completely preserved. The following steps outline the basics of such preservation which represents loads of work at considerable expense. Before beginning, consult with a mechanic.

☐ Drain the engine oil and refill with MIL-C-6259 Type II oil. The aircraft should then be flown for 30 minutes, reaching, but not exceeding, normal oil and cylinder temperatures. Allow the engine to cool to ambient temperature.

☐ Do everything required in Temporary Storage except replacing the spark plugs.

☐ Install dehydrator plugs in each of the top spark plug holes and make sure that each plug is blue in color when installed. Protect and support the spark plug leads.

☐ If the engine is equipped with a pressure-type carburetor: Drain the carburetor by removing the drain and vapor vent plugs from the regulator and fuel control unit. With the mixture control in Rich position, inject lubricating oil into the fuel inlet, at a pressure not to exceed 10 p.s.i. (pounds per square inch), until oil flows from the vapor vent opening. Allow excess oil to drain, plug the inlet, and tighten the drain and vapor vent plugs. Wire the throttle in the open position, place bags of desiccant in the intake, and seal the opening with moisture-resistant paper and tape, or a cover plate.

☐ Place a bag of desiccant in the exhaust pipes and seal the openings with moisture-resistant tape.

☐ Seal the cold-air inlet to the heater muff with moisture-resistant tape to exclude moisture and foreign objects.

☐ Seal the engine breather by inserting a dehydrator plug in the breather hose and clamping in place.

☐ Lubricate all airframe items.

☐ Remove the battery and store it in a cool, dry place.

☐ Place covers over the windshield and rear windows.

☐ Engines, with propellers installed, that are preserved for storage in accordance with this section should have a tag affixed to the propeller in a conspicuous place with the following notation on the tag:

DO NOT TURN PROPELLER—ENGINE PRESERVED
PRESERVATION DATE _____

Periodic examinations are necessary for aircraft placed in indefinite storage. Engines should have the cylinder dehydrator plugs visually inspected every 15 days and replaced as soon as the color indicates unsafe conditions for storage. If the dehydrator plugs have changed color on one-half or more of the cylinders, all desiccant material on the engine should be replaced.

The cylinder bores of all engines prepared for indefinite storage should be resprayed with a corrosion-preventive mixture every six months; more frequently if a bore inspection shows corrosion has started. Before spraying, the engine should be checked for corrosion by inspecting the interior of at least one cylinder on each engine through the spark plug hole. If the cylinder shows rust, spray the cylinder with corrosion preventive oil and turn the prop over six times, then respray all cylinders. Remove at least one rocker box cover from each engine and inspect the valve mechanism. Replace all desiccant packets and dehydrator plugs at this time.

Return to service

Preparation of the airplane for a return to service requires an inspection by a mechanic. The following steps are also necessary:

- ☐ Remove the aircraft from the blocks and check the tires for proper inflation.
- ☐ Check the nose strut for proper inflation.
- ☐ Remove all covers and plugs, and inspect the interior of the airframe for debris and foreign matter.
- ☐ Clean and inspect the exterior of the aircraft.
- ☐ Remove the cylinder dehydrator plugs, tape,and desiccant bags used to preserve the engine.
- ☐ Drain the corrosive preventive mixture and fill with recommended lubricating oil.
- ☐ If the carburetor has been preserved with oil, drain it by removing the drain and vapor vent plugs from the regulator and fuel control unit. With the mixture control in rich position, inject service-type gasoline into the fuel inlet, at a pressure not to exceed 10 p.s.i., until all of the oil is flushed from the carburetor. Re-install the carburetor plugs and attach the fuel line.
- ☐ With the bottom plugs removed, rotate the propeller to clear excess preservative oil from the cylinders. Re-install the spark plugs and rotate the propeller by hand through compression strokes of all cylinders to check for possible liquid lock.
- ☐ Install the battery.

☐ Thoroughly clean and visually inspect the airplane.
☐ Start the engine in the normal manner.
☐ Test flight per airframe manufacturer's instructions.

Disclaimer: The aforementioned procedures are generic recommendations applicable to many general aviation aircraft. For particulars on a specific airplane, check the service manual.

Lots of work

As you can see, nonuse of an airplane can be complicated and expensive. My recommendation for an airplane owner not planning to use his plane for a period in excess of three months is to sell it. You are not getting your money's worth from the airplane, and the lack of use will cost you maintenance dollars in the long run.

CLEANING THE AIRPLANE

Normal upkeep of any airplane requires cleanliness. Cleaning means everything from wash and wax of the exterior to proper car of the interior. The results will be a sharp-looking airplane that you can be proud of.

Cleaning the exterior

Exterior care of an airplane is not only important in the sense of appearance and value, but in safety as well. While cleaning the airplane you will notice small imperfections and minor damage, which can be corrected before they become big problems. Complete washing with automotive-type cleaners will produce acceptable results and be less expensive than using aircraft cleaners. Automotive wax will also provide adequate protection for painted or unpainted surfaces. The term wax (for our purposes) means new space-age silicone preparations called sealers.

Inside cleaning. The interior of an airplane is seen by everyone, including the pilot and his passengers. It is also used by everyone and therefore is a problem to keep clean. My recommendation is a very thorough cleaning by use of standard automobile cleaning methods.

Cleaning aids. Purchasing specialty cleaning products with the word a-i-r-p-l-a-n-e as part of the product name or description can be very expensive. The following items are available at most grocery stores or automotive supply houses, are reasonable in cost, and work well:

Spray cleaner is a heavy duty cleaner for the hard-to-remove stuff. Keep it away from the windshield, instruments, and painted surfaces.

Engine cleaner degreases the engine area and oleo struts. It dissolves grease and can be washed off with water. When using it in the engine compartment, cover the magnetos and alternator with plastic bags to keep the cleaner and rinse water out. Engine cleaner is also good for cleaning the plane's belly. It is reasonably safe on painted surfaces if rinsed per instructions.

Spray lubricant made with silicon stops squeaks and eases movement. It's good on cables, controls, seat runners, and doors. Keep it off the windows.

Rubbing compound cleans away exhaust stains. Use it carefully or you could remove more than just stains.

Touch-up paint may be difficult to find since many airplane colors are unavailable in small quantities for touch-up use. However, don't despair because any good automotive supply house (and some department stores) have inexpensive cans of spray paint to match almost any automotive color. Try to find one that closely matches your airplane's paint color. Remember that a touch-up is just that, not a complete re-paint job, and don't expect it to be more. Touching-up small blemishes and chips protects the airframe and improves the appearance slightly.

Spray furniture wax is invaluable for use on hard plastic surfaces such as instrument panels and other vinyl-covered objects.

Liquid resin rubber/vinyl cleaners are excellent for upholstery and other flexible surfaces. The surfaces will look and smell like new but may be very slippery.

Vacuum cleaners are essential for cleaning an airplane. Sweeping will not do the job.

Note that no window cleaners were mentioned. This is one area where you should only use products designed for cleaning airplane windows. Automotive and household products contain chemicals that are harmful to the plastics used in aviation.

AIRCRAFT THEFT

Theft of airplanes and equipment is something the owner must guard against at all times. Not just in the South and Southwest where airplanes are stolen for drug running, but in all areas of the country.

Theft prevention

An owner can do several things to protect his investment from thieves. Among these are the use of various devices designed to prevent the operation of the ignition switch, throttle, controls, or a combination of them. On the exterior of the airplane, special wheel locks or propeller locks may be installed. However, no device will provide complete protection. The determined thief will counter the measures and steal the airplane. The idea is to make the airplane undesirable to the thief because it will take too much time to fly away and thieves prefer not to linger for very long.

Equipment thefts have been on the upswing for several years, and no doubt will continue. This is a problem seen more near large urban areas than at small country airports. Contributing factors could be that better equipped and more sophisticated aircraft are concentrated in a smaller area (one airport) and that there are more thieves in metropolitan areas. Both factors probably go hand-in-hand.

A type of thievary presently occurring involves the theft of radio equipment with the thief replacing that stolen with similar but other stolen equipment. You could go on for months or years and never notice the swap that had been made. This delay can make tracing equipment ownership nearly impossible.

Certain preventive measures will aid in the prevention of equipment theft:

- Mark installed equipment (avionics) with a driver's or pilot's license number.
- Park in well-lighted areas. The dark corner of a deserted airport affords little protection for the airplane.
- Use covers inside the windows to keep prying eyes out.
- Use a *radio alert* burglar alarm. These systems have been installed at a few airports with great success. Ask the FBO if it is available.
- Photograph the instrument panel. This will show what equipment was installed, preventing any quibbling with the insurance company in the event of a loss.
- Keep your logbooks in a secure place. There are no requirements for them to be kept in the airplane, only that they be made available for inspection upon request. Many owners keep copies in the plane.
- Maintain a list of serial numbers and other data pertaining to your plane's equipment.

Destruction

A sad problem the airplane owner faces today is the outright destruction of equipment that is protected by anti-theft devices or markings. If the thief can't have it, they feel you shouldn't either. This, of course, applies to cars, boats, and nearly everything we work hard for.

How to report airplane theft

In the event your airplane is stolen, you must report the loss to the proper authorities as soon as possible. The less delay when reporting, the greater the chances of prompt recovery of the aircraft.

1. Immediately report the theft to the local law enforcement agency with jurisdiction over the airport. This will cause the aircraft's registration number to be entered into the NCIC (National Crime Information Center) computer data base. It will also cause a notice of the theft (called "a lookout") to be flashed among local jurisdictions.

2. Request the officer taking the report to notify the nearest FAA Flight Service Station of the theft. This will alert the air traffic control system of the theft and the information will be sent to all airports and centers.
3. Notify your insurance company of the loss.

Part II

Used airplane fleet

The following pages contain the photographs and specifications for most of the used airplanes you will find on today's market. There are, however, a few makes and models that have not been included due to their scarcity. You will notice that, with few exceptions, the airplanes included have an average value of under $60,000.

Specifications and performance information are as accurate as possible, having come from the FAA, manufacturers, and owner organizations. However, keep in mind that each airplane is an individual example of the art, and may or may not meet the exact data presented. Additionally, many older airplanes have been modified to perform well beyond original performance data.

Complete performance data is not presented for every make and model due to the typically small changes in the specifications and performance data from year to year; significant changes are noted.

7

Two-place airplanes

MOST PILOTS ARE QUITE FAMILIAR with two-place airplanes. After all, the majority of us learned to fly in a two-place trainer.

Two-placers come in two basic styles: tandem seating (one person sits behind the other) and side-by-side (both occupants sit beside each other, often quite snugly).

For most of these airplanes the key word is simplicity. They have small, efficient engines, few moving parts, and minimal required maintenance, all totaling up to lower costs.

Some of the older two-placers, due to their age and type of construction (tube and fabric), are considered to be representative of a bygone era. Examples are the Piper J3, Aeronca 7AC, and the Taylorcraft BC-12D. But wait a minute, today's manufacturers are again producing airplanes of those types. In fact, the Christen Husky was introduced in 1987 (very similar to the Super Cub), the Super Cub was produced into the middle 1980s, and the Taylorcraft was brought back into production in 1991. Well, I guess you can see that these old classic airplanes are not so old after all. They represent good solid flying, and pilots still want that, even if the airplanes happen to be 40 years old.

Most modern two-place airplanes are all metal in construction and can give reasonable speed performance and represent loads of affordable simple flying fun. Some models are aerobatic approved.

Other two-place airplanes are as modern as today; some even with many of the complexities found on larger airplanes: retractable landing gear, variable-pitch props, large engines, and more. The all-metal Swift, from the 1940s is such an example.

You will, no doubt, notice that many of these airplanes have the nosewheel "on the tail. " This is called *conventional landing gear*. There was a time when all airplanes had conventional landing gear, now most have tricycle gear. Arguments rage about which is better, and I suppose the question will never be settled. The point is that anyone can be competent with either. So, never forsake an airplane just because it has conventional gear. You can learn to handle it.

AERONCA

Aeronca airplanes were among the most popular trainers of the postwar period. Although not many are seen today as trainers, they do make inexpensive sport planes.

All Aeronca two-place airplanes are of tube and fabric design. The airframe is made of a welded steel tube structure that is covered with fabric. The wings are also covered with fabric. Coverings were originally Grade-A cotton cloth; today, most examples are covered with one of the new synthetic products.

Aeroncas are fun and easy to fly and are among the least expensive airplanes to operate. Although rather slow by today's standards, you can see what you're flying over. All Aeroncas (with one exception) have conventional landing gear, but don't let that scare you because they're honest little airplanes that display few bad habits.

Planes in the 7 Champ series were based upon the WWII TA Defender and the L3 Liaison plane. The 7AC had the A-65 Continental 65-hp engine. Although some were built with Franklin or Lycoming engines, most today have the Continental. The 7ACs, often referred to as Airknockers, were produced from 1945 through 1948. All were painted yellow, with red trim. According to historical records, Aeronca once produced 56 Champs in one day. The usual time to build one was 291 man-hours. The original price was $2,999.

The 7CCM with the 90-hp Continental engine was introduced in 1948. It had a slightly larger fin than the 7AC and a few minor structural changes. The military configuration of this plane was the L-16B.

The 7EC was the last try for Aeronca. Major changes included a Continental C-90-12F engine, electrical system, and metal propeller.

All told, more than 7,200 Champs were built before production was halted. There are many around and rare is the small airport where you would not see at least one.

Aeronca also built the 11 Chief series with a wider body than the Champ which seated two, side-by-side. Like the Champ, it was powered by a Continental A-65 engine. An updated version, the 11CC Super Chief powered by a Continental C-85-8F with a metal propeller, was introduced in 1947.

As with so many of the postwar era planes, a good design was hard to kill. Aeronca was a good design and in 1954 the Champion Aircraft Company of Osceola, Wisconsin, was formed reintroducing the Aeronca 7EC model as the champion Traveler. The new 7EC was upholstered, carpeted, and had a propeller spinner.

A tricycle gear version, called the 7FC Tri-Traveler, was built for a short period of time. There is nothing unusual about these fine little planes, just an Airknocker with a nosewheel. Unfortunately, their popularity was never that of the Piper or Cessna competition.

A new Champ series started with the 7GC in 1959. These planes were produced with various engines. All display good short field capabilities.

- 7GC, 1959, Lycoming 140-hp engine
- 7GCB, 1960–64, Lycoming 150-hp engine
- 7GCBC, long-wing version of 7GCB (with flaps)

Citabria airplanes emerged in 1964. Citabria is "airbatic" spelled backwards. They, like their predecessors, have been very popular planes. Of course model numbers changed with engines:

- 7ECA, 1964–65, Continental 100-hp
- 7ECA, 1966–71, Lycoming 115-hp
- 7GCAA, 1965–77, Lycoming 150-hp
- 7KCAB, 1967–77, Lycoming 150-hp, (fuel injected)

Bellanca, another old name in airplane manufacturing, merged with Champion in 1970. They continued producing the Champion line, then attempted to introduce a very low-cost airplane, the 7ACA. It was built to sell for $4,995 and had a two-cylinder Franklin 60-hp engine. It was never popular, and few exist today.

The Decathlon 8KCAB series, with a newly designed wing and bigger engine, was introduced in 1971. The new wing featured near-symmetrical airfoil, shorter span, and wider cord than the Citabria wing. This, coupled with the 6G positive and 5G negative flight load limits, and the inverted engine system, made the Decathlon perfect for aerobatics. It was available in 150-hp or 180-hp.

The last entry from Bellanca was the 8GCBC Scout. It is a strong-hearted workhorse built for pipeline/power line patrol and ranching; several fish and game departments also fly them.

Look for these airplanes under Aeronca, Champion, and Bellanca (Figs. 7-1 through 7-6).

Fig. 7-1. Aeronca 7AC Champ.

Make: Aeronca   Model: 7AC Champ
Year: 1945 – 48
Engine
    Make: Continental (Lycoming and Franklin alternates)
    Model: A-65
    Horsepower: 65
    TBO: 1800 hours
Speeds
    Maximum: 95 mph
    Cruise: 86 mph
    Stall: 38 mph
Fuel capacity: 13 gallons
Rate of climb: 370 fpm
Transitions
    Takeoff over 50-foot obstacle: NA
    Ground run: 630 feet
    Landing over 50-foot obstacle: NA
    Ground roll: 880 feet
Weights
    Gross: 1220 pounds
    Empty: 740 pounds
Seats: Two tandem
Dimensions
    Length: 21 feet 6 inches
    Height: 7 feet
    Span: 35 feet

Make: Aeronca   Model: 7CCM Champ
Year: 1947 – 50
Engine
    Make: Continental
    Model: C-90
    Horsepower: 90
    TBO: 1800 hours
Speeds
    Maximum: 103 mph
    Cruise: 90 mph
    Stall: 42 mph
Fuel capacity: 19 gallons
Rate of climb: 650 fpm
Transitions
    Takeoff over 50-foot obstacle: NA
    Ground run: 475 feet
    Landing over 50-foot obstacle: NA
    Ground roll: 850 feet

Weights
    Gross: 1300 pounds
    Empty: 810 pounds
Seats: Two tandem
Dimensions
    Length: 21 feet 6 inches
    Height: 7 feet
    Span: 35 feet

Fig. 7-2. Aeronca 11AC Chief.

Make: Aeronca   Model: 11AC Chief
Year: 1946 – 47
Engine
    Make: Continental
    Model: C-65
    Horsepower: 65
    TBO: 1800 hours
Speeds
    Maximum: 90 mph
    Cruise: 83 mph
    Stall: 38 mph
Fuel capacity: 15 gallons
Rate of climb: 360 fpm
Transitions
    Takeoff over 50-foot obstacle: NA
    Ground run: 580 feet
    Landing over 50-foot obstacle: NA
    Ground roll: 880 feet
Weights
    Gross: 1250 pounds
    Empty: 786 pounds

Seats: Two side by side
Dimensions
    Length: 20 feet 4 inches
    Height: 7 feet
    Span: 36 feet 1 inch

Make: Aeronca   Model: 11CC Super Chief
Year: 1947–49
Engine
    Make: Continental
    Model: C-85
    Horsepower: 85
    TBO: 1800 hours
Speeds
    Maximum: 102 mph
    Cruise: 95 mph
    Stall: 40 mph
Fuel capacity: 15 gallons
Rate of climb: 600 fpm
Transitions
    Takeoff over 50-foot obstacle: NA
    Ground run: 720 feet
    Landing over 50-foot obstacle: NA
    Ground roll: 880 feet
Weights
    Gross: 1350 pounds
    Empty: 820 pounds
Seats: Two side by side
Dimensions
    Length: 20 feet 7 inches
    Height: 7 feet
    Span: 36 feet 1 inch

Make: Champion   Model: 7-EC/FC (90) Traveler/Tri-Traveler
Year: 1955–62
Engine
    Make: Continental
    Model: C-90
    Horsepower: 90
    TBO: 1800 hours
Speeds
    Maximum: 135 mph
    Cruise: 105 mph
    Stall: 44 mph
Fuel capacity: 24 gallons
Rate of climb: 700 fpm

Fig. 7-3. Champion Tri-Traveler.

Transitions
    Takeoff over 50-foot obstacle: 980 feet
    Ground run: 630 feet
    Landing over 50-foot obstacle: 755 feet
    Ground roll: 400 feet
Weights
    Gross: 1450 pounds
    Empty: 860 pounds
Seats: Two tandem
Dimensions
    Length: 21 feet 6 inches
    Height: 7 feet 2 inches
    Span: 35 feet 2 inches

Make: Champion   Model: 7-EC/FC (150) Traveler/Tri-Traveler
Year: 1961–62
Engine
    Make: Continental
    Model: O-320
    Horsepower: 150
    TBO: 2000 hours
Speeds
    Maximum: 135 mph
    Cruise: 125 mph
    Stall: 44 mph
Fuel capacity: 24 gallons
Rate of climb: 900 fpm

Transitions
     Takeoff over 50-foot obstacle: 630 feet
     Ground run: 375 feet
     Landing over 50-foot obstacle: 755 feet
     Ground roll: 400 feet
Weights
     Gross: 1500 pounds
     Empty: 968 pounds
Seats: Two tandem
Dimensions
     Length: 21 feet 6 inches
     Height: 7 feet 2 inches
     Span: 35 feet 2 inches

Fig. 7-4. Champion 7ECA.

Make: Champion   Model: 7-ECA (100) Citabria
Year: 1964–65
Engine
     Make: Continental
     Model: O-200
     Horsepower: 100
     TBO: 1800 hours
Speeds
     Maximum: 117 mph
     Cruise: 112 mph
     Stall: 51 mph
Fuel capacity: 35 gallons
Rate of climb: 650 fpm
Transitions
     Takeoff over 50-foot obstacle: 890 feet
     Ground run: 480 feet

Landing over 50-foot obstacle: 755 feet
Ground roll: 400 feet
Weights
Gross: 1650 pounds
Empty: 980 pounds
Seats: Two tandem
Dimensions
Length: 22 feet 7 inches
Height: 6 feet 7 inches
Span: 33 feet 5 inches

Make: Champion   Model: 7-ECA (115) Citabria
Year: 1966 – 84
Engine
Make: Lycoming
Model: O-235
Horsepower: 115
TBO: 2000 hours
Speeds
Maximum: 119 mph
Cruise: 114 mph
Stall: 51 mph
Fuel capacity: 35 gallons
Rate of climb: 725 fpm
Transitions
Takeoff over 50-foot obstacle: 716 feet
Ground run: 450 feet
Landing over 50-foot obstacle: 775 feet
Ground roll: 400 feet
Weights
Gross: 1650 pounds
Empty: 1060 pounds
Seats: Two tandem
Dimensions
Length: 22 feet 7 inches
Height: 6 feet 7 inches
Span: 33 feet 5 inches

Make: Champion   Model: 7GC series
Year: 1959 – 84
Engine
Make: Lycoming
Model: O-320 (O-290-A2B 1959 only)
Horsepower: 150 (140 1959 only)
TBO: 2000 hours (1500 1959 only)

Speeds
    Maximum: 130 mph
    Cruise: 128 mph
    Stall: 45 mph
Fuel capacity: NA
Rate of climb: 1145 fpm
Transitions
    Takeoff over 50-foot obstacle: 475 feet
    Ground run: 296 feet
    Landing over 50-foot obstacle: 690 feet
    Ground roll: 310 feet
Weights
    Gross: 1650 pounds
    Empty: 1150 pounds
Seats: Two tandem
Dimensions
    Length: 22 feet 8 inches
    Height: 6 feet 7 inches
    Span: 34 feet 3 inches

Make: Champion   Model: 7KCAB Citabria
Year: 1967–77
Engine
    Make: Lycoming
    Model: IO-320-E2A
    Horsepower: 150
    TBO: 2000 hours
Speeds
    Maximum: 133 mph
    Cruise: 125 mph
    Stall: 50 mph
Fuel capacity: 39 gallons
Rate of climb: 1120 fpm
Transitions
    Takeoff over 50-foot obstacle: 535 feet
    Ground run: 375 feet
    Landing over 50-foot obstacle: 755 feet
    Ground roll: 400 feet
Weights
    Gross: 1650 pounds
    Empty: 1060 pounds
Seats: Two tandem
Dimensions
    Length: 22 feet 8 inches
    Height: 6 feet 7 inches
    Span: 33 feet 5 inches

Make: Bellanca   Model: 7-ACA Champ
Year: 1971–72
Engine
    Make: Franklin
    Model: 2A-120-B
    Horsepower: 60
    TBO: 1500 hours
Speeds
    Maximum: 98 mph
    Cruise: 83 mph
    Stall: 39 mph
Fuel capacity: 13 gallons
Rate of climb: 400 fpm
Transitions
    Takeoff over 50-foot obstacle: 900 feet
    Ground run: 525 feet
    Landing over 50-foot obstacle: NA
    Ground roll: 300 feet
Weights
    Gross: 1220 pounds
    Empty: 750 pounds
Seats: Two tandem
Dimensions
    Length: 21 feet 9 inches
    Height: 7 feet
    Span: 35 feet 1 inch

Miller Flying Service

Fig. 7-5. Bellanca 8-KCAB Decathlon.

Make: Bellanca   Model: 8-KCAB (150) Decathlon
Year: 1971 – 80
Engine
    Make: Lycoming
    Model: IO-320 (opt. C/S propeller)
    Horsepower: 150
    TBO: 2000 hours
Speeds
    Maximum: 147 mph
    Cruise: 137 mph
    Stall: 54 mph
Fuel capacity: 40 gallons
Rate of climb: 1000 fpm
Transitions
    Takeoff over 50-foot obstacle: 1450 feet
    Ground run: 840 feet
    Landing over 50-foot obstacle: 1462 feet
    Ground roll: 668 feet
Weights
    Gross: 1800 pounds
    Empty: 1260 pounds
Seats: Two tandem
Dimensions
    Length: 22 feet 11 inches
    Height: 7 feet 8 inches
    Span: 32 feet

Make: Bellanca   Model: 8-KCAB (180) Decathlon
Year: 1977 – 84
Engine
    Make: Lycoming
    Model: AEIO-360-H1A
    Horsepower: 180
    TBO: 1400 hours
Speeds
    Maximum: 158 mph
    Cruise: 150 mph
    Stall: 54 mph
Fuel capacity: 40 gallons
Rate of climb: 1230 fpm
Transitions
    Takeoff over 50-foot obstacle: 1310 feet
    Ground run: 710 feet
    Landing over 50-foot obstacle: 1462 feet
    Ground roll: 668 feet

Weights
    Gross: 1800 pounds
    Empty: 1315 pounds
Seats: Two tandem
Dimensions
    Length: 22 feet 11 inches
    Height: 7 feet 8 inches
    Span: 32 feet

Fig. 7-6. Bellanca 8-GCBC Scout.

Make: Bellanca   Model: 8-GCBC Scout
Year: 1974 – 84
Engine
    Make: Lycoming
    Model: O-360-C2E (opt. C/S propeller)
    Horsepower: 180
    TBO: 2000 hours
Speeds
    Maximum: 135 mph
    Cruise: 122 mph
    Stall: 52 mph
Fuel capacity: 35 gallons
Rate of climb: 1080 fpm

Transitions
    Takeoff over 50-foot obstacle: 1090 feet
    Ground run: 510 feet
    Landing over 50-foot obstacle: 1245 feet
    Ground roll: 400 feet
Weights
    Gross: 2150 pounds
    Empty: 1315 pounds
Seats: Two tandem
Dimensions
    Length: 23 feet 10 inches
    Height: 8 feet 8 inches
    Span: 36 feet 2 inches

BEECHCRAFT

Beech Aircraft Corporation, although not well known for their two-seat airplanes, has produced two of importance. Both are modern-type aircraft.

The most recent two-place Beechcraft is the Skipper, a low-wing, all-metal, tricycle-gear airplane. Naturally, it's quite up-to-date in design and appearance, having been introduced in 1979. Its wings are unusually sleek owing to their honeycomb ribs and bonded skin construction. No rivets are used on the wing surfaces. The Skipper is often confused with the Piper Tomahawk (PA-38), because of similarity in the general shape of the planes.

Declining general aviation sales in the early 1980s essentially forced the Skipper out of production. None were built in 1981 and a complete production halt soon followed.

The remaining member of the Beech two-place family is the T-34 Mentor (Beech Model 45). This tandem-seat, low-wing, all-metal airplane saw extensive service with the military as a trainer. Many pilots consider them war birds, due to their prolonged military history. They were produced from 1948 until 1958.

Until recently, most civilian T-34s were flying with the Civil Air Patrol or military-sponsored flight clubs, with only a few finding their way into the civilian market. Although Mentors are now readily available on the used market, they command a premium price. No longer supported by Beech for parts and service, they are expensive to own, pretty to look at, and amazing to fly. Late models are powered with the 285-hp Continental IO-520 engine.

Generally, you will see good examples of T-34s at airshows. Just look for the military yellow color that many are painted (Figs. 7-7 and 7-8).

Beechcraft

Fig. 7-7. Beechcraft 77 Skipper.

Make: Beechcraft   Model: 77 Skipper
Year: 1979 – 81
Engine
    Make: Lycoming

Model: O-235-L2C
Horsepower: 115
TBO: 2000 hours
Speeds
    Maximum: 122 mph
    Cruise: 112 mph
    Stall: 54 mph
Fuel capacity: 29 gallons
Rate of climb: 720 fpm
Transitions
    Takeoff over 50-foot obstacle: 1280 feet
    Ground run: 780 feet
    Landing over 50-foot obstacle: 1313 feet
    Ground roll: 670 feet
Weights
    Gross: 1675 pounds
    Empty: 1103 pounds
Seats: Two side by side
Dimensions
    Length: 24 feet
    Height: 6 feet 11 inches
    Span: 30 feet

Fig. 7-8. Beechcraft T-34 Mentor in military type colors.

Make: Beech   Model: T-34 Mentor (225-hp)
Engine
    Make: Continental
    Model: O-470
    Horsepower: 225
    TBO: 1500 hours

Speeds
    Maximum: 189 mph
    Cruise: 173 mph
    Stall: 54 mph
Fuel capacity: NA
Rate of climb: 1120 fpm
Transitions
    Takeoff over 50-foot obstacle: 1200 feet
    Ground run: NA
    Landing over 50-foot obstacle: 960 feet
    Ground roll: NA
Weights
    Gross: 2975 pounds
    Empty: 2246 pounds
Seats: Two tandem
Dimensions
    Length: 25 feet 11 inches
    Height: 9 feet 7 inches
    Span: 32 feet 10 inches

Make: Beech   Model: T-34 Mentor (285-hp)
Engine
    Make: Continental
    Model: IO-520
    Horsepower: 285
    TBO: 1700 hours
Speeds
    Maximum: 202 mph
    Cruise: 184 mph
    Stall: 54 mph
Fuel capacity: 80 gallons
Rate of climb: 1130 fpm
Transitions
    Takeoff over 50-foot obstacle: 1044 feet
    Ground run: 820 feet
    Landing over 50-foot obstacle: 735 feet
    Ground roll: 420 feet
Weights
    Gross: 3200 pounds
    Empty: 2170 pounds
Seats: Two tandem
Dimensions
    Length: 25 feet 11 inches
    Height: 9 feet 6 inches
    Span: 32 feet 10 inches

CESSNA

The first Cessna two-placer appeared in 1946 as the Model 120. The 120 was a metal-fuselage airplane with fabric-covered wings. Naturally, it was a taildragger. The seating, as in all the Cessna two-placers, was side-by-side. Control wheels graced the instrument panel.

The Model 140 that followed was a deluxe version of the 120 with with an electrical system, flaps, and a plushier cabin. Many 120s have been updated to look like 140s with the addition of extra side windows and electrical systems.

The 140A was the last Cessna two-place airplane for almost a decade. It was all-metal and had a Continental C-90 engine. It's interesting to note that the 140A airplane sold new for $3,695 and now commands more than triple that price. Production ceased in 1950 after more than 7,000 120s, 140s, and 140As were manufactured.

Cessna introduced a new two-place trainer airplane in 1959. Starting life as a tricycle gear version of the 140A, the Model 150 was destined to become the most popular training aircraft ever made. There are few pilots who have never flown a 150.

Always being improved, the 150 underwent numerous changes between 1959 until 1977, including the following improvements:

- Omni-vision (rear windows) in 1964
- Swept tail in 1966
- Aerobat model in 1970

The Aerobat 150A, stressed to 6Gs positive and 3Gs negative, has been economically popular for aerobatic training.

Cessna rolled out the 152 in 1978. The 152 is nearly identical to the 150; the biggest change is the Lycoming O-235 engine, which burns 100 low-lead fuel.

A used Cessna 150 or 152 is possibly the best buy in today's two-place used airplane market. If carefully selected and well cared for, you should not lose money on the airplane when sold. Nor should you have problems selling it (Figs. 7-9 through 7-13).

Make: Cessna   Model: 120 and 140
Year: 1946–50
Engine
    Make: Continental
    Model: C-90
    Horsepower: 90
    TBO: 1800 hours
Speeds
    Maximum: 125 mph
    Cruise: 115 mph
    Stall: 45 mph
Fuel capacity: 25 gallons

Fig. 7-9. Cessna 140.

Rate of climb: 680 fpm
Transitions
    Takeoff over 50-foot obstacle: 1850 feet
    Ground run: 650 feet
    Landing over 50-foot obstacle: 1530 feet
    Ground roll: 460 feet
Weights
    Gross: 1500 pounds
    Empty: 850 pounds
Seats: Two side by side
Dimensions
    Length: 20 feet 9 inches
    Height: 6 feet 3 inches
    Span: 32 feet 8 inches

Fig. 7-10. Cessna 1959 150.

Fig. 7-11. Cessna 1972 150.

Fig. 7-12. Cessna 150 Aerobat.

Make: Cessna   Model: 150
Year: 1959 – 77
Engine
    Make: Continental
    Model: O-200
    Horsepower: 100
    TBO: 1800 hours
Speeds
    Maximum: 125 mph

Cruise: 122 mph
Stall: 48 mph
Fuel capacity: 26 gallons
Rate of climb: 670 fpm
Transitions
    Takeoff over 50-foot obstacle: 1385 feet
    Ground run: 735 feet
    Landing over 50-foot obstacle: 1075 feet
    Ground roll: 445 feet
Weights
    Gross: 1600 pounds
    Empty: 1060 pounds
Seats: Two side by side
Dimensions
    Length: 23 feet 9 inches
    Height: 8 feet 9 inches
    Span: 32 feet 8 inches

Cessna

Fig. 7-13. Cessna 1983 152.

Make: Cessna   Model: 152
Year: 1978 – 85
Engine
    Make: Lycoming
    Model: O-235-L2C
    Horsepower: 110
    TBO: 2000 hours
Speeds
    Maximum: 127 mph
    Cruise: 123 mph
    Stall: 50 mph
Fuel capacity: 26 gallons

Rate of climb: 715 fpm
Transitions
    Takeoff over 50-foot obstacle: 1340 feet
    Ground run: 725 feet
    Landing over 50-foot obstacle: 1200 feet
    Ground roll: 475 feet
Weights
    Gross: 1670 pounds
    Empty: 1129 pounds
Seats: Two side by side
Dimensions
    Length: 24 feet 1 inch
    Height: 8 feet 6 inches
    Span: 33 feet 2 inches

CHRISTEN

Christen Industries introduced a "blank-sheet-of-paper" airplane in 1987 called the Husky, a two-place airplane, resembling the Piper Super Cub. Perhaps this similarity is correct, as the airplane was designed to fill the gap that opened when Piper stopped building Super Cubs.

Airplanes such as the Husky are used extensively by the United States Border Patrol, U.S. Forest Service, various state fish and game commissions, law enforcement agencies, pipeline and power line patrol companies, and ranchers.

It is doubtful that a large number of Husky airplanes will appear on the used market for a long time, due to their newness and low production numbers. However, a Husky—being new— should be considered an alternative to purchasing an aging Super Cub.

On March 19, 1991, Aviat, Inc. purchased the rights to produce the Husky A-1. The 1991 base price was $65,625 (Fig. 7-14).

Christen Industries

Fig. 7-14. Christen Huskey.

Make: Christen (Aviat)   Model: Husky A-1
Year: 1987 – up
Engine
    Make: Lycoming
    Model: O-360-C1G
    Horsepower: 180
    TBO: 2000 hours
Speeds
    Maximum: 145 mph
    Cruise: 140 mph
    Stall: 42 mph

Fuel capacity: 52 gallons
Rate of climb: 1500 fpm
Transitions
    Takeoff over 50-foot obstacle: NA
    Ground run: 200 feet
    Landing over 50-foot obstacle: NA
    Ground roll: 350 feet
Weights
    Gross: 1800 pounds
    Empty: 1190 pounds
Seats: Two tandem
Dimensions
    Length: 22 feet 7 inches
    Height: 6 feet 7 inches
    Span: 35 feet 6 inches

ERCOUPE

Ercoupes were designed to be the most fool-proof airplanes ever built. Originally they only had a control wheel for all directional maneuvering. The control wheel operated the ailerons and rudder via control interconnections and even steered the nosewheel. No coordination was required to make turns.

Originally, the single control wheel design was limited in the amount of travel, or authority, to avoid entering into a stall. Being unable to enter a stall made the original Ercoupe "spin proof," a fact that led to issuance of limited class pilot licenses in the late 1940s when spin training was still required.

Many Ercoupes have been modified to include rudder pedals and in later production years rudder pedals became a factory option.

The first Ercoupes had metal fuselages and fabric-covered wings; later models were all-metal. All Ercoupes have tricycle landing gear. One popular feature is the fighter-like canopy that may be opened during flight.

Crosswind landings are unique. The trailing beam main gear takes the shock of the crabbed landing, then makes any directional correction. This is not as novel as you might think; the Boeing 707 lands the same way, unable to drop a wing during crosswind landings due to low engine-to-ground clearance. Early Ercoupe model numbers indicated engine horsepower:

- 415C, 65 hp
- 415D, 75 hp
- 415G, 85 hp

Ercoupe was the original name, but several companies have been associated with the airplane's production. Forney Aircraft Company of Fort Collins, Colorado, became the owner of the production rights in 1956. Forney produced the F1, which was powered by a Continental C-90-12 engine, until 1960. Alon Inc., of McPhearson, Kansas, purchased the Ercoupe production rights in the mid-1960s after Forney gave up. They introduced the A-2 as a 90-hp aircraft with optional rudder pedals and sliding canopy for $7,825.

Alon gave up in 1967 and sold the production rights to Mooney Aircraft of Kerrville, Texas. Mooney produced the A-2 as the A-2A. Mooney completely redesigned the Ercoupe in 1968 and called it the M-10 Cadet. It didn't sell well and was quickly discontinued.

Interestingly, the Ercoupe was designed to be safe. Stalls were very minimal, and spins were impossible. A placard reads: "This Airplane Characteristically Incapable of Spinning." Yet, when Mooney introduced the Cadet, stalls and spins were also introduced.

The last remnants of the Ercoupe went the way of so many other good things in life when production ceased in 1970, probably for all time. More than 5,000 Ercoupes were manufactured (including Forney, Alon, and Mooney). A large number of these fine little planes are still flying, no doubt due to their small thirst for fuel, low used prices, and low taxation of pilot skills.

A mechanic who is familiar with Ercoupes should examine an airplane prior to purchase. Remember, some of the Ercoupes are nearly 50 years old (Figs. 7-15 through 7-17).

Fig. 7-15. Ercoupe 415.

Make: Ercoupe   Model: 415
Year: 1946–49
Engine
    Make: Continental
    Model: C-75-12(F)
    Horsepower: 75
    TBO: 1800 hours
Speeds
    Maximum: 125 mph
    Cruise: 114 mph
    Stall: 56 mph
Fuel capacity: 24 gallons
Rate of climb: 550 fpm
Transitions
    Takeoff over 50-foot obstacle: 2250 feet
    Ground run: 560 feet
    Landing over 50-foot obstacle: 1750 feet
    Ground roll: 350 feet
Weights
    Gross: 1400 pounds
    Empty: 815 pounds
Seats: Two side by side
Dimensions
    Length: 20 feet 9 inches
    Height: 5 feet 11 inches
    Span: 30 feet

Make: Forney   Model: F1
Year: 1957 – 60
Engine
    Make: Continental
    Model: C-90-12F
    Horsepower: 90
    TBO: 1800 hours
Speeds
    Maximum: 130 mph
    Cruise: 120 mph
    Stall: 56 mph
Fuel capacity: 24 gallons
Rate of climb: 600 fpm
Transitions
    Takeoff over 50-foot obstacle: 2100 feet
    Ground run: 500 feet
    Landing over 50-foot obstacle: 1750 feet
    Ground roll: 600 feet
Weights
    Gross: 1400 pounds
    Empty: 890 pounds
Seats: Two side by side
Dimensions
    Length: 20 feet 9 inches
    Height: 5 feet 11 inches
    Span: 30 feet

Fig. 7-16. Alon A2.

Make: Alon   Model: A-2 and Mooney A2-A
Year: 1965 – 68
Engine
    Make: Continental
    Model: C-90-16F

Horsepower: 90
TBO: 1800 hours
Speeds
Maximum: 128 mph
Cruise: 124 mph
Stall: 56 mph
Fuel capacity: 24 gallons
Rate of climb: 640 fpm
Transitions
Takeoff over 50-foot obstacle: 2100 feet
Ground run: 540 feet
Landing over 50-foot obstacle: 1750 feet
Ground roll: 650 feet
Weights
Gross: 1450 pounds
Empty: 930 pounds
Seats: Two side by side
Dimensions
Length: 20 feet 2 inches
Height: 5 feet 11 inches
Span: 30 feet

Ercoupe Pilot's Assn.

Fig. 7-17. Mooney M-10 Cadet.

Make: Mooney   Model: M-10 Cadet
Year: 1969–70
Engine
Make: Continental
Model: C-90
Horsepower: 90
TBO: 1800 hours

Speeds
    Maximum: 118 mph
    Cruise: 110 mph
    Stall: 46 mph
Fuel capacity: 24 gallons
Rate of climb: 835 fpm
Transitions
    Takeoff over 50-foot obstacle: 1953 feet
    Ground run: 534 feet
    Landing over 50-foot obstacle: 1015 feet
    Ground roll: 431 feet
Weights
    Gross: 1450 pounds
    Empty: 950 pounds
Seats: Two side by side
Dimensions
    Length: 20 feet 8 inches
    Height: 7 feet 8 inches
    Span: 30 feet

GULFSTREAM

Jim Bede is a name often associated with small airplane design and novel methods of airplane construction. His two-place airplane first flew as the AA-1, manufactured by American Aviation.

The wings were manufactured by a process of bonding the metal skins to the frame with special adhesive, heat, and pressure—no rivets. The intention was to create a low drag, sleek wing. Unfortunately, there have been problems with the bonding process, so some airplanes of this type airplane you see may have rivets in the wings for extra skin attachment strength.

The Gulfstream airplanes are known for their responsiveness and cruise considerably faster than the Cessna 150. They are referred to as a pilot's airplane and are often called mini-fighters. They are also hot and unforgiving of pilot inattention, landing fast, and need a lot of room for takeoff.

The AA-1, AA-1B, Trainer, and TR-2 have the same airframe and basic engine combination:

- Lycoming O-235-C2C 108-hp engine from 1969–1976
- Lycoming O-235-L2C 115-hp for AA-1C, T-Cat, and Lynx

Due to confusion about the manufacturers identity, you may see these airplanes advertised as Gulfstream American, Grumman American, or American Aviation (Fig. 7-18).

FLETCHAIR, Inc./Photo by G. Miller

Fig. 7-18. Gulfstream American AA-1.

Make: Gulfstream   Model: AA-1, AA-1B, TR-2 Trainer
Year: 1969–76

Engine
  Make: Lycoming
  Model: O-235-C2C
  Horsepower: 108
  TBO: 2000 hours
Speeds
  Maximum: 138 mph
  Cruise: 124 mph
  Stall: 60 mph
Fuel capacity: 24 gallons
Rate of climb: 710 fpm
Transitions
  Takeoff over 50-foot obstacle: 1590 feet
  Ground run: 890 feet
  Landing over 50-foot obstacle: 1100 feet
  Ground roll: 410 feet
Weights
  Gross: 1500 pounds
  Empty: 1000 pounds
Seats: Two side by side
Dimensions
  Length: 19 feet 3 inches
  Height: 6 feet 9 inches
  Span: 24 feet 5 inches

Make: Gulfstream   Model: AA-1C T-Cat/Lynx
Year: 1977–78
Engine
  Make: Lycoming
  Model: O-235-L2C
  Horsepower: 115
  TBO: 2000 hours
Speeds
  Maximum: 145 mph
  Cruise: 135 mph
  Stall: 60 mph
Fuel capacity: 22 gallons
Rate of climb: 700 fpm
Transitions
  Takeoff over 50-foot obstacle: 1590 feet
  Ground run: 890 feet
  Landing over 50-foot obstacle: 1125 feet
  Ground roll: 425 feet
Weights
  Gross: 1600 pounds
  Empty: 1066 pounds

Seats: Two side by side
Dimensions
    Length: 19 feet 3 inches
    Height: 7 feet 6 inches
    Span: 24 feet 5 inches

LUSCOMBE

Luscombe two-seat airplanes are noted as having one of the strongest airframe and wing structures ever manufactured. They also have a reputation for having some of the poorest ground handling characteristics of any small plane.

The first point is true, the second is no doubt a story spread by those who don't really know better. Luscombes can be touchy on landings due to the narrow-track landing gear, but if the pilot stays on his toes he'll have no problems (the same applies to all conventional-gear airplanes).

Luscombes were produced from 1946 through 1949 by the Luscombe Airplane Corporation of Dallas, Texas. In the early 1950s, Texas Engineering and Manufacturing Company (TEMCO) built the Luscombe 8F version. In 1955 Silvaire Aircraft Corporation was formed in Fort Collins, Colorado. Silvaire produced only the 8F. All production stopped in 1960 with 6,057 Series-8 Luscombes manufactured.

Like most other makes of airplanes, the various models indicated the engine horsepower:

- 8A, Continental 65-hp engine
- 8B, Lycoming 65-hp engine
- 8C/D, Continental 75-hp engine
- 8E, Continental 85-hp engine
- 8F, Continental 90-hp engine

Due to superior handling qualities, a Luscombe purchaser is cautioned to carefully inspect for damage caused by over stress from aerobatics (Figs. 7-19 and 7-20).

Fig. 7-19. Luscombe 8A.

Make: Luscombe   Model: 8A
Year: 1946–49
Engine
    Make: Continental
    Model: A-65
    Horsepower: 65
    TBO: 1800 hours
Speeds
    Maximum: 112 mph
    Cruise: 102 mph
    Stall: 48 mph
Fuel capacity: 14 gallons
Rate of climb: 550 fpm
Transitions
    Takeoff over 50-foot obstacle: 1950 feet
    Ground run: 1050 feet
    Landing over 50-foot obstacle: 1540 feet
    Ground roll: 450 feet
Weights
    Gross: 1260 pounds
    Empty: 665 pounds
Seats: Two side by side
Dimensions
    Length: 19 feet 8 inches
    Height: 6 feet 1 inch
    Span: 34 feet 7 inches

Make: Luscombe   Model: 8E
Year: 1946–47
Engine
    Make: Continental
    Model: C-85
    Horsepower: 85
    TBO: 1800 hours
Speeds
    Maximum: 122 mph
    Cruise: 112 mph
    Stall: 48 mph
Fuel capacity: 25 gallons
Rate of climb: 800 fpm
Transitions
    Takeoff over 50-foot obstacle: 1875 feet
    Ground run: 650 feet
    Landing over 50-foot obstacle: 1540 feet
    Ground roll: 450 feet

Weights
    Gross: 1400 pounds
    Empty: 810 pounds
Seats: Two side by side
Dimensions
    Length: 19 feet 8 inches
    Height: 6 feet 1 inch
    Span: 34 feet 7 inches

Fig. 7-20. Luscombe 8F.

Make: Luscombe   Model: 8F
Year: 1948 – 60
Engine
    Make: Continental
    Model: C-90
    Horsepower: 90
    TBO: 1800 hours
Speeds
    Maximum: 128 mph
    Cruise: 120 mph
    Stall: 48 mph
Fuel capacity: 25 gallons
Rate of climb: 900 fpm
Transitions
    Takeoff over 50-foot obstacle: 1850 feet
    Ground run: 550 feet
    Landing over 50-foot obstacle: 1540 feet
    Ground roll: 450 feet

Weights
    Gross: 1400 pounds
    Empty: 870 pounds
Seats: Two side by side
Dimensions
    Length: 20 feet
    Height: 6 feet 3 inches
    Span: 35 feet

PIPER

No other name is more often associated with small airplanes than Piper. Many people refer to every small airplane as a Piper Cub.

The most famous of the Cub series is the J3, first introduced in 1939 and manufactured until World War II, then again after the war. Production rates rose to the point of one airplane every 10 minutes. Production ended in 1947 after building 14,125 J3 Cubs.

The J4 Cub Coupe, built before the war, used many J3 parts, which kept costs of design and production to a minimum. None were built after the war.

The J5 Cub Cruiser, also introduced prior to the war, seated three persons and, like the J4, shared many J3 parts. The pilot sat in a single bucket seat up front with a bench seat for two in the rear. After the war, the J5-C and PA-12 appeared as outgrowths of the J5. All of this series are underpowered by today's standards and none will fly three adults on a real hot day unless the original engine has been replaced with something larger.

The "J" in the early Piper model numbers indicated Walter C. Jamouneau, Piper's chief engineer. Later the PA designator was used to indicate Piper Aircraft.

In 1947, the PA-11 Cub Special replaced the J3. The engine was completely enclosed by a cowling and the PA-11 could be soloed from the front seat, unlike the J3 which requires solo flight from the rear seat.

The PA-15 was introduced as the Vagabond in 1948 and was about an basic an airplane as you can get. It had a 65-hp Lycoming O-145 engine and seated two side-by-side. The main landing gear was solid, with the only shock-absorbing action coming from the pilot's finesse during landings.

Soon the PA-17, also called the Vagabond, came out as an upgraded PA-15 with such niceties as bungee-type landing gear, floor mats, and the Continental A-65 engine, which is supposed to have considerably more pep than the Lycoming O-145.

The PA-18 Super Cub, although built with a completely redesigned airframe, shows its true heritage by outwardly resembling a J3. Production started in 1949 and more than 9,000 Super Cubs were built with a variety of engines from 90- to 150-hp.

The last two-place Piper airplane of tube-and-fabric design was the PA-22-108 Colt. It was really a two-seat, flapless version of the very popular four-place Tri-Pacer, powered with a 108-hp Lycoming engine. The Colt was meant to be used as a trainer.

Piper did build a modern trainer, the PA-38 Tomahawk. It's an all-metal, low-wing, tricycle-gear airplane. Unfortunately, it has been the victim of numerous ADs and, due to economic problems in the aviation market, was only built for a few years (Figs. 7-21 through 7-27).

Make: Piper   Model: J3 Cub
Year: 1939 – 47
Engine
    Make: Continental

Fig. 7-21. Piper J3 Cub.

Model: A-65
Horsepower: 65
TBO: 1800 hours
Speeds
    Maximum: 87 mph
    Cruise: 75 mph
    Stall: 38 mph
Fuel capacity: 9 gallons
Rate of climb: 450 fpm
Transitions
    Takeoff over 50-foot obstacle: 730 feet
    Ground run: 370 feet
    Landing over 50-foot obstacle: 470 feet
    Ground roll: 290 feet
Weights
    Gross: 1220 pounds
    Empty: 680 pounds
Seats: Two tandem
Dimensions
    Length: 22 feet 4 inches
    Height: 6 feet 8 inches
    Span: 35 feet 2 inches

Make: Piper   Model: J4 Cub Coupe
Year: 1939 – 41
Engine
    Make: Continental

Fig. 7-22. Piper J4 Cub.

          Model: A-65
          Horsepower: 65
          TBO: 1800 hours
Speeds
          Maximum: 95 mph
          Cruise: 80 mph
          Stall: 42 mph
Fuel capacity: 25 gallons
Rate of climb: 450 fpm
Transitions
          Takeoff over 50-foot obstacle: 750 feet
          Ground run: 370 feet
          Landing over 50-foot obstacle: 480 feet
          Ground roll: 300 feet
Weights
          Gross: 1301 pounds
          Empty: 650 pounds
Seats: Two side by side
Dimensions
          Length: 22 feet 6 inches
          Height: 6 feet 10 inches
          Span: 36 feet 2 inches

Make: Piper   Model: J5
Year: 1941
Engine
          Make: Continental
          Model: A-75

Horsepower: 75
TBO: 1800 hours
Speeds
Maximum: 95 mph
Cruise: 80 mph
Stall: 43 mph
Fuel capacity: 25 gallons
Rate of climb: 400 fpm
Transitions
Takeoff over 50-foot obstacle: 1250 feet
Ground run: 750 feet
Landing over 50-foot obstacle: 900 feet
Ground roll: 400 feet
Weights
Gross: 1450 pounds
Empty: 820 pounds
Seats: Three
Dimensions
Length: 22 feet 6 inches
Height: 6 feet 10 inches
Span: 35 feet 6 inches

Make: Piper   Model: J5C
Year: 1946
Engine
Make: Lycoming
Model: O-235
Horsepower: 100
TBO: 2000 hours
Speeds
Maximum: 110 mph
Cruise: 95 mph
Stall: 45 mph
Fuel capacity: 20 gallons
Rate of climb: 650 fpm
Transitions
Takeoff over 50-foot obstacle: 1050 feet
Ground run: 650 feet
Landing over 50-foot obstacle: 950 feet
Ground roll: 450 feet
Weights
Gross: 1550 pounds
Empty: 860 pounds
Seats: Three
Dimensions
Length: 22 feet 6 inches

Height: 6 feet 10 inches
Span: 35 feet 6 inches

Make: Piper   Model: PA-11 Cub Special (65)
Year: 1947 – 49
Engine
    Make: Continental
    Model: A-65
    Horsepower: 65
    TBO: 1800 hours
Speeds
    Maximum: 100 mph
    Cruise: 87 mph
    Stall: 38 mph
Fuel capacity: 18 gallons
Rate of climb: 550 fpm
Transitions
    Takeoff over 50-foot obstacle: 730 feet
    Ground run: 370 feet
    Landing over 50-foot obstacle: 470 feet
    Ground roll: 290 feet
Weights
    Gross: 1220 pounds
    Empty: 730 pounds
Seats: Two tandem
Dimensions
    Length: 22 feet 4 inches
    Height: 6 feet 8 inches
    Span: 35 feet 2 inches

Make: Piper   Model: PA-11 Cub Special (90)
Year: 1948 – 49
Engine
    Make: Continental
    Model: C-90
    Horsepower: 90
    TBO: 1800 hours
Speeds
    Maximum: 112 mph
    Cruise: 100 mph
    Stall: 40 mph
Fuel capacity: 18 gallons
Rate of climb: 900 fpm
Transitions
    Takeoff over 50-foot obstacle: 475 feet
    Ground run: 250 feet

Landing over 50-foot obstacle: 550 feet
Ground roll: 290 feet
Weights
Gross: 1220 pounds
Empty: 750 pounds
Seats: Two tandem
Dimensions
Length: 22 feet 4 inches
Height: 6 feet 8 inches
Span: 35 feet 2 inches

Fig. 7-23. Piper PA-12 Cruiser.

Make: Piper   Model: PA-12
Year: 1946 – 47
Engine
Make: Lycoming
Model: O-235
Horsepower: 100 (some have 108 hp)
TBO: 2000 hours
Speeds
Maximum: 115 mph
Cruise: 105 mph
Stall: 49 mph
Fuel capacity: 30 gallons
Rate of climb: 650 fpm
Transitions
Takeoff over 50-foot obstacle: 720 feet
Ground run: 410 feet
Landing over 50-foot obstacle: 470 feet
Ground roll: 360 feet

Weights
    Gross: 1500 pounds
    Empty: 855 pounds
Seats: Three
Dimensions
    Length: 23 feet 1 inch
    Height: 6 feet 9 inches
    Span: 35 feet 6 inches

Fig. 7-24. Piper PA-17 Vagabond.

Make: Piper   Model: PA-15/17 Vagabond
Year: 1948 – 50
Engine
    Make: Continental (Lycoming on PA-15)
    Model: A-65
    Horsepower: 65
    TBO: 1800 hours
Speeds
    Maximum: 100 mph
    Cruise: 90 mph
    Stall: 45 mph
Fuel capacity: 12 gallons
Rate of climb: 510 fpm
Transitions
    Takeoff over 50-foot obstacle: 1572 feet
    Ground run: 800 feet
    Landing over 50-foot obstacle: 1280 feet
    Ground roll: 450 feet
Weights
    Gross: 1100 pounds

Empty: 620 pounds
Seats: Two side by side
Dimensions
    Length: 18 feet 7 inches
    Height: 6 feet
    Span: 29 feet 3 inches

Fig. 7-25. Piper PA-18 Super Cub.

Make: Piper   Model: PA-18 Super Cub (90)
Year: 1950 – 61
Engine
    Make: Continental
    Model: C-90
    Horsepower: 90
    TBO: 1800 hours
Speeds
    Maximum: 112 mph
    Cruise: 100 mph
    Stall: 42 mph
Fuel capacity: 18 gallons
Rate of climb: 700 fpm
Transitions
    Takeoff over 50-foot obstacle: 1150 feet
    Ground run: 400 feet
    Landing over 50-foot obstacle: 800 feet
    Ground roll: 385 feet
Weights
    Gross: 1500 pounds
    Empty: 800 pounds

Seats: Two tandem
Dimensions
 Length: 22 feet 5 inches
 Height: 6 feet 6 inches
 Span: 35 feet 3 inches

Make: Piper   Model: PA-18 Super Cub (125)
Year: 1951 – 52
Engine
 Make: Lycoming
 Model: O-290-D
 Horsepower: 125
 TBO: 2000 hours
Speeds
 Maximum: 125 mph
 Cruise: 112 mph
 Stall: 41 mph
Fuel capacity: NA
Rate of climb: 940 fpm
Transitions
 Takeoff over 50-foot obstacle: 650 feet
 Ground run: 420 feet
 Landing over 50-foot obstacle: 725 feet
 Ground roll: 350 feet
Weights
 Gross: 1500 pounds
 Empty: 845 pounds
Seats: Two tandem
Dimensions
 Length: 22 feet 5 inches
 Height: 6 feet 6 inches
 Span: 35 feet 3 inches

Make: Piper   Model: PA-18 Super Cub (150)
Year: 1955 – 83
Engine
 Make: Lycoming
 Model: O-320-A2A
 Horsepower: 150
 TBO: 2000 hours
Speeds
 Maximum: 130 mph
 Cruise: 115 mph
 Stall: 43 mph
Fuel capacity: 36 gallons
Rate of climb: 960 fpm

Transitions
    Takeoff over 50-foot obstacle: 500 feet
    Ground run: 200 feet
    Landing over 50-foot obstacle: 725 feet
    Ground roll: 350 feet
Weights
    Gross: 1750 pounds
    Empty: 930 pounds
Seats: Two tandem
Dimensions
    Length: 22 feet 5 inches
    Height: 6 feet 6 inches
    Span: 35 feet 3 inches

Fig. 7-26. Piper PA-22 Colt.

Make: Piper   Model: PA-22-108 Colt
Year: 1961–63
Engine
    Make: Lycoming
    Model: O-235-C1B
    Horsepower: 108
    TBO: 2000 hours
Speeds
    Maximum: 120 mph
    Cruise: 108 mph
    Stall: 54 mph
Fuel capacity: 36 gallons

Rate of climb: 610 fpm
Transitions
    Takeoff over 50-foot obstacle: 1500 feet
    Ground run: 950 feet
    Landing over 50-foot obstacle: 1250 feet
    Ground roll: 500 feet
Weights
    Gross: 1650 pounds
    Empty: 940 pounds
Seats: Two side by side
Dimensions
    Length: 20 feet
    Height: 6 feet 3 inches
    Span: 30 feet

Fig. 7-27. Piper PA-38 Tomahawk.

Make: Piper   Model: PA-38 Tomahawk
Year: 1978 – 82
Engine
    Make: Lycoming
    Model: O-235-L2C
    Horsepower: 112
    TBO: 2000 hours
Speeds
    Maximum: 125 mph
    Cruise: 122 mph
    Stall: 54 mph
Fuel capacity: 30 gallons
Rate of climb: 720 fpm

Transitions
    Takeoff over 50-foot obstacle: 1340 feet
    Ground run: 810 feet
    Landing over 50-foot obstacle: 1520 feet
    Ground roll: 710 feet
Weights
    Gross: 1670 pounds
    Empty: 1128 pounds
Seats: Two side by side
Dimensions
    Length: 23 feet 1 inch
    Height: 9 feet 1 inch
    Span: 34 feet

SWIFT

The Swift airplane was far ahead of other two-seat airplanes of its era. Built of all-metal construction, it had retractable conventional landing gear, a variable pitch prop, and flew very fast.

First introduced in the immediate post-World War II era, the factory was at one time cranking out Swifts on a 24-hour basis and in one 6-month period pushed 833 planes out the door. This was the bulk of those ever manufactured; the total number of Swifts built is around 1,500.

The first Swifts were powered with 85-hp engines; however, nearly all of those have since been repowered with larger engines. The B models were equipped with a 125-hp engine, and many of these have also been modified by adding larger engines up to 225 hp.

Swifts were built strong—stressed to 7.2 Gs positive and 4.4 Gs negative. They are real hot rods and take plenty of pilot skill to safely handle.

Although no longer in production, new parts are still manufactured and sold by Univair Aircraft (Fig. 7-28).

Fig. 7-28. Swift GC-B1.

Make: Swift   Model: GC1B
Year: 1946–50
Engine
    Make: Continental
    Model: C-125
    Horsepower: 125
    TBO: 1800 hours
Speeds
    Maximum: 150 mph
    Cruise: 140 mph
    Stall: 50 mph
Fuel capacity: 30 gallons

Rate of climb: 1000 fpm
Transitions
    Takeoff over 50-foot obstacle: 1185 feet
    Ground run: 830 feet
    Landing over 50-foot obstacle: 880 feet
    Ground roll: 650 feet
Weights
    Gross: 1710 pounds
    Empty: 1125 pounds
Seats: Two side by side
Dimensions
    Length: 20 feet 9 inches
    Height: 6 feet 1 inch
    Span: 29 feet 3 inches

TAYLORCRAFT

Taylorcraft airplanes started as part of Piper Aircraft. Originally, C. Gilbert Taylor was in business with William Piper; however, there was a parting of the ways and Mr. Taylor set about on his own. Although built at the same time as the Piper Cub series, the Taylor airplanes never enjoyed Cub-like popularity.

Taylorcraft's BC-12 was introduced in 1941 but it saw a short production run due to the start of WWII. After the war, Taylorcraft, like all the other aircraft companies, restarted production. The new plane was the BC-12D, an updated version of the prewar BC-12.

Despite the wider side-by-side seating fuselage, and its inherent extra wind resistance, the BC-12D can outpace a J3 Cub by better than 20 mph. The cockpit had dual control wheels, but brakes only on the pilot's side. About 3,000 BC-12Ds were built before production stopped in 1950.

By late 1950, the Taylorcraft Aviation Corporation, of Alliance, Ohio, was a thing of the past, and a new company, Taylorcraft Inc., began in Conway, Pennsylvania. This company introduced the Model 19, called the Sportsman, which was powered with an 85-hp Continental engine. About 200 of these planes were built before Taylorcraft Aviation folded in 1957. Between then and 1965 the Univair Corporation of Aurora, Colorado, built and sold parts for the Taylorcrafts. Univair did not build complete airplanes.

Production was restarted in 1965 at Alliance, Ohio, with the Taylorcraft Model F-19 powered by a Continental O-200 engine. In 1980, the Continental engine was dropped in favor of the 118-hp Lycoming, which called for a new model number, the F-21. Other than slight updating, little has changed from the BC-12D airplanes, showing that it is difficult to improve upon something as time-proven as the postwar T-craft airplanes.

A Taylorcraft in good condition is about the most efficient (cheap) airplane you can fly because they only burn a little over four gallons of fuel per hour (Figs. 7-29 and 7-30).

Fig. 7-29. Taylorcraft BC-12D.

Make: Taylorcraft   Model: BC-12D
Year: 1946 – 47
Engine
    Make: Continental
    Model: A-65-8A
    Horsepower: 65
    TBO: 1800 hours
Speeds
    Maximum: 100 mph
    Cruise: 95 mph
    Stall: 38 mph
Fuel capacity: 18 gallons
Rate of climb: 500 fpm
Transitions
    Takeoff over 50-foot obstacle: 700 feet
    Ground run: 350 feet
    Landing over 50-foot obstacle: 450 feet
    Ground roll: 300 feet
Weights
    Gross: 1200 pounds
    Empty: 730 pounds
Seats: Two side by side
Dimensions
    Length: 21 feet 9 inches
    Height: 6 feet 10 inches
    Span: 36 feet

Make: Taylorcraft   Model: F-19
Year: 1974 – 79
Engine
    Make: Continental
    Model: O-200
    Horsepower: 100
    TBO: 1800 hours
Speeds
    Maximum: 127 mph
    Cruise: 115 mph
    Stall: 43 mph
Fuel capacity: 24 gallons
Rate of climb: 775 fpm
Transitions
    Takeoff over 50-foot obstacle: 350 feet
    Ground run: 200 feet
    Landing over 50-foot obstacle: 350 feet
    Ground roll: 275 feet

Weights
    Gross: 1500 pounds
    Empty: 900 pounds
Seats: Two side by side
Dimensions
    Length: 22 feet 1 inch
    Height: 6 feet 10 inches
    Span: 36 feet

Fig. 7-30. Taylorcraft F-21.

Make: Taylorcraft   Model: F-21 & F-21A/B
Year: 1980 – 90
Engine
    Make: Lycoming
    Model: O-235-L2C
    Horsepower: 118
    TBO: 2000 hours
Speeds
    Maximum: 125 mph
    Cruise: 120 mph
    Stall: 43 mph
Fuel capacity: 40 gallons
Rate of climb: 875 fpm
Transitions
    Takeoff over 50-foot obstacle: 350 feet
    Ground run: 275 feet
    Landing over 50-foot obstacle: 350 feet
    Ground roll: 275 feet

Weights
　　Gross: 1500 pounds
　　Empty: 1040 pounds
Seats: Two side by side
Dimensions
　　Length: 22 feet 3 inches
　　Height: 6 feet 6 inches
　　Span: 36 feet

VARGA

The Varga is an all-metal, military-looking airplane that closely resembles the Beech T-34 Mentor in outward appearance, albeit much smaller. It first appeared in 1977 and was produced until 1982.

First built by Morrisey, then Shinn, before becoming the Varga, it has tricycle landing gear and tandem seating under a "green-house" style canopy. A limited number were produced as tail draggers and some of the tri-gears planes were converted to tail draggers. Two models, 150 hp and 180 hp, were built (Fig. 7-31).

Fig. 7-31. Varga 2150.

Make: Varga   Model: 2150 Kachina
Year: 1977 – 80
Engine
    Make: Lycoming
    Model: O-320-A2C
    Horsepower: 150
    TBO: 2000 hours
Speeds
    Maximum: 135 mph
    Cruise: 120 mph
    Stall: 52 mph
Fuel capacity: 33 gallons
Rate of climb: 910 fpm

Transitions
    Takeoff over 50-foot obstacle: NA
    Ground run: 440 feet
    Landing over 50-foot obstacle: NA
    Ground roll: 450 feet
Weights
    Gross: 1817 pounds
    Empty: 1125 pounds
Seats: Two tandem
Dimensions
    Length: 21 feet 3 inches
    Height: 7 feet
    Span: 30 feet

Make: Varga   Model: 2180
Year: 1981–82
Engine
    Make: Lycoming
    Model: O-360-A4AD
    Horsepower: 180
    TBO: 2000 hours
Speeds
    Maximum: 150 mph
    Cruise: 133 mph
    Stall: 52 mph
Fuel capacity: 33 gallons
Rate of climb: 1310 fpm
Transitions
    Takeoff over 50-foot obstacle: NA
    Ground run: 400 feet
    Landing over 50-foot obstacle: NA
    Ground roll: 450 feet
Weights
    Gross: 1817 pounds
    Empty: 1175 pounds
Seats: Two tandem
Dimensions
    Length: 21 feet 3 inches
    Height: 7 feet
    Span: 30 feet

8

Four-place easy fliers

THE FOUR-PLACE "EASY" FLIER AIRPLANE is by far the most airplane for the money. Over the years many have been produced by different companies, but there are only two basic designs: high-wing and low-wing.

This class of airplane can provide adequate transportation for most personal and business needs. There are few complexities about this group of airplanes. All have fixed landing gear, all have engines of less than 200 hp, and most come with fixed-pitch propellers (although a few have optional constant-speed props). They are, as a group, easily found, inexpensively maintained, quickly sold, and tolerant of any new equipment needed to fulfill most flying requirements. The majority of these planes are of all-metal construction, have tricycle landing gear, and are easy to fly.

A few classics belong in the category of "easy fliers," also, including the fabric-covered Stinsons, Tri-Pacers, and Pacers.

AERO COMMANDER

The Aero Commander Darter started life as the Volaire, and was made in Aliquippa, Pennsylvania. Only a few were made before Aero Commander, a division of Rockwell International, bought the design.

The airplane appears very similar to the Cessna 172, is all metal, and has similar performance data. It was aimed at the Cessna 172 market, but failed and was soon removed from production.

Volaires were underpowered with only 135-hp engines. The model 100 Darters have a 150-hp engine.

The biggest drawback to these planes is the scarcity of parts. Additionally, the braking system uses a single-handle control, which is far less maneuverable than the more familiar toe brakes found in most similar type airplanes.

Aero Commander built a larger version of the 100, called the Lark, powered with a 180-hp engine. It was to compete with the Cessna 182; like the low-power version, it did not prove to be popular either. Although sharing a model number with the Darter, the Lark does not visually resemble the Darter. All production halted in 1971.

Aero Commanders of this group may be found under Aero Commander, Rockwell, or Volaire in classified advertisements (Figs. 8-1 and 8-2).

Fig. 8-1. Aero Commander 100 Darter.

Make: Aero Commander   Model: 100 Darter
Year: 1965 – 69
Engine
    Make: Lycoming
    Model: O-320-A2B (O-290 if Volaire version)
    Horsepower: 150 (135 if O-290 engine)
    TBO: 2000 hours
Speeds
    Maximum: 133 mph
    Cruise: 128 mph
    Stall: 55 mph
Fuel capacity: 44 gallons
Rate of climb: 785 fpm
Transitions
    Takeoff over 50-foot obstacle: 1550 feet
    Ground run: 870 feet
    Landing over 50-foot obstacle: 1215 feet
    Ground roll: 6550 feet
Weights
    Gross: 2250 pounds
    Empty: 1280 pounds
Seats: Four
Dimensions
    Length: 22 feet 6 inches

Height: 9 feet 4 inches
Span: 35 feet

Fig. 8-2. Aero Commander 100 Lark.

Make: Aero Commander   Model: 100 Lark
Year: 1968–71
Engine
    Make: Lycoming
    Model: O-360-A2F
    Horsepower: 180
    TBO: 2000 hours
Speeds
    Maximum: 138 mph
    Cruise: 132 mph
    Stall: 60 mph
Fuel capacity: 44 gallons
Rate of climb: 750 fpm
Transitions
    Takeoff over 50-foot obstacle: 1575 feet
    Ground run: 875 feet
    Landing over 50-foot obstacle: 1280 feet
    Ground roll: 675 feet
Weights
    Gross: 2450 pounds
    Empty: 1450 pounds
Seats: Four
Dimensions
    Length: 24 feet 9 inches
    Height: 10 feet 1 inch
    Span: 35 feet

BEECHCRAFT

The typical Beech four-place "easy flier" is of low-wing design and all-metal construction. All have large roomy cabins and give the appearance of more plane than they really are. Although they are stoutly constructed and are usually well equipped with avionics, resale values remain low because of a general lack of popularity.

As with most manufacturers, Beech used an assortment of engines during various production runs:

- 1963, Lycoming 160-hp
- 1964, Continental 165-hp fuel-injected
- 1968, Lycoming 180-hp

To further confuse identification, the Model 23s were built under different model names:

- 1963, Model 23 Musketeer
- 1964–65, Model A23 II Musketeer
- 1966–67, Model A23 IIIA Custom
- 1968–69, Model B23 Custom
- 1970–71, Model C23 Custom
- 1972–83, Model C23 Sundowner

In 1964, Beech introduced the A23-19 as a four-place airplane. It really should be considered a two- or four-place airplane, meaning that if you carry four adult persons on board, you will carry only partial fuel (due to gross weight limitations). An optional aerobatic version was available.

The 23-24 was introduced in 1966 as the Super III, was equipped with a 200-hp Lycoming fuel-injected engine, and easily carried four adults and full fuel.

Performance-wise, these planes cruise slow, are underpowered for their size, and have low safety ratings from NTSB (see Appendix B). They are also expensive to maintain and poorly supported by Beechcraft (Figs. 8-3 through 8-5).

Make: Beechcraft   Model: 23 Musketeer
Year: 1963
Engine
    Make: Lycoming
    Model: O-320-D2B
    Horsepower: 160
    TBO: 2000 hours
Speeds
    Maximum: 144 mph
    Cruise: 135 mph
    Stall: 62 mph
Fuel capacity: 60 gallons

Fig. 8-3. Beechcraft B-23 Musketeer.

Rate of climb: 710 fpm
Transitions
    Takeoff over 50-foot obstacle: 1320 feet
    Ground run: 925 feet
    Landing over 50-foot obstacle: 1260 feet
    Ground roll: 640 feet
Weights
    Gross: 2300 pounds
    Empty: 1300 pounds
Seats: Four
Dimensions
    Length: 25 feet
    Height: 8 feet 3 inches
    Span: 32 feet 9 inches

Make: Beechcraft   Model: A23 II and IIIA Musketeer
Year: 1964 – 68
Engine
    Make: Continental
    Model: IO-346-A
    Horsepower: 165
    TBO: 1500 hours
Speeds
    Maximum: 146 mph
    Cruise: 138 mph
    Stall: 58 mph
Fuel capacity: 60 gallons
Rate of climb: 728 fpm
Transitions
    Takeoff over 50-foot obstacle: 1460 feet

Ground run: 990 feet
Landing over 50-foot obstacle: 1260 feet
Ground roll: 640 feet
Weights
Gross: 2350 pounds
Empty: 1375 pounds
Seats: Four
Dimensions
Length: 25 feet
Height: 8 feet 3 inches
Span: 32 feet 9 inches

Make: Beechcraft   Model: 23 B and C Custom
Year: 1968–71
Engine
Make: Lycoming
Model: O-360-A4K
Horsepower: 180
TBO: 2000 hours
Speeds
Maximum: 151 mph
Cruise: 143 mph
Stall: 60 mph
Fuel capacity: 60 gallons
Rate of climb: 820 fpm
Transitions
Takeoff over 50-foot obstacle: 1380 feet
Ground run: 950 feet
Landing over 50-foot obstacle: 1275 feet
Ground roll: 640 feet
Weights
Gross: 2450 pounds
Empty: 1416 pounds
Seats: Four
Dimensions
Length: 25 feet
Height: 8 feet 3 inches
Span: 32 feet 9 inches

Make: Beechcraft   Model: C23 Sundowner
Year: 1972–83
Engine
Make: Lycoming
Model: O-360-A4G
Horsepower: 180
TBO: 2000 hours

Fig. 8-4. Beechcraft C-23 Sundowner.

Speeds
    Maximum: 147 mph
    Cruise: 133 mph
    Stall: 59 mph
Fuel capacity: 57 gallons
Rate of climb: 792 fpm
Transitions
    Takeoff over 50-foot obstacle: 1955 feet
    Ground run: 1130 feet
    Landing over 50-foot obstacle: 1484 feet
    Ground roll: 700 feet
Weights
    Gross: 2450 pounds
    Empty: 1494 pounds
Seats: Four
Dimensions
    Length: 25 feet 9 inches
    Height: 8 feet 3 inches
    Span: 32 feet 9 inches

Make: Beechcraft   Model: A23-24 Super III
Year: 1966 – 69
Engine
    Make: Lycoming
    Model: O-360-A2B
    Horsepower: 200
    TBO: 1800 hours

Speeds
    Maximum: 158 mph
    Cruise: 150 mph
    Stall: 61 mph
Fuel capacity: 60 gallons
Rate of climb: 880 fpm
Transitions
    Takeoff over 50-foot obstacle: 1380 feet
    Ground run: 950 feet
    Landing over 50-foot obstacle: 1300 feet
    Ground roll: 660 feet
Weights
    Gross: 2550 pounds
    Empty: 1410 pounds
Seats: Four
Dimensions
    Length: 25 feet
    Height: 8 feet 3 inches
    Span: 32 feet 9 inches

Fig. 8-5. Beechcraft 23-19 Sport.

Make: Beechcraft   Model: 23-19/19A Sport and Sport III
Year: 1966 – 67
Engine
    Make: Lycoming
    Model: O-320-E2C
    Horsepower: 150
    TBO: 2000 hours
Speeds
    Maximum: 140 mph

Cruise: 131 mph
Stall: 56 mph
Fuel capacity: 60 gallons
Rate of climb: 700 fpm
Transitions
    Takeoff over 50-foot obstacle: 1320 feet
    Ground run: 885 feet
    Landing over 50-foot obstacle: 1220 feet
    Ground roll: 590 feet
Weights
    Gross: 2250 pounds
    Empty: 1374 pounds
Seats: Four (not with full fuel)
Dimensions
    Length: 25 feet 1 inch
    Height: 8 feet 2 inches
    Span: 32 feet 7 inches

Make: Beechcraft   Model: B-19 Sport
Year: 1968 – 78
Engine
    Make: Lycoming
    Model: O-320-E2C
    Horsepower: 150
    TBO: 2000 hours
Speeds
    Maximum: 127 mph
    Cruise: 123 mph
    Stall: 57 mph
Fuel capacity: 57 gallons
Rate of climb: 680 fpm
Transitions
    Takeoff over 50-foot obstacle: 1635 feet
    Ground run: 1030 feet
    Landing over 50-foot obstacle: 1690 feet
    Ground roll: 825 feet
Weights
    Gross: 2150 pounds
    Empty: 1414 pounds
Seats: Four
Dimensions
    Length: 25 feet 9 inches
    Height: 8 feet 3 inches
    Span: 32 feet 9 inches

CESSNA

The modern Cessna line of four-place airplanes started in 1948 with the model 170, which had a metal fuselage and a fabric-covered wing with conventional landing gear. 170-B models are all-metal, including the wings.

A good 170 will take you just about anywhere and do so economically. Although considered a classic, based upon the years of production, the 170 is as modern as today.

No doubt you can see the resemblance between the 170 and the 172. The advent of the nosewheel rang the death knell for the 170 and in 1956 production of the model 170 ceased, while production of 172s, continued into the 1980s when all of general aviation faltered. The 172 has seen many refinements since entering production in 1956:

- 1960, swept-back tail
- 1963, omni-vision
- 1964, electric flaps
- 1968, Lycoming O-320-E2D engine
- 1970, conical wing tips
- 1971, tubular landing gear
- 1977, the O-320-H2AD low lead 160-hp engine
- 1981, Lycoming O-320-D2J engine

The 172 is also known as the Skyhawk or Skyhawk 100, depending upon factory installed equipment. In 1977, the 172 Hawk XP was introduced with an IO-360-KB 195-hp fuel-injected Continental engine.

Cessna brought out the 175 Skylark in 1958 with a GO-300 Continental engine. It never achieved the popularity of the 172 due to chronic engine problems. The 175s GO-300 engine is geared and develops higher horsepower by operating at higher rpms, which leads to early wear problems. Some 175s have had the GO-300 engine replaced with an O-320 or O-360 and can represent good buys because they are stigmatized by the 175 model number.

Cessna 177 Cardinals appeared in 1968. The first 177s were underpowered with only a 150-hp Lycoming engine; 1969 models, and later, have 180-hp engines. A new airfoil in 1970 attempted to improve low-speed handling. Some models have constant-speed propellers. Cardinals remained in production until 1978.

Cessna airplanes in the "easy flier" category represent the most airplane for the money. They are proven safe airplanes that will not drag you to the bank for maintenance and parts. If the plane is properly cared for, your initial investment will easily be returned upon resale. Often a good profit can be made (Figs. 8-6 through 8-11).

Make: Cessna   Model: 170 (all)
Year: 1948 – 56
Engine
    Make: Continental

Fig. 8-6. Cessna 1956 170B.

Model: C-145-2
Horsepower: 145
TBO: 1800 hours
Speeds
    Maximum: 135 mph
    Cruise: 120 mph
    Stall: 52 mph
Fuel capacity: 42 gallons
Rate of climb: 660 fpm
Transitions
    Takeoff over 50-foot obstacle: 1820 feet
    Ground run: 700 feet
    Landing over 50-foot obstacle: 1145 feet
    Ground roll: 500 feet
Weights
    Gross: 2200 pounds
    Empty: 1260 pounds
Seats: Four
Dimensions
    Length: 25 feet
    Height: 6 feet 5 inches
    Span: 36 feet

Make: Cessna   Model: 172 Skyhawk
Year: 1956 – 67
Engine
    Make: Continental
    Model: O-300 A (D after 1960)
    Horsepower: 145
    TBO: 1800 hours
Speeds
    Maximum: 138 mph

Fig. 8-7. Cessna 1956 172.

    Cruise: 130 mph
    Stall: 49 mph
Fuel capacity: 42 gallons
Rate of climb: 645 fpm
Transitions
    Takeoff over 50-foot obstacle: 1525 feet
    Ground run: 865 feet
    Landing over 50-foot obstacle: 1250 feet
    Ground roll: 520 feet
Weights
    Gross: 2300 pounds
    Empty: 1260 pounds
Seats: Four
Dimensions
    Length: 26 feet 6 inches
    Height: 8 feet 11 inches
    Span: 36 feet 2 inches

Make: Cessna   Model: 172 Skyhawk
Year: 1968 – 76
Engine:
    Make: Lycoming
    Model: O-320-E2D
    Horsepower: 150
    TBO: 2000 hours
Speeds
    Maximum: 139 mph

Fig. 8-8. Cessna 1968 Skyhawk.

Cruise: 131 mph
Stall: 49 mph
Fuel capacity: 42 gallons
Rate of climb: 645 fpm
Transitions
    Takeoff over 50-foot obstacle: 1525 feet
    Ground run: 865 feet
    Landing over 50-foot obstacle: 1250 feet
    Ground roll: 520 feet
Weights
    Gross: 2300 pounds
    Empty: 1265 pounds
Seats: Four
Dimensions
    Length: 26 feet 6 inches
    Height: 8 feet 11 inches
    Span: 36 feet 2 inches

Make: Cessna   Model: 172 Skyhawk
Year: 1977 – 80
Engine
    Make: Lycoming
    Model: O-320-H2AD
    Horsepower: 160
    TBO: 2000 hours
Speeds
    Maximum: 141 mph
    Cruise: 138 mph
    Stall: 51 mph

Fuel capacity: 43 gallons
Rate of climb: 700 fpm
Transitions
    Takeoff over 50-foot obstacle: 1825 feet
    Ground run: 890 feet
    Landing over 50-foot obstacle: 1280 feet
    Ground roll: 540 feet
Weights
    Gross: 2400 pounds
    Empty: 1414 pounds
Seats: Four
Dimensions
    Length: 26 feet 6 inches
    Height: 8 feet 11 inches
    Span: 36 feet 2 inches

Make: Cessna   Model: 172P II
Year: 1981 – 86
Engine
    Make: Lycoming
    Model: O-320-D2J
    Horsepower: 160
    TBO: 2000 hours
Speeds
    Maximum: 141 mph
    Cruise: 138 mph
    Stall: 53 mph
Fuel capacity: 43 gallons
Rate of climb: 700 fpm
Transitions
    Takeoff over 50-foot obstacle: 1625 feet
    Ground run: 890 feet
    Landing over 50-foot obstacle: 1280 feet
    Ground roll: 540 feet
Weights
    Gross: 2400 pounds
    Empty: 1454 pounds
Seats: Four
Dimensions
    Length: 26 feet 11 inches
    Height: 8 feet 10 inches
    Span: 35 feet 10 inches

Make: Cessna   Model: 172 Skyhawk XP
Year: 1977 – 81

Fig. 8-9. Cessna 1978 Hawk XP II.

Engine
    Make: Continental
    Model: IO-360-K (KB after 1977)
    Horsepower: 195
    TBO: 1500 hours (2000 on KB)
Speeds
    Maximum: 153 mph
    Cruise: 150 mph
    Stall: 54 mph
Fuel capacity: 52 gallons
Rate of climb: 870 fpm
Transitions
    Takeoff over 50-foot obstacle: 1360 feet
    Ground run: 800 feet
    Landing over 50-foot obstacle: 1345 feet
    Ground roll: 635 feet
Weights
    Gross: 2550 pounds
    Empty: 1546 pounds
Seats: Four
Dimensions
    Length: 26 feet 6 inches
    Height: 8 feet 11 inches
    Span: 36 feet 2 inches

Make: Cessna   175 Skylark and Powermatic
Year: 1958 – 62
Engine
    Make: Continental

Fig. 8-10. Cessna 1959 Skylark 175.

    Model: GO-300-E
    Horsepower: 175
    TBO: 1200 hours
Speeds
    Maximum: 139 mph
    Cruise: 131 mph
    Stall: 50 mph
Fuel capacity: 52 gallons
Rate of climb: 850 fpm
Transitions
    Takeoff over 50-foot obstacle: 1340 feet
    Ground run: 735 feet
    Landing over 50-foot obstacle: 1155 feet
    Ground roll: 590 feet
Weights
    Gross: 2300 pounds
    Empty: 1330 pounds
Seats: Four
Dimensions
    Length: 25 feet
    Height: 8 feet 5 inches
    Span: 36 feet

Make: Cessna   Model: 177 Cardinal (150)
Year: 1968
Engine
    Make: Lycoming
    Model: O-320-E2D

Fig. 8-11. Cessna Cardinal 177.

Horsepower: 150
TBO: 2000 hours
Speeds
    Maximum: 144 mph
    Cruise: 134 mph
    Stall: 53 mph
Fuel capacity: 49 gallons
Rate of climb: 670 fpm
Transitions
    Takeoff over 50-foot obstacle: 1575 feet
    Ground run: 845 feet
    Landing over 50-foot obstacle: 1135 feet
    Ground roll: 400 feet
Weights
    Gross: 2350 pounds
    Empty: 1415 pounds
Seats: Four
Dimensions
    Length: 27 feet 3 inches
    Height: 8 feet 7 inches
    Span: 35 feet 7 inches

Make: Cessna   Model: 177 Cardinal (180)
Year: 1969–78
Engine
    Make: Lycoming
    Model: O-360-A1F6 (A1F6D after 1975)
    Horsepower: 180
    TBO: 2000 hours (1800 on A1F6D w/o mod)

Speeds
    Maximum: 150 mph
    Cruise: 139 mph
    Stall: 53 mph
Fuel capacity: 50 gallons
Rate of climb: 840 fpm
Transitions
    Takeoff over 50-foot obstacle: 1400 feet
    Ground run: 750 feet
    Landing over 50-foot obstacle: 1220 feet
    Ground roll: 600 feet
Weights
    Gross: 2500 pounds
    Empty: 1430 pounds
Seats: Four
Dimensions
    Length: 27 feet 3 inches
    Height: 8 feet 7 inches
    Span: 35 feet 7 inches

GULFSTREAM

Gulfstream built two airplanes in the four-place "easy flier" category, the AA5 and AA5A, under three names. The AA5 and AA5A Traveler and Cheetah models are powered by a 150-hp engine and the AA5B Tiger has a 180-hp engine.

Gulfstream airplanes are unusual because they have space-age wing construction using no rivets to hold the skin in place. Adhesive holds the skin to the honeycombed wing ribs. As with the two-place airplanes of similar construction, some rivets have been used to halt delamination.

Gulfstreams have a sliding canopy. Entry is gained by a step over the sidewall of the cabin and onto the seat, which allows for a complete cabin interior wash down if opened during a rainstorm.

Directional control is via differential braking and a swiveling nosewheel. They are good performers, although somewhat hot on landings. They have a short propeller clearance and are not recommended for soft field work. The laminated landing gear is noted for its strength and ability to make botched landings look good.

Production stopped in 1979 but restarted in 1991 by American aircraft Corporation. The 1991 base price was $94,250 and a typically equipped airplane sold for about $103,000 (Figs. 8-12 and 8-13)

FLETCHAIR, Inc./Photo by G. Miller

Fig. 8-12. Gulfstream AA5 Cheetah.

Make: Gulfstream   Model: AA5/AA5A Traveler/Cheetah
Year: 1972–79
Engine
    Make: Lycoming
    Model: O-320-E2G
    Horsepower: 150
    TBO: 2000 hours

Speeds
    Maximum: 150 mph
    Cruise: 140 mph
    Stall: 58 mph
Fuel capacity: 38 gallons
Rate of climb: 660 fpm
Transitions
    Takeoff over 50-foot obstacle: 1600 feet
    Ground run: 880 feet
    Landing over 50-foot obstacle: 1100 feet
    Ground roll: 380 feet
Weights
    Gross: 2200 pounds
    Empty: 1200 pounds
Seats: Four
Dimensions
    Length: 22 feet
    Height: 8 feet
    Span: 32 feet 6 inches

Fig. 8-13. Gulfstream AA5 Tiger.

Make: Gulfstream   Model: AA5B Tiger
Year: 1975 – 91
Engine
    Make: Lycoming
    Model: O-360-A4K
    Horsepower: 180
    TBO: 2000 hours

Speeds
   Maximum: 170 mph
   Cruise: 160 mph
   Stall: 61 mph
Fuel capacity: 51 gallons
Rate of climb: 850 fpm
Transitions
   Takeoff over 50-foot obstacle: 1550 feet
   Ground run: 865 feet
   Landing over 50-foot obstacle: 1120 feet
   Ground roll: 410 feet
Weights
   Gross: 2400 pounds
   Empty: 1285 pounds
Seats: Four
Dimensions
   Length: 22 feet
   Height: 8 feet
   Span: 31 feet 6 inches

LUSCOMBE

The Luscombe Sedan is an all-metal high-wing airplane with conventional landing gear. Ahead of their time, the Sedans had a rear window, something Cessna didn't discover until 20 years later. The wide landing gear stance makes the Sedans unusually easy to handle.

Unfortunately, few Sedans were built and they are infrequently seen on the used market (Fig. 8-14).

Fig. 8-14. Luscombe 11 Sedan.

Make: Luscombe   Model: 11 Sedan
Year: 1948 – 50
Engine
    Make: Continental
    Model: C-165
    Horsepower: 165
    TBO: 1800 hours
Speeds
    Maximum: 140 mph
    Cruise: 130 mph
    Stall: 55 mph
Fuel capacity: 42 gallons
Rate of climb: 900 fpm
Transitions
    Takeoff over 50-foot obstacle: 1540 feet
    Ground run: 800 feet
    Landing over 50-foot obstacle: 1310 feet
    Ground roll: 500 feet
Weights
    Gross: 2280 pounds
    Empty: 1280 pounds

Seats: Four
Dimensions
    Length: 23 feet 6 inches
    Height: 6 feet 10 inches
    Span: 38 feet

MAULE

The Maule M-4 was conceived as a homebuilt called the Bee Dee M4. Rather than market it as a homebuilt, designer B.D. Maule decided to commercially produce the airplane himself.

Constructed of a fiberglass-covered tubular fuselage and with all-metal wings, Maule airplanes exhibit excellent short-field capabilities, yet have relatively good cruise speeds. They are fine examples in the art of matching engine power to wing design.

An interesting innovation from Maule is the addition of tricycle landing gear on their latest model M-7 series 180-hp planes. First introduced in 1989, it currently sells for a base price of $85,000.

Several additional models of Maule airplanes are available on the market, generally for use as utility airplanes, some having more engine power. They are included in chapter 10 (Figs. 8-15 and 8-16).

Fig. 8-15. Maule M4-145.

Make: Maule   Model: M-4 Jeteson
Year: 1962–67
Engine
    Make: Continental
    Model: O-300-A
    Horsepower: 145
    TBO: 1800 hours
Speeds
    Maximum: 180 mph
    Cruise: 150 mph
    Stall: 40 mph
Fuel capacity: 42 gallons
Rate of climb: 700 fpm
Transitions
    Takeoff over 50-foot obstacle: 900 feet
    Ground run: 700 feet
    Landing over 50-foot obstacle: 600 feet
    Ground roll: 450 feet

Weights
    Gross: 2100 pounds
    Empty: 1100 pounds
Seats: Four
Dimensions
    Length: 22 feet
    Height: 6 feet 2 inches
    Span: 29 feet 8 inches

Fig. 8-16. Maule M7-180.

Make: Maule   Model: M-7/180D
Year: 1989–91
Engine
    Make: Lycoming
    Model: O-360-C1F
    Horsepower: 180
    TBO: 2000 hours
Speeds
    Maximum: NA
    Cruise: 140 mph
    Stall: 404 mph
Fuel capacity: 70 gallons
Rate of climb: 1200 fpm
Transitions
    Takeoff over 50-foot obstacle: 600 feet
    Ground run: NA
    Landing over 50-foot obstacle: 500 feet
    Ground roll: NA
Weights
    Gross: 2500 pounds
    Empty: 1410 pounds
Seats: Four

Dimensions
    Length: 23 feet 6 inches
    Height: 8 feet 4 inches
    Span: 33 feet

PIPER

Piper started production of four-place airplanes with the Family Cruiser PA-14. It was small and underpowered. Only 236 Cruisers were manufactured before replacement by the PA-16 Clipper, a slightly larger plane.

In 1950, the PA-20 Pacer series appeared. Like the PA-14s and 16s, the original PA-20s were of tube and fabric construction and had conventional landing gear. They had small engines and did not display eye-dazzling performance numbers.

Evolution of the Pacer resulted in the Tri-Pacer, billed as an anyone-can-fly-it airplane because of tricycle landing gear. It became a success and soon the Tri-Pacer's sales far outstripped those of the Pacer. General aviation customers were demanding easier-to-handle airplanes and they found what they wanted in the Tri-Pacer. PA-22s, as Tri-Pacers are officially known, were built with several different engines. Power varied from 125- to 160-hp.

Piper introduced the PA-28 series in 1961. Unlike previous Piper products, this new airplane was of all-metal construction and had low wings. The PA-28 series is the backbone for all of Piper's all-metal single-engine products. All of the early PA-28 series have the "Hershey-bar" wing, making them very docile to handle.

Initially, the PA-28 was produced as the Model 140, powered with a 150-hp Lycoming engine. An optional version, PA-28 160 with a 160-hp engine, was also available.

In 1964, the Cherokee 140 was introduced as a two-to-four place trainer. Initially delivered with a 140-hp engine, the 150-hp Lycoming was available for increased load carrying. The Model 140, in slightly different versions, is called the Cruiser or Fliteliner and was produced from 1964 to 1977.

The PA-28 180 was built from 1963 until 1975 and is a true four-place airplane, able to carry four adults and full fuel. Later called the Challenger or Archer, it had a 180-hp engine.

In 1974, Piper changed the wing design of the entire PA-28 series. The Warrior wing, providing increased load carrying abilities and very gentle stall characteristics, was added to the Challenger and Archer fuselage and designated the Model 151. It had a 150-hp engine and was built from 1974 through 1977. It was replaced by the Model 161 with a 160-hp low-lead engine in late 1977. The PA-28 181 was introduced in 1976 as the Archer II with a 180-hp Lycoming engine.

Piper airplanes have always been reliable and affordable. They make good purchases that are easy to fly and economical to maintain (Figs. 8-17 through 8-23).

Make: Piper   Model: PA-14 Cruiser
Year: 1948–49
Engine
    Make: Lycoming
    Model: O-235-C1

Horsepower: 115
TBO: 2000 hours
Speeds
    Maximum: 123 mph
    Cruise: 110 mph
    Stall: 46 mph
Fuel capacity: 38 gallons
Rate of climb: 540 fpm
Transitions
    Takeoff over 50-foot obstacle: 1770 feet
    Ground run: 720 feet
    Landing over 50-foot obstacle: 1410 feet
    Ground roll: 470 feet
Weights
    Gross: 1850 pounds
    Empty: 1020 pounds
Seats: Four
Dimensions
    Length: 23 feet 2 inches
    Height: 6 feet 7 inches
    Span: 35 feet 6 inches

Fig. 8-17. Piper PA-16.

Make: Piper   Model: PA-16 Clipper
Year: 1949
Engine
    Make: Lycoming

Model: O-235-C1
Horsepower: 115
TBO: 2000 hours
Speeds
    Maximum: 125 mph
    Cruise: 112 mph
    Stall: 50 mph
Fuel capacity: 36 gallons
Rate of climb: 580 fpm
Transitions
    Takeoff over 50-foot obstacle: 1910 feet
    Ground run: 720 feet
    Landing over 50-foot obstacle: 1440 feet
    Ground roll: 600 feet
Weights
    Gross: 1650 pounds
    Empty: 850 pounds
Seats: Four
Dimensions
    Length: 20 feet 1 inch
    Height: 6 feet 2 inches
    Span: 29 feet 3 inches

Fig. 8-18. Piper PA-20 Pacer.

Make: Piper   Model: PA-20 Pacer
Year: 1951–52
Engine
    Make: Lycoming
    Model: O-290-D
    Horsepower: 125
    TBO: 2000 hours
Speeds
    Maximum: 134 mph

Cruise: 119 mph
Stall: 47 mph
Fuel capacity: 36 gallons
Rate of climb: 550 fpm
Transitions
Takeoff over 50-foot obstacle: 1725 feet
Ground run: 1210 feet
Landing over 50-foot obstacle: 1280 feet
Ground roll: 780 feet
Weights
Gross: 1800 pounds
Empty: 970 pounds
Seats: Four
Dimensions
Length: 20 feet 4 inches
Height: 6 feet 1 inch
Span: 29 feet 3 inches

Make: Piper   Model: PA-20 Pacer
Year: 1952–54
Engine
Make: Lycoming
Model: O-290-D2 (opt. C/S propeller)
Horsepower: 135
TBO: 1500 hours
Speeds
Maximum: 139 mph
Cruise: 125 mph
Stall: 48 mph
Fuel capacity: 36 gallons
Rate of climb: 620 fpm
Transitions
Takeoff over 50-foot obstacle: 1600 feet
Ground run: 1120 feet
Landing over 50-foot obstacle: 1280 feet
Ground roll: 780 feet
Weights
Gross: 1920 pounds
Empty: 1020 pounds
Seats: Four
Dimensions
Length: 20 feet 4 inches
Height: 6 feet 1 inch
Span: 29 feet 3 inches

Fig. 8-19. Piper PA-22 Tri-Pacer.

Make: Piper   Model: PA-22 Tri-Pacer
Year: 1951–52
Engine
     Make: Lycoming
     Model: O-290-D
     Horsepower: 125
     TBO: 2000 hours
Speeds
     Maximum: 134 mph
     Cruise: 130 mph
     Stall: 48 mph
Fuel capacity: 36 gallons
Rate of climb: 550 fpm
Transitions
     Takeoff over 50-foot obstacle: 1600 feet
     Ground run: 1120 feet
     Landing over 50-foot obstacle: 1280 feet
     Ground roll: 650 feet
Weights
     Gross: 1850 pounds
     Empty: 1060 pounds
Seats: Four
Dimensions
     Length: 20 feet 4 inches

Height: 8 feet 3 inches
Span: 29 feet 3 inches

Make: Piper   Model: PA-22 Tri-Pacer
Year: 1952–54
Engine
    Make: Lycoming
    Model: O-290-D2
    Horsepower: 135
    TBO: 1500 hours
Speeds
    Maximum: 137 mph
    Cruise: 132 mph
    Stall: 48 mph
Fuel capacity: 36 gallons
Rate of climb: 620 fpm
Transitions
    Takeoff over 50-foot obstacle: 1550 feet
    Ground run: 1080 feet
    Landing over 50-foot obstacle: 1280 feet
    Ground roll: 650 feet
Weights
    Gross: 1850 pounds
    Empty: 1060 pounds
Seats: Four
Dimensions
    Length: 20 feet 4 inches
    Height: 8 feet 3 inches
    Span: 29 feet 3 inches

Make: Piper   Model: PA-22 Tri-Pacer
Year: 1955–60
Engine
    Make: Lycoming
    Model: O-320-A1A
    Horsepower: 150
    TBO: 2000 hours
Speeds
    Maximum: 139 mph
    Cruise: 132 mph
    Stall: 49 mph
Fuel capacity: 36 gallons
Rate of climb: 725 fpm
Transitions
    Takeoff over 50-foot obstacle: 1500 feet
    Ground run: 1050 feet

Landing over 50-foot obstacle: 1280 feet
Ground roll: 650 feet
Weights
    Gross: 2000 pounds
    Empty: 1100 pounds
Seats: Four
Dimensions
    Length: 20 feet 4 inches
    Height: 8 feet 3 inches
    Span: 29 feet 3 inches

Make: Piper   Model: PA-22 Tri-Pacer
Year: 1958–60
Engine
    Make: Lycoming
    Model: O-320-B2A
    Horsepower: 160
    TBO: 2000 hours
Speeds
    Maximum: 141 mph
    Cruise: 133 mph
    Stall: 48 mph
Fuel capacity: 36 gallons
Rate of climb: 800 fpm
Transitions
    Takeoff over 50-foot obstacle: 1480 feet
    Ground run: 1035 feet
    Landing over 50-foot obstacle: 1280 feet
    Ground roll: 650 feet
Weights
    Gross: 2000 pounds
    Empty: 1110 pounds
Seats: Four
Dimensions
    Length: 20 feet 5 inches
    Height: 8 feet 3 inches
    Span: 29 feet 3 inches

Make: Piper   Model: PA-28 140
Year: 1964–77
Engine
    Make: Lycoming
    Model: O-320-E2A
    Horsepower: 150
    TBO: 2000 hours

Fig. 8-20. Piper PA-28 140 Cruiser.

Speeds
    Maximum: 139 mph
    Cruise: 130 mph
    Stall: 53 mph
Fuel capacity: 36 gallons
Rate of climb: 660 fpm
Transitions
    Takeoff over 50-foot obstacle: 1750 feet
    Ground run: 800 feet
    Landing over 50-foot obstacle: 1890 feet
    Ground roll: 535 feet
Weights
    Gross: 2150 pounds
    Empty: 1205 pounds
Seats: Four
Dimensions
    Length: 23 feet 3 inches
    Height: 7 feet 3 inches
    Span: 30 feet

Make: Piper   Model: PA-28 Cherokee
Year: 1962 – 67
Engine
    Make: Lycoming
    Model: O-320-B2B
    Horsepower: 160
    TBO: 2000 hours
Speeds
    Maximum: 141 mph

Cruise: 132 mph
Stall: 55 mph
Fuel capacity: 36 gallons
Rate of climb: 700 fpm
Transitions
    Takeoff over 50-foot obstacle: 1700 feet
    Ground run: 775 feet
    Landing over 50-foot obstacle: 1890 feet
    Ground roll: 550 feet
Weights
    Gross: 2200 pounds
    Empty: 1210 pounds
Seats: Four
Dimensions
    Length: 23 feet 3 inches
    Height: 7 feet 3 inches
    Span: 30 feet

Fig. 8-21. Piper PA-28 180 Challenger.

Make: Piper   Model: PA-28 Challenger/Archer
Year: 1963 – 75
Engine
    Make: Lycoming
    Model: O-360-A3A
    Horsepower: 180
    TBO: 2000 hours
Speeds
    Maximum: 150 mph
    Cruise: 141 mph
    Stall: 57 mph
Fuel capacity: 50 gallons

Rate of climb: 720 fpm
Transitions
    Takeoff over 50-foot obstacle: 1620 feet
    Ground run: 725 feet
    Landing over 50-foot obstacle: 1150 feet
    Ground roll: 600 feet
Weights
    Gross: 2400 pounds
    Empty: 1225 pounds
Seats: Four
Dimensions
    Length: 23 feet 3 inches
    Height: 7 feet 3 inches
    Span: 30 feet

Make: Piper   Model: PA-28-151 Warrior
Year: 1974 – 77
Engine
    Make: Lycoming
    Model: O-320-E3D
    Horsepower: 150
    TBO: 2000 hours
Speeds
    Maximum: 134 mph
    Cruise: 126 mph
    Stall: 58 mph
Fuel capacity: 48 gallons
Rate of climb: 649 fpm
Transitions
    Takeoff over 50-foot obstacle: 1760 feet
    Ground run: 1065 feet
    Landing over 50-foot obstacle: 1115 feet
    Ground roll: 595 feet
Weights
    Gross: 2325 pounds
    Empty: 1301 pounds
Seats: Four
Dimensions
    Length: 23 feet 8 inches
    Height: 7 feet 3 inches
    Span: 35 feet

Make: Piper   Model: PA-28-161 Warrior
Year: 1977 – 90
Engine
    Make: Lycoming

Fig. 8-22. Piper PA-28 161 Warrior II.

Model: O-320-D3G
Horsepower: 160
TBO: 2000 hours
Speeds
    Maximum: 145 mph
    Cruise: 140 mph
    Stall: 57 mph
Fuel capacity: 48 gallons
Rate of climb: 710 fpm
Transitions
    Takeoff over 50-foot obstacle: 1490 feet
    Ground run: 975 feet
    Landing over 50-foot obstacle: 1115 feet
    Ground roll: 595 feet
Weights
    Gross: 2325 pounds
    Empty: 1353 pounds
Seats: Four
Dimensions
    Length: 23 feet 8 inches
    Height: 7 feet 3 inches
    Span: 35 feet

Make: Piper   Model: PA-28-181 Archer II
Year: 1976 – 90

Fig. 8-23. Piper PA-28 181 Archer II.

Engine
    Make: Lycoming
    Model: O-360-A4M
    Horsepower: 180
    TBO: 2000 hours
Speeds
    Maximum: 154 mph
    Cruise: 148 mph
    Stall: 61 mph
Fuel capacity: 48 gallons
Rate of climb: 735 fpm
Transitions
    Takeoff over 50-foot obstacle: 1625 feet
    Ground run: 870 feet
    Landing over 50-foot obstacle: 1390 feet
    Ground roll: 925 feet
Weights
    Gross: 2550 pounds
    Empty: 1413 pounds
Seats: Four
Dimensions
    Length: 23 feet 8 inches
    Height: 7 feet 3 inches
    Span: 35 feet

STINSON

All Stinson airplanes, for our purpose, were built of tube and fabric; however, many have since been metalized, that is, covered with a metal skin in place of the fabric. All have conventional landing gear.

Franklin engines, heavy case and light case, were used on these airplanes. Only the heavy-case engine is acceptable because the light case did not stand up well. It is very unlikely you would ever encounter a light-case engine at this time.

The 108-1 models had 150-hp engines and model 108-2 and 108-3 had 165-hp engines. Many have been modified by changing to Lycoming or Continental engines ranging from 200- to 250-hp. Stinsons make good seaplanes and are often seen in western Canada and Alaska in float configuration.

Piper bought out Stinson in 1948 and continued to produce the Model 108s, however, the numbers built by Piper were few and production was soon halted. Any Stinson with a serial number above 4231 is a Piper airplane.

Although long out of production, new parts are available. They are roomy and strong airplanes (Fig. 8-24)

Fig. 8-24. Stinson 108.

Make: Stinson   Model: 108-1
Year: 1946 – 47
Engine
    Make: Franklin
    Model: 6A4-150-B23
    Horsepower: 150
    TBO: 1200 hours
Speeds
    Maximum: 130 mph
    Cruise: 117 mph
    Stall: 57 mph

Fuel capacity: 50 gallons
Rate of climb: 700 fpm
Transitions
    Takeoff over 50-foot obstacle: 1750 feet
    Ground run: 945 feet
    Landing over 50-foot obstacle: 1400 feet
    Ground roll: 940 feet
Weights
    Gross: 2230 pounds
    Empty: 1206 pounds
Seats: Four
Dimensions
    Length: 24 feet
    Height: 7 feet
    Span: 33 feet 11 inches

Make: Stinson   Model: 108-2/3 Voyager and Station Wagon
Year: 1947–48
Engine
    Make: Franklin
    Model: 6A4-165-B3
    Horsepower: 165
    TBO: 1200 hours
Speeds
    Maximum: 133 mph
    Cruise: 125 mph
    Stall: 61 mph
Fuel capacity: 50 gallons
Rate of climb: 750 fpm
Transitions
    Takeoff over 50-foot obstacle: 1400 feet
    Ground run: 980 feet
    Landing over 50-foot obstacle: 1680 feet
    Ground roll: 940 feet
Weights
    Gross: 2400 pounds
    Empty: 1300 pounds
Seats: Four
Dimensions
    Length: 24 feet
    Height: 7 feet
    Span: 33 feet 11 inches

9

Complex airplanes

COMPLEX AIRPLANES REPRESENT THE PINNACLE of single-engine aircraft design and capabilities. They are real people movers and are used extensively by businessmen and families requiring fast and reliable transportation.

Complex airplane cruise speeds are higher, ranges are longer, and load capacities are greater than simpler four-place airplanes. They have more powerful engines and more features, such as retractable landing gear and constant-speed propellers. Many complex airplanes offer up to six-place seating.

Purchase and maintenance expenses of these airplanes are considerably higher than for the simpler planes. However, if you can justify this class of airplane, then the expenses will not be out of line.

Most of these airplanes are IFR-equipped. Perhaps this is an indication of business usage, where reliable transportation is a requirement rather than a pleasure.

Airplane ownership may offer tax advantages for a business. Consulting an accountant is recommended if you are going to use an airplane for business purposes.

AERO COMMANDER

Aero Commander produced two series of complex single-engine airplanes: Meyers and the 112/114.

The Meyers 200 is a sleek, low-wing, very fast airplane. The cabin is smaller than the older Beech Bonanzas but not too cramped for the average family. It was first produced with a 260-hp engine. Models built after 1964 have a 285-hp engine. Production ceased in 1967.

The model 112s came out in 1972 and were powered with a 200-hp fuel-injected engine. The manufacturer claimed that the cabin was the most spacious in its class. The 112TC Alpine with a turbo-charged 210-hp engine debuted in 1976.

The same airplane, except powered with a 260-hp fuel-injected engine, is called the Model 114 Gran Turismo. It was built from 1976 to 1979.

Search for these planes under Meyers, Aero Commander, Rockwell, and Gulfstream in classified ads (Figs. 9-1 and 9-2).

Fig. 9-1. Aero Commander 200 Myers.

Make: Aero Commander   Model: 200 A/B/C Meyers
Year: 1959 – 64
Engine
    Make: Continental
    Model: IO-470-D
    Horsepower: 260
    TBO: 1500 hours
Speeds
    Maximum: 216 mph
    Cruise: 195 mph
    Stall: 62 mph
Fuel capacity: 40 gallons
Rate of climb: 1245 fpm
Transitions
    Takeoff over 50-foot obstacle: 1260 feet
    Ground run: 1010 feet
    Landing over 50-foot obstacle: 1150 feet
    Ground roll: 850 feet
Weights
    Gross: 3000 pounds
    Empty: 1975 pounds
Seats: Four
Dimensions
    Length: 24 feet 4 inches
    Height: 8 feet 6 inches
    Span: 30 feet 5 inches

Make: Aero Commander   Model: 200 D Meyers
Year: 1965 – 67
Engine
    Make: Continental
    Model: IO-520 A
    Horsepower: 285
    TBO: 1700 hours
Speeds
    Maximum: 215 mph
    Cruise: 210 mph
    Stall: 64 mph
Fuel capacity: 40 gallons
Rate of climb: 1450 fpm
Transitions
    Takeoff over 50-foot obstacle: 1150 feet
    Ground run: 900 feet
    Landing over 50-foot obstacle: 1150 feet
    Ground roll: 850 feet
Weights
    Gross: 3000 pounds
    Empty: 1990 pounds
Seats: Four
Dimensions
    Length: 24 feet 4 inches
    Height: 8 feet 6 inches
    Span: 30 feet 5 inches

Fig. 9-2. Aero Commander 112.

Make: Rockwell   Model: 112
Year: 1972 – 77

Engine
  Make: Lycoming
  Model: IO-360-C1B6
  Horsepower: 200
  TBO: 1800 hours
Speeds
  Maximum: 175 mph
  Cruise: 165 mph
  Stall: 61 mph
Fuel capacity: 60 gallons
Rate of climb: 1000 fpm
Transitions
  Takeoff over 50-foot obstacle: 1460 feet
  Ground run: 880 feet
  Landing over 50-foot obstacle: 1310 feet
  Ground roll: 680 feet
Weights
  Gross: 2550 pounds
  Empty: 1530 pounds
Seats: Four
Dimensions
  Length: 24 feet 11 inches
  Height: 8 feet 5 inches
  Span: 32 feet 9 inches

Make: Rockwell   Model: 112 Alpine
Year: 1976 – 79
Engine
  Make: Lycoming
  Model: TO-360-C1B6D
  Horsepower: 210
  TBO: 1400 hours
Speeds
  Maximum: 196 mph
  Cruise: 187 mph
  Stall: 61 mph
Fuel capacity: 60 gallons
Rate of climb: 900 fpm
Transitions
  Takeoff over 50-foot obstacle: 1750 feet
  Ground run: 930 feet
  Landing over 50-foot obstacle: 1250 feet
  Ground roll: 680 feet
Weights
  Gross: 2950 pounds
  Empty: 2035 pounds

Seats: Four
Dimensions
     Length: 24 feet 11 inches
     Height: 8 feet 5 inches
     Span: 32 feet 9 inches

Make: Rockwell   Model: 114 Gran Turismo
Year: 1976–79
Engine
     Make: Lycoming
     Model: IO-540-T3B5D
     Horsepower: 260
     TBO: 2000 hours
Speeds
     Maximum: 191 mph
     Cruise: 181 mph
     Stall: 63 mph
Fuel capacity: 68 gallons
Rate of climb: 1030 fpm
Transitions
     Takeoff over 50-foot obstacle: 2150 feet
     Ground run: NA
     Landing over 50-foot obstacle: 1200 feet
     Ground roll: NA
Weights
     Gross: 3260 pounds
     Empty: 2070 pounds
Seats: Four
Dimensions
     Length: 24 feet 11 inches
     Height: 8 feet 5 inches
     Span: 32 feet 9 inches

BEECHCRAFT

The name Beechcraft goes back further, historically, than most other manufacturers found in this book. Many early Beech airplanes are not relevant to this book. However, one large single-engine plane Beech built is not only historic, it is also a capable people mover.

The Staggerwing Beech was built from the 1930s through the 1940s, a bygone era, and are classics in the truest sense of the word. Of tube and fabric construction, the cabin is larger than any airplane in the same class today. Its engine was a radial and although expensive to maintain, it makes the right sound (you'll know it when you hear it and never forget it). Staggerwings are very expensive to purchase, and even more expensive to operate and maintain.

The V-tailed Model 35 Bonanza has probably captured the imagination of more pilots, and non-pilots, over the years than any other light plane. The basic style has been utilized for over 45 years. It is the most thought-of airplane when the name Beechcraft is mentioned.

The first Model 35 had a 185-hp engine, a wooden prop, and seated four people. Many improvements and refinements have been made down through the years, but a Bonanza is still a Bonanza. The Model 35 remained in production through the early 1980s. The final models were powered with a 285-hp engine and seated six. Today, it's difficult to find an early Model 35 in stock configuration. Most have been updated with regard to appearance, avionics, and, of course, power.

The Model 33 Debonair was introduced in 1960. It was a four-seat conventional tail airplane powered with a 225-hp engine. An optional 285-hp version became available in 1966. The Debonair was dropped in 1968; however, the Model 33 continues as a Bonanza.

Beechcraft introduced the Sierra in 1970 as the model 24R. It had a 200-hp engine, constant-speed prop, and retractable landing gear. The Sierra was the top of a special line of airplanes built for the Beech Aero Centers. The Aero Centers were set up to sell and rent the lower end of Beech products.

Beech airplanes generally are thought of as the best of the crop. They are tough and hold their values well, but, as with anything complex, they are expensive to maintain (Figs. 9-4 through 9-9).

Make: Beechcraft   Model: D17S Staggerwing (unofficial name)
Year: 1937–48
Engine
    Make: Pratt & Whitney
    Model: R-985
    Horsepower: 450
    TBO: NA
Speeds
    Maximum: 212 mph
    Cruise: 202 mph
    Stall: 60 mph

Fig. 9-3. Beechcraft 17 Staggerwing.

Fuel capacity: 124 gallons
Rate of climb: 1500 fpm
Transitions
    Takeoff over 50-foot obstacle: 1130 feet
    Ground run: 610 feet
    Landing over 50-foot obstacle: 980 feet
    Ground roll: 750 feet
Weights
    Gross: 4250 pounds
    Empty: 2540 pounds
Seats: Four
Dimensions
    Length: 26 feet 10 inches
    Height: 8 feet
    Span: 32 feet

Make: Beechcraft   Model: 24R Sierra
Year: 1970 – 83
Engine
    Make: Lycoming
    Model: IO-360-A1B6
    Horsepower: 200
    TBO: 1800 hours

Fig. 9-4. Beechcraft 24R Sierra.

Speeds
   Maximum: 170 mph
   Cruise: 162 mph
   Stall: 66 mph
   Fuel capacity: 59 gallons
Rate of climb: 862 fpm
Transitions
   Takeoff over 50-foot obstacle: 1980 feet
   Ground run: 1260 feet
   Landing over 50-foot obstacle: 1670 feet
   Ground roll: 752 feet
Weights
   Gross: 2750 pounds
   Empty: 1610 pounds
Seats: Four
Dimensions
   Length: 25 feet 9 inches
   Height: 8 feet 3 inches
   Span: 32 feet 9 inches

Make: Beechcraft   Model: 33 Debonair/Bonanza
Year: 1960 – 70
Engine
   Make: Continental
   Model: IO-470-J
   Horsepower: 225
   TBO: 1500 hours
Speeds
   Maximum: 195 mph
   Cruise: 185 mph

Fig. 9-5. Beechcraft F33A Bonanza.

Beechcraft

Stall: 60 mph
Fuel capacity: 50 gallons
Rate of climb: 960 fpm
Transitions
    Takeoff over 50-foot obstacle: 1235 feet
    Ground run: 940 feet
    Landing over 50-foot obstacle: 1282 feet
    Ground roll: 635 feet
Weights
    Gross: 3000 pounds
    Empty: 1745 pounds
    Seats: Four-Five
Dimensions
    Length: 25 feet 6 inches
    Height: 8 feet 3 inches
    Span: 32 feet 10 inches

Make: Beechcraft   Model: 33 Debonair/Bonanza
Year: 1966 – 90
Engine
    Make: Continental
    Model: IO-520-BA
    Horsepower: 285
    TBO: 1700 hours

Speeds
    Maximum: 208 mph
    Cruise: 200 mph
    Stall: 63 mph
Fuel capacity: 50 gallons
Rate of climb: 1136 fpm
Transitions
    Takeoff over 50-foot obstacle: 1873 feet
    Ground run: 1091 feet
    Landing over 50-foot obstacle: 1500 feet
    Ground roll: 795 feet
Weights
    Gross: 3400 pounds
    Empty: 1965 pounds
Seats: Five-Six
Dimensions
    Length: 25 feet 6 inches
    Height: 8 feet 3 inches
    Span: 33 feet 5 inches

Fig. 9-6. Beechcraft 35 Bonanza.

Make: Beechcraft   Model: 35-A35 Bonanza
Year: 1947–49
Engine
    Make: Continental
    Model: E-185-1
    Horsepower: 185 (205 and 225 optional)
    TBO: 1500 hours
Speeds
    Maximum: 184 mph
    Cruise: 172 mph
    Stall: 55 mph

Fuel capacity: 39 gallons
Rate of climb: 950 fpm
Transitions
    Takeoff over 50-foot obstacle: 1440 feet
    Ground run: 1200 feet
    Landing over 50-foot obstacle: 925 feet
    Ground roll: 580 feet
Weights
    Gross: 2550 pounds
    Empty: 1458 pounds
Seats: Four
Dimensions
    Length: 25 feet 1 inch
    Height: 6 feet 6 inches
    Span: 32 feet 9 inches

Make: Beechcraft   Model: B35 Bonanza
Year: 1950
Engine
    Make: Continental
    Model: E-185-8
    Horsepower: 196
    TBO: 1500 hours
Speeds
    Maximum: 184 mph
    Cruise: 170 mph
    Stall: 56 mph
Fuel capacity: 39 gallons
Rate of climb: 890 fpm
Transitions
    Takeoff over 50-foot obstacle: 1515 feet
    Ground run: 1275 feet
    Landing over 50-foot obstacle: 950 feet
    Ground roll: 625 feet
Weights
    Gross: 2650 pounds
    Empty: 1575 pounds
Seats: Four
Dimensions
    Length: 25 feet 1 inch
    Height: 6 feet 6 inches
    Span: 32 feet 9 inches

Make: Beechcraft   Model: C35/D35 Bonanza
Year: 1951-53

Engine
    Make: Continental
    Model: E-185-11
    Horsepower: 205
    TBO: 1500 hours
Speeds
    Maximum: 190 mph
    Cruise: 175 mph
    Stall: 55 mph
Fuel capacity: 39 gallons
Rate of climb: 1100 fpm
Transitions
    Takeoff over 50-foot obstacle: 1500 feet
    Ground run: 1250 feet
    Landing over 50-foot obstacle: 975 feet
    Ground roll: 625 feet
Weights
    Gross: 2700 pounds
    Empty: 1650 pounds
Seats: Four
Dimensions
    Length: 25 feet 1 inch
    Height: 6 feet 6 inches
    Span: 32 feet 9 inches

Make: Beechcraft   Model: E35/G35 Bonanza
Year: 1954–56
Engine
    Make: Continental
    Model: E-225-8
    Horsepower: 225
    TBO: 1500 hours
Speeds
    Maximum: 194 mph
    Cruise: 184 mph
    Stall: 55 mph
Fuel capacity: 39 gallons
Rate of climb: 1300 fpm
Transitions
    Takeoff over 50-foot obstacle: 1270 feet
    Ground run: 1060 feet
    Landing over 50-foot obstacle: 1025 feet
    Ground roll: 680 feet
Weights
    Gross: 2775 pounds
    Empty: 1722 pounds

Seats: Four
Dimensions
     Length: 25 feet 1 inch
     Height: 6 feet 6 inches
     Span: 32 feet 9 inches

Make: Beechcraft   Model: H35 Bonanza
Year: 1957
Engine
     Make: Continental
     Model: O-470-G
     Horsepower: 240
     TBO: 1500 hours
Speeds
     Maximum: 206 mph
     Cruise: 196 mph
     Stall: 57 mph
Fuel capacity: 39 gallons
Rate of climb: 1250 fpm
Transitions
     Takeoff over 50-foot obstacle: 1260 feet
     Ground run: 1050 feet
     Landing over 50-foot obstacle: 1050 feet
     Ground roll: 710 feet
Weights
     Gross: 2900 pounds
     Empty: 1833 pounds
Seats: Four
Dimensions
     Length: 25 feet 1 inch
     Height: 6 feet 6 inches
     Span: 32 feet 9 inches

Make: Beechcraft   Model: J35/M35 Bonanza
Year: 1958–60
Engine
     Make: Continental
     Model: O-470-C
     Horsepower: 250
     TBO: 1500 hours
Speeds
     Maximum: 210 mph
     Cruise: 195 mph
     Stall: 57 mph
Fuel capacity: 39 gallons
Rate of climb: 1250 fpm

Transitions
    Takeoff over 50-foot obstacle: 1185 feet
    Ground run: 950 feet
    Landing over 50-foot obstacle: 1050 feet
    Ground roll: 710 feet
Weights
    Gross: 2900 pounds
    Empty: 1820 pounds
Seats: Four
Dimensions
    Length: 25 feet 1 inch
    Height: 6 feet 6 inches
    Span: 32 feet 9 inches

Fig. 9-7. Beechcraft N35 Bonanza.

Make: Beechcraft   Model: N35/P35 Bonanza
Year: 1961 – 63
Engine
    Make: Continental
    Model: IO-470-N
    Horsepower: 260
    TBO: 1500 hours
Speeds
    Maximum: 205 mph
    Cruise: 190 mph
    Stall: 60 mph
Fuel capacity: 49 gallons
Rate of climb: 1150 fpm
Transitions
    Takeoff over 50-foot obstacle: 1260 feet
    Ground run: 1050 feet
    Landing over 50-foot obstacle: 1100 feet
    Ground roll: 650 feet

Weights
    Gross: 3125 pounds
    Empty: 1855 pounds
Seats: Five
Dimensions
    Length: 25 feet 1 inch
    Height: 6 feet 6 inches
    Span: 32 feet 9 inches

Fig. 9-8. Beechcraft V35B Bonanza.

Make: Beechcraft   Model: S35/V35 Bonanza
Year: 1965 – 84
Engine
    Make: Continental
    Model: IO-520-B
    Horsepower: 285
    TBO: 1700 hours
Speeds
    Maximum: 210 mph
    Cruise: 203 mph
    Stall: 63 mph
Fuel capacity: 50 gallons
Rate of climb: 1136 fpm
Transitions
    Takeoff over 50-foot obstacle: 1320 feet
    Ground run: 965 feet
    Landing over 50-foot obstacle: 1177 feet
    Ground roll: 647 feet
Weights
    Gross: 3400 pounds

Empty: 1970 pounds
Seats: Five-Six
Dimensions
    Length: 25 feet 1 inch
    Height: 6 feet 6 inches
    Span: 32 feet 9 inches

Make: Beechcraft   Model: V35 Turbo Bonanza
Year: 1966–70
Engine
    Make: Continental
    Model: TSIO-520-D
    Horsepower: 285
    TBO: 1400 hours
Speeds
    Maximum: 240 mph
    Cruise: 224 mph
    Stall: 63 mph
Fuel capacity: 50 gallons
Rate of climb: 1225 fpm
Transitions
    Takeoff over 50-foot obstacle: 1320 feet
    Ground run: 950 feet
    Landing over 50-foot obstacle: 1177 feet
    Ground roll: 647 feet
Weights
    Gross: 3400 pounds
    Empty: 2027 pounds
Seats: Six
Dimensions
    Length: 25 feet 1 inch
    Height: 6 feet 6 inches
    Span: 32 feet 9 inches

Make: Beechcraft   Model: 36/A36 Bonanza
Year: 1968–83
Engine
    Make: Continental
    Model: IO-520-BB
    Horsepower: 285
    TBO: 1700 hours
Speeds
    Maximum: 206 mph
    Cruise: 193 mph
    Stall: 60 mph

Fig. 9-9. Beechcraft A36 Bonanza.

Fuel capacity: 74 gallons
Rate of climb: 1030 fpm
Transitions
    Takeoff over 50-foot obstacle: 2040 feet
    Ground run: 1140 feet
    Landing over 50-foot obstacle: 1450 feet
    Ground roll: 840 feet
Weights
    Gross: 3600 pounds
    Empty: 2295 pounds
Seats: Six
Dimensions
    Length: 27 feet 6 inches
    Height: 8 feet 5 inches
    Span: 33 feet 6 inches

BELLANCA

Bellanca airplanes have been good performers throughout the years, but there aren't as many as the more popular makes.

Bellanca has been in and out of business several times. This is no mark against the airplanes themselves, however. Northern Aircraft Company, Downer Aircraft, Inter-Aire, Bellanca Sales, and Miller Flying Service have all been associated with manufacturing Bellanca airplanes at one time or another.

The Bellanca fuselage is fabric-covered and the wings are of wooden construction. This type of construction may be part of the reason for the general lack of popularity of these planes. Bellanca wings are said to be the strongest in the industry.

The tail configurations have changed considerably over the years of production. Prior to 1964, Bellancas originally had three surfaces, and were similar in appearance to the Lockheed Constellation. Later models have standard tails with a single vertical surface.

A used Bellanca, in good condition, can be a lot of airplane for the dollar. They are fast and roomy, but beware of the plane requiring recovery, as that is a sure way to spend several thousand dollars (Figs. 9-10 and 9-11).

Make: Bellanca   Model: 14–19 Cruisemaster
Year: 1950–51
Engine
      Make: Lycoming
      Model: O-435-A
      Horsepower: 190
      TBO: 1200 hours
Speeds
      Maximum: 200 mph
      Cruise: 180 mph
      Stall: 44 mph
Fuel capacity: 40 gallons
Rate of climb: 1250 fpm
Transitions
      Takeoff over 50-foot obstacle: 1270 feet
      Ground run: 850 feet
      Landing over 50-foot obstacle: 1025 feet
      Ground roll: 450 feet
Weights
      Gross: 2600 pounds
      Empty: 1575 pounds
Seats: Four
Dimensions
      Length: 23 feet
      Height: 6 feet 2 inches
      Span: 34 feet 2 inches

Make: Bellanca   Model: 14–19–2 Cruisemaster
Year: 1957–59
Engine
    Make: Continental
    Model: O-470-K
    Horsepower: 230
    TBO: 1500 hours
Speeds
    Maximum: 206 mph
    Cruise: 196 mph
    Stall: 46 mph
Fuel capacity: 40 gallons
Rate of climb: 1500 fpm
Transitions
    Takeoff over 50-foot obstacle: 1025 feet
    Ground run: 760 feet
    Landing over 50-foot obstacle: 1150 feet
    Ground roll: 470 feet
Weights
    Gross: 2700 pounds
    Empty: 1640 pounds
Seats: Four
Dimensions
    Length: 23 feet
    Height: 6 feet 2 inches
    Span: 34 feet 2 inches

Miller Flying Service

Fig. 9-10. Bellanca 14-19-3B.

Make: Bellanca   Model: 14-19-3 (A-C)
Year: 1959 – 68
Engine
    Make: Continental
    Model: IO-470-F
    Horsepower: 260
    TBO: 1500 hours
Speeds
    Maximum: 208 mph
    Cruise: 203 mph
    Stall: 62 mph
Fuel capacity: 40 gallons
Rate of climb: 1500 fpm
Transitions
    Takeoff over 50-foot obstacle: 1000 feet
    Ground run: 340 feet
    Landing over 50-foot obstacle: 800 feet
    Ground roll: 400 feet
Weights
    Gross: 3000 pounds
    Empty: 1850 pounds
Seats: Four
Dimensions
    Length: 23 feet 6 inches
    Height: 6 feet 5 inches
    Span: 34 feet 2 inches

Make: Bellanca   Model: 17 – 30 Viking
Year: 1967 – 70
Engine
    Make: Continental
    Model: IO-520-K1A
    Horsepower: 300
    TBO: 1700
Speeds
    Maximum: 192 mph
    Cruise: 188 mph
    Stall: 62 mph
Fuel capacity: 58 gallons
Rate of climb: 1840 fpm
Transitions
    Takeoff over 50-foot obstacle: 908 feet
    Ground run: 450 feet
    Landing over 50-foot obstacle: 1050 feet
    Ground roll: 575 feet

Fig. 9-11. Bellanca Viking.

Weights
    Gross: 3200 pounds
    Empty: 1900 pounds
Seats: Four
Dimensions
    Length: 23 feet 7 inches
    Height: 7 feet 4 inches
    Span: 34 feet 2 inches

Make: Bellanca   Model: 17 – 30 A/B
Year: 1970 – 90
Engine
    Make: Continental
    Model: IO-520-K1A
    Horsepower: 300
    TBO: 1700
Speeds
    Maximum: 208 mph
    Cruise: 202 mph
    Stall: 70 mph
Fuel capacity: 68 gallons
Rate of climb: 1210 fpm

Transitions
    Takeoff over 50-foot obstacle: 1420 feet
    Ground run: NA
    Landing over 50-foot obstacle: 1340 feet
    Ground roll: NA
Weights
    Gross: 3325 pounds
    Empty: 2185 pounds
Seats: Four
Dimensions
    Length: 26 feet 4 inches
    Height: 7 feet 4 inches
    Span: 34 feet 2 inches

Make: Bellanca   Model: 17 – 31/A
Year: 1969 – 78
Engine
    Make: Continental
    Model: IO-540-K1E5
    Horsepower: 300
    TBO: 2000
Speeds
    Maximum: 200 mph
    Cruise: 190 mph
    Stall: 70 mph
Fuel capacity: 68 gallons
Rate of climb: 1170 fpm
Transitions
    Takeoff over 50-foot obstacle: 1420 feet
    Ground run: 980
    Landing over 50-foot obstacle: 1340 feet
    Ground roll: 835
Weights
    Gross: 3325 pounds
    Empty: 2247 pounds
Seats: Four
Dimensions
    Length: 26 feet 4 inches
    Height: 7 feet 4 inches
    Span: 34 feet 2 inches

Make: Bellanca   Model: 17 – 31 TC/ATC (turbo)
Year: 1969 – 79
Engine
    Make: Continental
    Model: IO-520-K1A (Rayjay Turbo charging)

Horsepower: 300
TBO: 1700
Speeds
    Maximum: 222 mph
    Cruise: 215 mph
    Stall: 62 mph
Fuel capacity: 72 gallons
Rate of climb: 1800 fpm
Transitions
    Takeoff over 50-foot obstacle: 890 feet
    Ground run: 460 feet
    Landing over 50-foot obstacle: 1100 feet
    Ground roll: 575 feet
Weights
    Gross: 3200 pounds
    Empty: 2010 pounds
Seats: Four
Dimensions
    Length: 23 feet 7 inches
    Height: 7 feet 4 inches
    Span: 34 feet 2 inches

CESSNA

Along with the Beech Staggerwing, another airplane suitable for this chapter is of historical interest: the Cessna 190. The 190 and subsequent 195 airplanes, although produced later than the Beech Staggerwings, are also powered with radial engines. They are very roomy, can land nearly anywhere, and their metal construction makes them less expensive to maintain than the Staggerwing.

Cessna's 180, covered in the next chapter, was the evolutionary ancestor of the popular Cessna 182. The 182 is a real workhorse, able to carry a full complement of passengers, fuel, and baggage. Although without retractable landing gear, it is considered a complex airplane because of gross weight and the 230-hp engine. Changes to the 182 help identification of the various year models:

- 1960, swept tail
- 1962, rear window
- 1972, tubular landing gear
- 1977, 100 octane engine

In 1960, the Model 210 Centurion entered production as a four-seat plane with a 260-hp engine and retractable gear; the engine increased to 285 hp in 1964.

Cessna added retractable landing gear to several planes seen in the "easy-flier" category including the 172-RG and the 177-RG. Additionally, even the 182 got retractable in the 182-RG model.

Generally, Cessna airplanes are well thought of, maintained without excess expense, and fly easily. The high wings afford excellent downward visibility (Figs. 9-12 through 9-17).

Fig. 9-12. Cessna 1949 195.

Make: Cessna   Model: 190/195
Year: 1947–54

Engine
    Make: Jacobs
    Model: R-755 (Continental R-670 240-hp in the 190)
    Horsepower: 245 to 300
    TBO: 1000 hours
Speeds
    Maximum: 176 mph
    Cruise: 170 mph
    Stall: 64 mph
Fuel capacity: 80 gallons
Rate of climb: 1050 feet
Transitions
    Takeoff over 50-foot obstacle: 1670 feet
    Ground run: NA
    Landing over 50-foot obstacle: 1495 feet
    Ground roll: NA
Weights
    Gross: 3350 pounds
    Empty: 2030 pounds
Seats: Five
Dimensions
    Length: 27 feet 3 inches
    Height: 7 feet 2 inches
    Span: 36 feet 2 inches

Cessna

Fig. 9-13. Cessna 1956 182.

Make: Cessna   Model: 182 Skylane
Year: 1956 – 86
Engine
    Make: Continental

Model: O-470 (O-470-U after 1976)
Horsepower: 230
TBO: 1500 hours
Speeds
    Maximum: 165 mph
    Cruise: 157 mph
    Stall: 57 mph
Fuel capacity: 56 gallons
Rate of climb: 890 fpm
Transitions
    Takeoff over 50-foot obstacle: 1350 feet
    Ground run: 705 feet
    Landing over 50-foot obstacle: 1350 feet
    Ground roll: 590 feet
Weights
    Gross: 2950 pounds
    Empty: 1595 pounds
Seats: Four
Dimensions
    Length: 28 feet 2 inches
    Height: 9 feet 2 inches
    Span: 35 feet 10 inches

Make: Cessna   Model: 210
Year: 1960 – 63
Engine
    Make: Continental
    Model: IO-470-E
    Horsepower: 260
    TBO: 1500 hours
Speeds
    Maximum: 198 mph
    Cruise: 189 mph
    Stall: 60 mph
Fuel capacity: 84 gallons
Rate of climb: 1270 fpm
Transitions
    Takeoff over 50-foot obstacle: 1210 feet
    Ground run: 695 feet
    Landing over 50-foot obstacle: 1110 feet
    Ground roll: 725 feet
Weights
    Gross: 3000 pounds
    Empty: 1780 pounds
Seats: Four

Dimensions
    Length: 27 feet 9 inches
    Height: 9 feet 9 inches
    Span: 36 feet 7 inches

Fig. 9-14. Cessna 1972 210 Centurion.

Make: Cessna   Model: 210 Centurion
Year: 1964 – 73
Engine
    Make: Continental
    Model: IO-520-A
    Horsepower: 285
    TBO: 1700 hours
Speeds
    Maximum: 200 mph
    Cruise: 188 mph
    Stall: 65 mph
Fuel capacity: 84 gallons
Rate of climb: 860 fpm
Transitions
    Takeoff over 50-foot obstacle: 1900 feet
    Ground run: 1100 feet
    Landing over 50-foot obstacle: 1500 feet
    Ground roll: 765 feet
Weights
    Gross: 3800 pounds
    Empty: 2134 pounds
Seats: Six
Dimensions
    Length: 27 feet 9 inches
    Height: 9 feet 9 inches
    Span: 36 feet 7 inches

Make: Cessna   Model: 210 Turbo Centurion
Year: 1974–76
Engine
    Make: Continental
    Model: TSIO-520
    Horsepower: 300
    TBO: 1400 hours
Speeds
    Maximum: 200 mph
    Cruise: 196 mph
    Stall: 65 mph
Fuel capacity: 84 gallons
Rate of climb: 1060 fpm
Transitions
    Takeoff over 50-foot obstacle: 2050 feet
    Ground run: 1215 feet
    Landing over 50-foot obstacle: 1585
    Ground roll: 815 feet
Weights
    Gross: 3850 pounds
    Empty: 2220 pounds
Seats: Six
Dimensions
    Length: 28 feet 2 inches
    Height: 9 feet 8 inches
    Span: 36 feet 9 inches

Fig. 9-15. Cessna 1983 172 Cutlass RG.

Make: Cessna   Model: 172-RG
Year: 1980–85
Engine
    Make: Lycoming
    Model: O-360-F1A6

Horsepower: 180
TBO: 2000 hours
Speeds
    Maximum: 167 mph
    Cruise: 161 mph
    Stall: 58 mph
Fuel capacity: 66 gallons
Rate of climb: 800 fpm
Transitions
    Takeoff over 50-foot obstacle: 1775 feet
    Ground run: 1060 feet
    Landing over 50-foot obstacle: 1340 feet
    Ground roll: 625 feet
Weights
    Gross: 2650 pounds
    Empty: 1555 pounds
Seats: Four
Dimensions
    Length: 27 feet 5 inches
    Height: 8 feet 10 inches
    Span: 35 feet 10 inches

Fig. 9-16. Cessna 177 Cardinal RG.

Make: Cessna   Model: 177-RG Cardinal
Year: 1971–78
Engine
    Make: Lycoming
    Model: IO-360-A1B6D
    Horsepower: 200
    TBO: 1800 hours
Speeds
    Maximum: 180 mph
    Cruise: 171 mph

Stall: 57 mph
Fuel capacity: 60 gallons
Rate of climb: 925 fpm
Transitions
    Takeoff over 50-foot obstacle: 1585 feet
    Ground run: 890 feet
    Landing over 50-foot obstacle: 1350 feet
    Ground roll: 730 feet
Weights
    Gross: 2800 pounds
    Empty: 1645 pounds
Seats: Four
Dimensions
    Length: 27 feet 3 inches
    Height: 8 feet 7 inches
    Span: 35 feet 6 inches

Fig. 9-17. Cessna 1983 182 Skylane RG.

Make: Cessna   Model 182-RG
Year: 1978 – 86
Engine
    Make: Lycoming
    Model: O-540-J3C5D
    Horsepower: 235
    TBO: 2000 hours
Speeds
    Maximum: 184 mph
    Cruise: 180 mph
    Stall: 58 mph
Fuel capacity: 56 gallons
Rate of climb: 1140 fpm

Transitions
    Takeoff over 50-foot obstacle: 1570 feet
    Ground run: 820 feet
    Landing over 50-foot obstacle: 1320 feet
    Ground roll: 600 feet
Weights
    Gross: 3100 pounds
    Empty: 1750 pounds
Seats: Four
Dimensions
    Length: 28 feet 7 inches
    Height: 8 feet 11 inches
    Span: 35 feet 10 inches

LAKE

If the thought of having lunch in a quiet sheltered cove of a lake or a river is a turn-on, then perhaps the Lake amphibian is for you. Amphibian means that this plane is equally at home on land or on water. You can take off from a paved runway, fly hundreds of miles, and land on a secluded lake.

Many pilots consider amphibian aircraft to be lackluster in performance. They should consider the size of the engine and the fact this is a four-place airplane, then look at the performance data. The Lake is no slouch and performs as well or better than plenty of land-bound airplanes.

First produced with a 180-hp engine in 1960 as the LA-4, this aircraft was updated to 200-hp in 1970 and renamed the Buccaneer. The latest version, the Renegade, is powered with a 250-hp engine.

Lake owners can take advantage of something seldom found in general aviation—factory service. This includes affordable refurbishing, repairs, and updating (Fig. 9-18).

Fig. 9-18. Lake Amphibian.

Make: Lake   Model: LA-4
Year: 1960–71
Engine
    Make: Lycoming
    Model: O-360-A1A
    Horsepower: 180
    TBO: 2000 hours
Speeds
    Maximum: 135 mph
    Cruise: 131 mph
    Stall: 51 mph
Fuel capacity: 40 gallons

Rate of climb: 800 fpm
Transitions (add 40 percent on water)
    Takeoff over 50-foot obstacle: 1275 feet
    Ground run: 650 feet
    Landing over 50-foot obstacle: 900 feet
    Ground roll: 475 feet
Weights
    Gross: 2400 pounds
    Empty: 1550 pounds
Seats: Four
Dimensions
    Length: 24 feet 11 inches
    Height: 9 feet 4 inches
    Span: 38 feet

Make: Lake   Model: LA-4 200/200EP Buccaneer
Year: 1972–88
Engine
    Make: Lycoming
    Model: IO-360-A1B
    Horsepower: 200
    TBO: 1800 hours
Speeds
    Maximum: 154 mph
    Cruise: 150 mph
    Stall: 54 mph
Fuel capacity: 40 gallons
Rate of climb: 1200 fpm
Transitions (add 40 percent on water)
    Takeoff over 50-foot obstacle: 1100 feet
    Ground run: 600 feet
    Landing over 50-foot obstacle: 900 feet
    Ground roll: 475 feet
Weights
    Gross: 2690 pounds
    Empty: 1555 pounds
Seats: Four
Dimensions
    Length: 24 feet 11 inches
    Height: 9 feet 4 inches
    Span: 38 feet

Make: Lake   Model: LA-250 Renegade
Year: 1983–91
Engine
    Make: Lycoming

Model: IO-540-C4B5
Horsepower: 250
TBO: 2800 hours
Speeds
    Maximum: NA
    Cruise: 140 mph
    Stall: 61 mph
Fuel capacity: 85 gallons
Rate of climb: 900 fpm
Transitions (add 40 percent on water)
    Takeoff over 50-foot obstacle: NA
    Ground run: 980 feet
    Landing over 50-foot obstacle: NA
    Ground roll: NA
Weights
    Gross: 3050 pounds
    Empty: 1850 pounds
Seats: Six
Dimensions
    Length: 28 feet 1 inch
    Height: 10 feet
    Span: 38 feet

MOONEY

Mooney airplanes are best known for their ability to extract maximum performance from available horsepower with minimum fuel consumption.

All, except a few very early versions, have retractable landing gear. The first Mooney retractables used a Johnson bar to manually retract and extend the gear; later versions were equipped with electrically operated landing gear.

Mooney airplanes have undergone many power and name changes over the years, often leading to considerable confusion:

- M-20, 55 – 57 150-hp (laminated wood wing and tail surfaces)
- M-20A, 58 – 60 180-hp
- M-20B/C Mark 21, 58 – 78 180-hp all-metal (Ranger)
- M-20E Chaparral, 64 – 75 200-hp (Super 21)
- M-20F Executive 21, 67 – 77 200-hp (10 inches longer than the M-20E)
- M-20G Mark 21, 68 – 70 180-hp all-metal (Statesman)
- M-20J Mooney 210, 77 – 91 200-hp (sloped windshield)
- M-20K Mooney 231, 79 – 85 210-hp (turbocharged)

Mooney built the M-22 Mustang, a pressurized five-seat plane, from 1967 to 1970. Approximately 26 were sold.

A real plus for Mooney airplanes is factory support. The company is still in the business of making airplanes, an enviable position in general aviation today (Figs. 9-19 through 9-24).

Fig. 9-19. Mooney M20.

Make: Mooney   Model: M-20
Year: 1955–57
Engine
    Make: Lycoming
    Model: O-320
    Horsepower: 150
    TBO: 2000 hours
Speeds
    Maximum: 171 mph
    Cruise: 165 mph
    Stall: 57 mph
Fuel capacity: 35 gallons
Rate of climb: 900 fpm
Transitions
    Takeoff over 50-foot obstacle: 1150 feet
    Ground run: 850 feet
    Landing over 50-foot obstacle: 1100 feet
    Ground roll: 600 feet
Weights
    Gross: 2450 pounds
    Empty: 1415 pounds
Seats: Four
Dimensions
    Length: 23 feet 1 inch
    Height: 8 feet 3 inches
    Span: 35 feet

Fig. 9-20. Mooney M20B.

Make: Mooney   Model: M-20 A/B/C/G
Year: 1958–78
Engine
    Make: Lycoming
    Model: O-360
    Horsepower: 180
    TBO: 2000 hours
Speeds
    Maximum: 185 mph
    Cruise: 180 mph
    Stall: 57 mph
Fuel capacity: 52 gallons
Rate of climb: 1010 fpm
Transitions
    Takeoff over 50-foot obstacle: 1525 feet
    Ground run: 890 feet
    Landing over 50-foot obstacle: 1365 feet
    Ground roll: 550 feet
Weights
    Gross: 2575 pounds
    Empty: 1525 pounds
Seats: Four
Dimensions
    Length: 23 feet 2 inches
    Height: 8 feet 4 inches
    Span: 35 feet

Fig. 9-21. Mooney M20E.

Make: Mooney   Model: M-20 E/F
Year: 1965 – 77
Engine
    Make: Lycoming
    Model: IO-360-A1A
    Horsepower: 200
    TBO: 1800 hours
Speeds
    Maximum: 190 mph
    Cruise: 184 mph
    Stall: 57 mph
Fuel capacity: 52 gallons
Rate of climb: 1125 fpm
Transitions
    Takeoff over 50-foot obstacle: 1550 feet
    Ground run: 760 feet
    Landing over 50-foot obstacle: 1550 feet
    Ground roll: 595 feet
Weights
    Gross: 2575 pounds
    Empty: 1600 pounds
Seats: Four
Dimensions
    Length: 23 feet 2 inches
    Height: 8 feet 4 inches
    Span: 35 feet

Make: Mooney   Model: M-20J 201
Year: 1977 – 91
Engine
    Make: Lycoming
    Model: IO-360-A3B6D
    Horsepower: 200
    TBO: 1800 hours
Speeds
    Maximum: 202 mph
    Cruise: 195 mph
    Stall: 63 mph
Fuel capacity: 64 gallons
Rate of climb: 1030 fpm
Transitions
    Takeoff over 50-foot obstacle: 1517 feet
    Ground run: 850 feet
    Landing over 50-foot obstacle: 1610 feet
    Ground roll: 770 feet

Fig. 9-22. Mooney M20E Chaparral.

Weights
    Gross: 2740 pounds
    Empty: 1640 pounds
Seats: Four
Dimensions
    Length: 24 feet 8 inches
    Height: 8 feet 4 inches
    Span: 36 feet 1 inch

Make: Mooney   Model: Mark 20K 231
Year: 1979 – 85
Engine
    Make: Continental
    Model: TSIO-360-GBA
    Horsepower: 210
    TBO: 1800 hours
Speeds
    Maximum: 231 mph
    Cruise: 220 mph
    Stall: 66 mph
Fuel capacity: 75 gallons
Rate of climb: 1080 fpm

Fig. 9-23. Mooney 201/231.

Transitions
    Takeoff over 50-foot obstacle: 2060 feet
    Ground run: 1220 feet
    Landing over 50-foot obstacle: 2280 feet
    Ground roll: 1147 feet
Weights
    Gross: 2900 pounds
    Empty: 1800 pounds
Seats: Four
Dimensions
    Length: 25 feet 5 inches
    Height: 8 feet 4 inches
    Span: 36 feet 1 inch

Fig. 9-24. Mooney M-22 Mustang.

Make: Mooney   Model: Mark 22 Mustang
Year: 1967–70
Engine
    Make: Lycoming
    Model: TSIO-541-A1A
    Horsepower: 310
    TBO: 1300 hours
Speeds
    Maximum: 250 mph
    Cruise: 230 mph
    Stall: 69 mph
Fuel capacity: 92 gallons
Rate of climb: 1120 fpm
Transitions
    Takeoff over 50-foot obstacle: 2079 feet
    Ground run: 1142 feet
    Landing over 50-foot obstacle: 1549 feet
    Ground roll: 958 feet
Weights
    Gross: 3680 pounds
    Empty: 2380 pounds
Seats: Five
Dimensions
    Length: 26 feet 1 inch
    Height: 9 feet 1 inch
    Span: 35 feet

NAVION

Of all the complex airplanes, there is no other like the Navion. It was placed into production by North American Aviation in 1946, just before the Beechcraft Bonanza came out. Sadly, though, the Navion has bounced around from one manufacturer to another in and out of production until 1976, never enjoying the popularity of the Bonanza.

The Navion is a strong and capable short-field plane; unimproved strips don't seem to bother it. Navions were built with 185-, 205-, and 225-hp engines. Rangemasters, a later model, were available with a 260- or 285-hp engine.

Few all-original Navions exist today, as most have been modified and updated. A wise purchaser will contact the American Navion Society (see Appendix E) and request their pamphlet about buying a used Navion before making a choice; they can also answer questions about modifications and difficulties (see Figs. 9-25 and 9-26).

Fig. 9-25. Navion.

Make: Navion   Model: NA
Year: 1946–51
Engine
    Make: Continental
    Model: E-185-3
    Horsepower: 205
    TBO: 1500 hours
Speeds
    Maximum: 163 mph
    Cruise: 148 mph
    Stall: 60 mph

Fuel capacity: 40 gallons
Rate of climb: 750 fpm
Transitions
    Takeoff over 50-foot obstacle: 1500 feet
    Ground run: 670 feet
    Landing over 50-foot obstacle: 1300 feet
    Ground roll: 500 feet
Weights
    Gross: 2750 pounds
    Empty: 1700 pounds
Seats: Four
Dimensions
    Length: 27 feet 3 inches
    Height: 8 feet 7 inches
    Span: 33 feet 4 inches

Don Downie

Fig. 9-26. Navion Ranger.

Make: Navion   Model: Rangemaster
Year: 1961–75
Engine
    Make: Continental
    Model: IO-520-B
    Horsepower: 285
    TBO: 1700 hours
Speeds
    Maximum: 203 mph
    Cruise: 191 mph
    Stall: 55 mph
Fuel capacity: 40 gallons
Rate of climb: 1375 fpm
Transitions
    Takeoff over 50-foot obstacle: 950 feet
    Ground run: 740 feet

Landing over 50-foot obstacle: 980 feet
Ground roll: 760 feet

Weights
Gross: 3315 pounds
Empty: 2000 pounds

Seats: Four

Dimensions
Length: 27 feet 3 inches
Height: 8 feet 7 inches
Span: 33 feet 4 inches

PIPER

Piper entered the complex airplane market in 1958 with the PA-24 Comanche. It was an all-metal, low-wing craft that became popular as a market trend setter. Built with several different engines, production ceased in 1972 when Piper's Lock Haven, Pennsylvania, manufacturing facility was flooded during a hurricane.

Piper's PA-28/235 is a rugged and honest airplane, yet easy to fly and quite inexpensive to maintain. The 235 will carry a load equivalent to its weight and, in later versions, do it in style. The 235 was replaced by the 236 in 1979, renamed the Dakota, and is a meld of the Warrior wing and the Archer fuselage.

The large success of the PA-28 series no doubt moved Piper, as it had Cessna, to install retractable landing gear and aim toward a different market. Thus, in 1967 the PA-28R Arrow series arose as an extension to the Cherokee 180. The new Arrow had the same fuel burn as the Cherokee, yet cruised about 25 mph faster. Shown to be efficient, simplicity was also desired in these new retractables and even the responsibility of controlling the landing gear was removed from the pilot (automatic landing gear). Of course the basic airplane saw different configurations and names:

- 1969, 200-hp Arrow 200
- 1973, Arrow II/200 (five-place)
- 1977, Arrow III/201 (turbo version is T201)
- 1979, Arrow IV with T-tail
- 1990, PA-28R 201 conventional tail returns

In 1979, the PA-32R-300 Lance was introduced as a retractable version of the popular PA-32 Cherokee Six (see Chapter 10). The Lance first appeared with a conventional tail, and after the first half of 1978, with a T-tail. Many pilots/owners complained about the T-tail and its lack of authority at low speeds. In 1980, the conventional tail returned and the PA-32R-300 was renamed the Saratoga.

The last complex entry from Piper is the Malibu, a pressurized cabin-class single engine airplane, costing nearly $500,000 new. The Malibu has been the subject of numerous ADs involving airframe failure in turbulance.

Although not as popular as other manufacturer's airplanes, Piper complex airplanes offer fair values and an excellent selection of them can be found on today's market (Figs. 9-27 through 9-33).

Make: Piper   Model: PA-24/180
Year: 1958 – 64
Engine
    Make: Lycoming
    Model: O-360-A1A
    Horsepower: 180
    TBO: 2000 hours
Speeds
    Maximum: 167 mph

Cruise: 150 mph
Stall: 61 mph
Fuel capacity: 60 gallons
Rate of climb: 910 fpm
Transitions
    Takeoff over 50-foot obstacle: 2240 feet
    Ground run: 750 feet
    Landing over 50-foot obstacle: 1025 feet
    Ground roll: 600 feet
Weights
    Gross: 2550 pounds
    Empty: 1475 pounds
Seats: Four
Dimensions
    Length: 24 feet 9 inches
    Height: 7 feet 5 inches
    Span: 36 feet

Fig. 9-27. Piper PA-24 Comanche.

Make: Piper   Model: PA-24/250
Year: 1958 – 64
Engine
    Make: Lycoming
    Model: O-540-A1A5
    Horsepower: 250
    TBO: 2000 hours
Speeds
    Maximum: 190 mph
    Cruise: 181 mph
    Stall: 61 mph
Fuel capacity: 60 gallons

Rate of climb: 1350 fpm
Transitions
    Takeoff over 50-foot obstacle: 1650 feet
    Ground run: 750 feet
    Landing over 50-foot obstacle: 1025 feet
    Ground roll: 650 feet
Weights
    Gross: 2800 pounds
    Empty: 1690 pounds
Seats: Four
Dimensions
    Length: 24 feet 9 inches
    Height: 7 feet 5 inches
    Span: 36 feet

Make: Piper   Model: PA-24/260
Year: 1965–72
Engine
    Make: Lycoming
    Model: O-540 (IO-540 after 1969)
    Horsepower: 260
    TBO: 2000
Speeds
    Maximum: 195 mph
    Cruise: 185 mph
    Stall: 61 mph
Fuel capacity: 60 gallons
Rate of climb: 1320 fpm
Transitions
    Takeoff over 50-foot obstacle: 1400 feet
    Ground run: 820 feet
    Landing over 50-foot obstacle: 1200 feet
    Ground roll: 690 feet
Weights
    Gross: 3200 pounds
    Empty: 1773 pounds
Seats: Four
Dimensions
    Length: 25 feet 8 inches
    Height: 7 feet 3 inches
    Span: 36 feet

Make: Piper   Model: PA-24/235 Cherokee/Charger/Pathfinder
Year: 1964–77
Engine
    Make: Lycoming

Fig. 9-28. Piper PA-22/235 Cherokee.

Model: O-540-B4B5
Horsepower: 235
TBO: 2000 hours
Speeds
    Maximum: 166 mph
    Cruise: 156 mph
    Stall: 60 mph
Fuel capacity: 84 gallons
Rate of climb: 825 fpm
Transitions
    Takeoff over 50-foot obstacle: 1360 feet
    Ground run: 800 feet
    Landing over 50-foot obstacle: 1300 feet
    Ground roll: 680 feet
Weights
    Gross: 2900 pounds
    Empty: 1410 pounds
Seats: Four
Dimensions
    Length: 23 feet 6 inches
    Height: 7 feet 1 inch
    Span: 32 feet

Make: Piper   Model: PA-28/236 Dakota
Year: 1979 – 90
Engine
    Make: Lycoming
    Model: O-540-J3A5D
    Horsepower: 235
    TBO: 2000 hours

Fig. 9-29. Piper PA-28/236 Dakota.

Speeds
    Maximum: 170 mph
    Cruise: 159 mph
    Stall: 64 mph
Fuel capacity: 72 gallons
Rate of climb: 1110 fpm
Transitions
    Takeoff over 50-foot obstacle: 1210 feet
    Ground run: 885 feet
    Landing over 50-foot obstacle: 1725 feet
    Ground roll: 825 feet
Weights
    Gross: 3000 pounds
    Empty: 1634 pounds
Seats: Four
Dimensions
    Length: 24 feet 8 inches
    Height: 7 feet 2 inches
    Span: 35 feet

Make: Piper   Model: PA-28R/180 Arrow
Year: 1967 – 71
Engine
    Make: Lycoming
    Model: IO-360-B1E
    Horsepower: 180
    TBO: 2000 hours
Speeds
    Maximum: 170 mph
    Cruise: 162 mph

Stall: 61 mph
Fuel capacity: 50 gallons
Rate of climb: 875 fpm
Transitions
    Takeoff over 50-foot obstacle: 1240 feet
    Ground run: 820 feet
    Landing over 50-foot obstacle: 1340 feet
    Ground roll: 770 feet
Weights
    Gross: 2500 pounds
    Empty: 1380 pounds
Seats: Four
Dimensions
    Length: 24 feet 2 inches
    Height: 8 feet
    Span: 30 feet

Fig. 9-30. Piper PA-28R Arrow 200.

Make: Piper   Model: PA-28R/200
Year: 1970-78
Engine
    Make: Lycoming
    Model: IO-360-C1C6
    Horsepower: 200
    TBO: 1800 hours
Speeds
    Maximum: 176 mph
    Cruise: 162 mph
    Stall: 63 mph
Fuel capacity: 50 gallons
Rate of climb: 831 fpm

Transitions
    Takeoff over 50-foot obstacle: 1580 feet
    Ground run: 780 feet
    Landing over 50-foot obstacle: 1350 feet
    Ground roll: 760 feet
Weights
    Gross: 2750 pounds
    Empty: 1601 pounds
Seats: Four
Dimensions
    Length: 24 feet 2 inches
    Height: 8 feet
    Span: 30 feet

Fig. 9-31. Piper PA-28R Turbo Arrow IV.

Make: Piper   Model: PA-28/200 Turbo Arrow
Year: 1977–78
Engine
    Make: Continental
    Model: TSIO-360-F
    Horsepower: 200
    TBO: 1400 hours
Speeds
    Maximum: 198 mph
    Cruise: 172 mph
    Stall: 63 mph
Fuel capacity: 50 gallons
Rate of climb: 940 fpm
Transitions
    Takeoff over 50-foot obstacle: 1620 feet
    Ground run: 1120 feet
    Landing over 50-foot obstacle: 1555 feet
    Ground roll: 645 feet

Weights
    Gross: 2900 pounds
    Empty: 1638 pounds
Seats: Four
Dimensions
    Length: 24 feet 2 inches
    Height: 8 feet
    Span: 30 feet

Fig. 9-32. Piper PA-32R 300 Lance.

Make: Piper   Model: PA-32R/300 Lance
Year: 1976 – 79
Engine
    Make: Lycoming
    Model: IO-540 (opt. TC)
    Horsepower: 300
    TBO: 2000 hours
Speeds
    Maximum: 180 mph
    Cruise: 176 mph
    Stall: 60 mph
Fuel capacity: 98 gallons
Rate of climb: 1000 fpm
Transitions
    Takeoff over 50-foot obstacle: 1660 feet
    Ground run: 960 feet
    Landing over 50-foot obstacle: 1708 feet
    Ground roll: 880 feet

Weights
    Gross: 3600 pounds
    Empty: 1980 pounds
Seats: Seven
Dimensions
    Length: 27 feet 9 inches
    Height: 9 feet
    Span: 32 feet 9 inches

Make: Piper   Model: PA-32R/301 Saratoga
Year: 1980 – 90
Engine
    Make: Lycoming
    Model: IO-540-K1G5
    Horsepower: 300
    TBO: 2000 hours
Speeds
    Maximum: 188 mph
    Cruise: 182 mph
    Stall: 66 mph
Fuel capacity: 102 gallons
Rate of climb: 1010 fpm
Transitions
    Takeoff over 50-foot obstacle: 1573 feet
    Ground run: 1013 feet
    Landing over 50-foot obstacle: 1612 feet
    Ground roll: 732 feet
Weights
    Gross: 3600 pounds
    Empty: 1999 pounds
Seats: Seven
Dimensions
    Length: 27 feet 8 inches
    Height: 8 feet 2 inches
    Span: 36 feet 2 inches

Make: Piper   Model: PA-32R/301T Saratoga
Year: 1980 – 90
Engine
    Make: Lycoming
    Model: TIO-540-K1G5
    Horsepower: 300
    TBO: 2000 hours
Speeds
    Maximum: 224 mph

Cruise: 203 mph
Stall: 65 mph
Fuel capacity: 102 gallons
Rate of climb: 1120 fpm
Transitions
    Takeoff over 50-foot obstacle: 1420 feet
    Ground run: 960 feet
    Landing over 50-foot obstacle: 1725 feet
    Ground roll: 732 feet
Weights
    Gross: 3600 pounds
    Empty: 2078 pounds
Seats: Seven
Dimensions
    Length: 28 feet 2 inches
    Height: 8 feet 2 inches
    Span: 36 feet 2 inches

Fig. 9-33. Piper PA-46 Malibu.

Make: Piper   Model: PA-46 Malibu
Year: 1984 – 90
Engine
    Make: Continental
    Model: TSIO-520-BE
    Horsepower: 310
    TBO: 2000 hours

Speeds
    Maximum: 269 mph
    Cruise: 235 mph
    Stall: 67 mph
Fuel capacity: 120 gallons
Rate of climb: 1143 fpm
Transitions
    Takeoff over 50-foot obstacle: 2025 feet
    Ground run: 1440 feet
    Landing over 50-foot obstacle: 1800 feet
    Ground roll: 1070 feet
Weights
    Gross: 4100 pounds
    Empty: 2460 pounds
Seats: Six
Dimensions
    Length: 28 feet 10 inches
    Height: 11 feet 4 inches
    Span: 43 feet

REPUBLIC

Republic Aviation was famous for its World War II P-47 Thunderbolt fighters and after the war entered the civilian aviation marketplace with the Seabee, a four-place amphibian. Few Seabees were produced and in 1948 production was halted for all time.

Seabees are stout aircraft, built to last. Most of those currently flying have been extensively modified—some even to twin engine—hence, performance data is sketchy. Today a good Seabee commands a high price, far more than the approximately $4,800 they sold for when new (Fig. 9-34).

Fig. 9-34. Republic Seabee.

Make: Republic   Model: RC-3 Seabee
Year: 1948
Engine
    Make: Franklin
    Model: 6A-215-G8F
    Horsepower: 215
    TBO: 1200
Speeds
    Maximum: 120 mph
    Cruise: 100 mph
    Stall: 58 mph
Fuel capacity: 75 gallons
Rate of climb: 700 fpm
Transitions
    Takeoff over 50-foot obstacle: NA

Ground run: NA
Landing over 50-foot obstacle: NA
Ground roll: NA
Weights
Gross: 3000 pounds
Empty: 2950 pounds
Seats: Four
Dimensions
Length: NA
Height: NA
Span: NA

10

Heavy-haulers

THE TERM "HEAVY-HAULER" refers to the capabilities of the described airplanes and includes carrying heavy loads—often exceeding that which they were designed to carry—ranging from people to livestock, and all the assorted possible hardware and cargo in between.

These planes will be found doing their everyday work in the outer reaches of the lower 48 states on ranches, reservations, or perhaps with the highway patrol. Alaska, Central American, Africa, and the Australian outback are typically home to these airplanes.

Heavy-haulers are built beefy, with ample power and large lifting capabilities. Most are high-wing planes, for clearance reasons as well as easier loading, and may be found on wheels, skis, or floats.

CESSNA

Cessna's 180 has become a legend; used everywhere that strength, reliability, and performance are required. From 1953 to 1981, when production ceased, the 180 remained essentially unchanged; equipped with a Continental 0-470 engine and conventional landing gear.

The 185 Skywagon, also with conventional gear, was introduced in 1961 with a 260-hp engine, updated in 1966 with a 300-hp engine. Both planes will accept an optional under-fuselage cargo carrier that will hold up to 300 pounds.

The 1963 Cessna 205 was introduced as a fixed-gear version of the 210. The 205 is basically a tricycle geared counterpart to the 185. It too can be fitted with the under-fuselage cargo carrier. The 205 was replaced in 1965 by the U206 Super Skywagon. The 206 has large double doors on the right side of the cabin to allow loading of awkward cargo items. It's powered with a 285-hp engine.

The P206 Super Skylane is a fancy version of the U206 that is designed to carry passengers. In 1969 the seven-place 207 Skywagon was introduced as an outgrowth of the 206 series.

Cessna's latest entry to the heavy-hauler market is the Caravan, a turbo-prop, single-engine plane designed for short hauls of light cargo. It is the largest and most costly of all the heavy-haulers, selling for slightly over $1 million.

Cessna has built an excellent reputation for work airplanes. They are seen all over the world, representing economy and dependability (Figs. 10-1 through 10-6).

Fig. 10-1. Cessna 1953 180.

Make: Cessna   Model: 180
Year: 1953 – 81
Engine
    Make: Continental
    Model: O-470-K
    Horsepower: 230
    TBO: 1500 hours
Speeds
    Maximum: 170 mph
    Cruise: 162 mph
    Stall: 58 mph
Fuel capacity: 55 gallons
Rate of climb: 1090 fpm
Transitions
    Takeoff over 50-foot obstacle: 1225 feet
    Ground run: 625 feet
    Landing over 50-foot obstacle: 1365 feet
    Ground roll: 480 feet
Weights
    Gross: 2800 pounds
    Empty: 1545 pounds
Seats: Four (Six after 1963)
Dimensions
    Length: 25 feet 9 inches
    Height: 7 feet 9 inches
    Span: 35 feet 10 inches

Make: Cessna   Model: 185 Skywagon (260)
Year: 1961 – 66
Engine
    Make: Continental
    Model: IO-470-F
    Horsepower: 260
    TBO: 1500 hours
Speeds
    Maximum: 176 mph
    Cruise: 167 mph
    Stall: 62 mph
Fuel capacity: 65 gallons
Rate of climb: 1000 fpm
Transitions
    Takeoff over 50-foot obstacle: 1510 feet
    Ground run: 650 feet
    Landing over 50-foot obstacle: 1265 feet
    Ground roll: 610 feet
Weights
    Gross: 3200 pounds
    Empty: 1520 pounds
Seats: Six
Dimensions
    Length: 25 feet 9 inches
    Height: 7 feet 9 inches
    Span: 35 feet 10 inches

Fig. 10-2. Cessna 1983 185 Skywagon.

Make: Cessna   Model: 185 Skywagon (300)
Year: 1966 – 85
Engine
    Make: Continental

Model: IO-520-D
Horsepower: 300
TBO: 1700 hours
Speeds
    Maximum: 178 mph
    Cruise: 169 mph
    Stall: 59 mph
Fuel capacity: 65 gallons
Rate of climb: 1010 fpm
Transitions
    Takeoff over 50-foot obstacle: 1365 feet
    Ground run: 770 feet
    Landing over 50-foot obstacle: 1400 feet
    Ground roll: 480 feet
Weights
    Gross: 3350 pounds
    Empty: 1585 pounds
Seats: Six
Dimensions
    Length: 25 feet 9 inches
    Height: 7 feet 9 inches
    Span: 35 feet 10 inches

Fig. 10-3. Cessna 1963 205.

Make: Cessna   Model: 205
Year: 1963 – 64
Engine
    Make: Continental
    Model: IO-470-S
    Horsepower: 260

TBO: 1500 hours
Speeds
    Maximum: 167 mph
    Cruise: 159 mph
    Stall: 57 mph
Fuel capacity: 65 gallons
Rate of climb: 965 fpm
Transitions
    Takeoff over 50-foot obstacle: 1465 feet
    Ground run: 685 feet
    Landing over 50-foot obstacle: 1510 feet
    Ground roll: 625 feet
Weights
    Gross: 3300 pounds
    Empty: 1750 pounds
Seats: Six
Dimensions
    Length: 27 feet 3 inches
    Height: 9 feet 7 inches
    Span: 36 feet 6 inches

Fig. 10-4. Cessna 1967 206 Super Skylane.

Make: Cessna   Model: U206/P206 Super Skylane/Skywagon
Year: 1965 – 86
Engine
    Make: Continental
    Model: IO-520 (turbocharging optional)
    Horsepower: 285
    TBO: 1700 hours (1400 if turbocharged)

Speeds
      Maximum: 174 mph
      Cruise: 164 mph
      Stall: 61 mph
Fuel capacity: 65 gallons
Rate of climb: 920 fpm
Transitions
      Takeoff over 50-foot obstacle: 1265 feet
      Ground run: 675 feet
      Landing over 50-foot obstacle: 1340 feet
      Ground roll: 735 feet
Weights
      Gross: 3600 pounds
      Empty: 1750 pounds
Seats: Six
Dimensions
      Length: 28 feet
      Height: 9 feet 7 inches
      Span: 35 feet 10 inches

Make: Cessna   Model: U206/P206 Super Skylane/Skywagon
Year: 1967 – 86
Engine
      Make: Continental
      Model: IO-520
      Horsepower: 300
      TBO: 1700 hours
Speeds
      Maximum: 179 mph
      Cruise: 169 mph
      Stall: 62 mph
Fuel capacity: 65 gallons
Rate of climb: 920 fpm
Transitions
      Takeoff over 50-foot obstacle: 1780 feet
      Ground run: 900 feet
      Landing over 50-foot obstacle: 1395 feet
      Ground roll: 735 feet
Weights
      Gross: 3600 pounds
      Empty: 2000 pounds
Seats: Six
Dimensions
      Length: 28 feet 3 inches
      Height: 9 feet 4 inches
      Span: 35 feet 10 inches

Fig. 10-5. Cessna 1982 207 Stationair.

Make: Cessna   Model: 207 Skywagon/Stationair
Year: 1969 – 84
Engine
    Make: Continental
    Model: IO-520 (turbocharging optional)
    Horsepower: 300
    TBO: 1700 (1400 if turbocharged)
Speeds
    Maximum: 168 mph
    Cruise: 159 mph
    Stall: 67 mph
Fuel capacity: 61 gallons
Rate of climb: 810 fpm
Transitions
    Takeoff over 50-foot obstacle: 1970 feet
    Ground run: 1100 feet
    Landing over 50-foot obstacle: 1500 feet
    Ground roll: 765 feet
Weights
    Gross: 3800 pounds
    Empty: 1890 pounds
Seats: Seven
Dimensions
    Length: 31 feet 9 inches
    Height: 9 feet 7 inches
    Span: 35 feet 10 inches

Make: Cessna   Model: 208 Caravan
Year: 1985 – 91

Fig. 10-6. Cessna Caravan I.

Engine
    Make: Pratt & Witney
    Model: PT6A-114
    Horsepower: 600 (shaft)
    TBO: 3500
Speeds
    Maximum: 210 mph
    Cruise: 200 mph
    Stall: 69 mph
Fuel capacity: 332 gallons
Rate of climb: 1215 fpm
Transitions
    Takeoff over 50-foot obstacle: 1665 feet
    Ground run: 970 feet
    Landing over 50-foot obstacle: 1550 feet
    Ground roll: 645 feet
Weights
    Gross: 7300 pounds
    Empty: 3800 pounds
Seats: Fourteen
Dimensions
    Length: 37 feet 7 inches
    Height: 14 feet 2 inches
    Span: 51 feet 8 inches

HELIO

The Helio Courier is a STOL (short take-off and landing) airplane designed to fly and remain fully controllable at speeds far slower than any other airplane. To accomplish this feat the wings have automatic Handley Page leading edge slats and electrically operated slotted flaps. Frise ailerons work in conjunction with the arc type spoilers, which project upwards from the wing.

Although a stall speed is listed in the specifications for Helios, the effect is that of mushing down in a parachute. The flaps extend nearly 75 percent of the length of the wings. A very few have tricycle landing gear, some from the factory and others via an STC.

Several different Helio models were produced; however, most were built for special purposes and government operations and are not usually to be found on the civilian market. Popular model numbers and years of production:

- H-395, 1957–65, 295-hp engine
- H-295, 1965–74, 295-hp engine (300 lb. increase in useful load)

The Helio is a specialized airplane not often seen at the local airport (Fig. 10-7).

Fig. 10-7. Helio Courier.

Make: Helio   Model: H-395/295 Super Courier
Year: 1957–74
Engine
    Make: Lycoming
    Model: GO-489
    Horsepower: 295
    TBO: 1400 hours
Speeds
    Maximum: 167 mph
    Cruise: 162 mph
    Stall: 30 mph (min. fully controllable speed)

Fuel capacity: 60 gallons
Rate of climb: 1250 fpm
Transitions
    Takeoff over 50-foot obstacle: 610 feet
    Ground run: 335 feet
    Landing over 50-foot obstacle: 520 feet
    Ground roll: 270 feet
Weights
    Gross: 3400 pounds
    Empty: 2080 pounds
Seats: Six
Dimensions
    Length: 31 feet
    Height: 8 feet 10 inches
    Span: 39 feet

MAULE

Maules are ruggedly constructed simple airplanes specifically designed for short-field operation. With all-metal wings and a fiberglass-covered tubular fuselage, they have few moving or complex parts and are therefore economically maintained.

Production started in 1962 with the M-4 (see Chapter 9), eventually built under several model names, each designating a different engine rating:

- 145-hp (see Chapter 9)
- 180-hp Astro Rocket
- 210-hp Rocket
- 220-hp Strata Rocket

In 1974, the M-5 Lunar Rocket series replaced the M-4 with its larger tail surfaces, a 30 percent increase in flap area, and a more powerful engine making them capable of carrying larger loads almost anywhere.

The M-6, with longer wings and a 235-hp engine was built from 1983 to 1985. Performance of the M-6 is remarkable; takeoff ground runs seem almost nonexistent and approaches are incredibly slow. Maule's most recent entry is the M-7, which is powered by a 180-hp engine, with an optional 235-hp engine available. A tricycle gear version of the M-7 180-hp is pictured in Chapter 8.

Maule aircraft have a reputation of having somewhat optimistic speed figures listed in their specifications, but are hard-working airplanes usable nearly anywhere (Figs. 10-8 through 10-11).

Make: Maule   Model: M-4/180 Astro Rocket
Year: 1970–71
Engine
    Make: Franklin
    Model: 6A-355-B1
    Horsepower: 180
    TBO: 2000 hours
Speeds
    Maximum: 170 mph
    Cruise: 155 mph
    Stall: 40 mph
Fuel capacity: 42 gallons
Rate of climb: 1000 fpm
Transitions
    Takeoff over 50-foot obstacle: 700 feet
    Ground run: 500 feet
    Landing over 50-foot obstacle: 600 feet
    Ground roll: 450 feet
Weights
    Gross: 2300 pounds

Empty: 1250 pounds
Seats: Four
Dimensions
    Length: 22 feet
    Height: 6 feet 2 inches
    Span: 30 feet 10 inches

Make: Maule   Model: M-4/210 Rocket
Year: 1965–73
Engine
    Make: Continental
    Model: IO-360-A
    Horsepower: 210
    TBO: 1500 hours
Speeds
    Maximum: 180 mph
    Cruise: 165 mph
    Stall: 40 mph
Fuel capacity: 42 gallons
Rate of climb: 1250 fpm
Transitions
    Takeoff over 50-foot obstacle: 650 feet
    Ground run: 430 feet
    Landing over 50-foot obstacle: 600 feet
    Ground roll: 390 feet
Weights
    Gross: 2300 pounds
    Empty: 1120 pounds
Seats: Four
Dimensions
    Length: 22 feet
    Height: 6 feet 2 inches
    Span: 30 feet 10 inches

Make: Maule   Model: M-4/220 Strata Rocket
Year: 1967–73
Engine
    Make: Franklin
    Model: 6A-350-C1
    Horsepower: 220
    TBO: 1500 hours
Speeds
    Maximum: 180 mph
    Cruise: 165 mph
    Stall: 40 mph
Fuel capacity: 42 gallons

Fig. 10-8. Maule M-4 220.

Maule

Rate of climb: 1250 fpm
Transitions
    Takeoff over 50-foot obstacle: 600 feet
    Ground run: 400 feet
    Landing over 50-foot obstacle: 600 feet
    Ground roll: 390 feet
Weights
    Gross: 2300 pounds
    Empty: 1220 pounds
Seats: Four
Dimensions
    Length: 22 feet
    Height: 6 feet 2 inches
    Span: 30 feet 10 inches

Make: Maule   Model: M-5/180 C
Year: 1979 – 88
Engine
    Make: Continental
    Model: O-360-C1F
    Horsepower: 180
    TBO: 2000 hours
Speeds
    Maximum: NA

Cruise: 156 mph
Stall: 38 mph
Fuel capacity: 40 gallons
Rate of climb: 900 fpm
Transitions
    Takeoff over 50-foot obstacle: 800 feet
    Ground run: 200 feet
    Landing over 50-foot obstacle: 600 feet
    Ground roll: NA
Weights
    Gross: 2300 pounds
    Empty: 1300 pounds
Seats: Four
Dimensions
    Length: 22 feet 9 inches
    Height: 6 feet 4 inches
    Span: 30 feet 10 inches

Fig. 10-9. Maule M-5 220C.

Make: Maule   Model: M-5/210 Lunar Rocket
Year: 1974–77
Engine
    Make: Continental
    Model: IO-360-D
    Horsepower: 210
    TBO: 1500 hours
Speeds
    Maximum: 180 mph
    Cruise: 158 mph
    Stall: 38 mph
Fuel capacity: 40 gallons
Rate of climb: 1250 fpm

Transitions
    Takeoff over 50-foot obstacle: 600 feet
    Ground run: 400 feet
    Landing over 50-foot obstacle: 600 feet
    Ground roll: 400 feet
Weights
    Gross: 2300 pounds
    Empty: 1350 pounds
Seats: Four
Dimensions
    Length: 22 feet 9 inches
    Height: 6 feet 4 inches
    Span: 30 feet 10 inches

Make: Maule   Model: M-5/235
Year: 1977 – 88
Engine
    Make: Lycoming
    Model: O-540-J1A5D
    Horsepower: 235
    TBO: 2000 hours
Speeds
    Maximum: 185 mph
    Cruise: 172 mph
    Stall: 38 mph
Fuel capacity: 40 gallons
Rate of climb: 1350 fpm
Transitions
    Takeoff over 50-foot obstacle: 600 feet
    Ground run: 400 feet
    Landing over 50-foot obstacle: 600 feet
    Ground roll: 400 feet
Weights
    Gross: 2300 pounds
    Empty: 1400 pounds
Seats: Four
Dimensions
    Length: 22 feet 9 inches
    Height: 6 feet 4 inches
    Span: 30 feet 10 inches

Make: Maule   Model: M-6/235 Super Rocket
Year: 1981 – 91
Engine
    Make: Lycoming
    Model: IO-540-J1A5D

Fig. 10-10. Maule M-6 235C.

Horsepower: 235
TBO: 2000 hours
Speeds
    Maximum: 180 mph
    Cruise: 148 mph
    Stall: 44 mph
Fuel capacity: 40 gallons
Rate of climb: 1900 fpm
Transitions
    Takeoff over 50-foot obstacle: 540 feet
    Ground run: 150 feet
    Landing over 50-foot obstacle: 440 feet
    Ground roll: 250 feet
Weights
    Gross: 2500 pounds
    Empty: 1450 pounds
Seats: Four
Dimensions
    Length: 23 feet 6 inches
    Height: 6 feet 4 inches
    Span: 33 feet 2 inches

Make: Maule   Model: M-7/180
Year: 1985 – 91
Engine
    Make: Lycoming
    Model: O-360-C1F
    Horsepower: 180
    TBO: 2000 hours

Speeds
    Maximum: 180 mph
    Cruise: 145 mph
    Stall: 40 mph
Fuel capacity: 70 gallons
Rate of climb: 1200 fpm
Transitions
    Takeoff over 50-foot obstacle: 600 feet
    Ground run: 125 feet
    Landing over 50-foot obstacle: 500 feet
    Ground roll: 275 feet
Weights
    Gross: 2500 pounds
    Empty: 1365 pounds
Seats: Four
Dimensions
    Length: 23 feet 6 inches
    Height: 6 feet 4 inches
    Span: 30 feet 10 inches

Fig. 10-11. Maule M-7 235.

Make: Maule   Model: M-7/235
Year: 1985 – 91
Engine
    Make: Lycoming
    Model: IO-540-W1A5D or O-540-J1A5D
    Horsepower: 235
    TBO: 2000 hours
Speeds
    Maximum: 180 mph
    Cruise: 160 mph
    Stall: 35 mph

Fuel capacity: 70 gallons
Rate of climb: 2000 fpm
Transitions
    Takeoff over 50-foot obstacle: 600 feet
    Ground run: 125 feet
    Landing over 50-foot obstacle: 500 feet
    Ground roll: 275 feet
Weights
    Gross: 2500 pounds
    Empty: 1500 pounds
Seats: Four
Dimensions
    Length: 23 feet 6 inches
    Height: 6 feet 4 inches
    Span: 33 feet 8 inches

PIPER

Piper only has two airplanes fitting the "heavy-hauler" category and both defy the rule of "high-wings only" for heavy-haulers.

First is the low-winged Cherokee Six, which was manufactured from 1965 to 1979. Removable seats allow this craft to carry cargo, a stretcher, or livestock. A 260-hp was standard, with a 300-hp engine available as an option.

The second example is the PA-32-301 Saratoga which replaced the Cherokee Six in 1980. It was built with a normally aspirated engine, although a turbo-charged engine was optionally available.

Both "heavy-hauler" type Pipers are easy to fly, will operate reliably, and require little maintenance (Figs. 10-12 and 10-13).

Make: Piper   Model: PA-32/260 Cherokee Six
Year: 1965–78
Engine
    Make: Lycoming
    Model: O-540-E4B5
    Horsepower: 260
    TBO: 2000 hours (1200 without modifications)
Speeds
    Maximum: 168 mph
    Cruise: 160 mph
    Stall: 63 mph
Fuel capacity: 50 gallons
Rate of climb: 760 fpm
Transitions
    Takeoff over 50-foot obstacle: 1360 feet
    Ground run: 810 feet
    Landing over 50-foot obstacle: 1000 feet
    Ground roll: 630 feet
Weights
    Gross: 3400 pounds
    Empty: 1699 pounds
Seats: Seven
Dimensions
    Length: 27 feet 9 inches
    Height: 7 feet 11 inches
    Span: 32 feet 9 inches

Make: Piper   Model: PA-32/300 Cherokee Six
Year: 1966–79
Engine
    Make: Lycoming
    Model: O-540-K1A5B

Fig. 10-12. Piper PA-32/300 Cherokee Six.

Horsepower: 300
TBO: 2000 hours
Speeds
    Maximum: 174 mph
    Cruise: 168 mph
    Stall: 63 mph
Fuel capacity: 50 gallons
Rate of climb: 1050 fpm
Transitions
    Takeoff over 50-foot obstacle: 1140 feet
    Ground run: 700 feet
    Landing over 50-foot obstacle: 1000 feet
    Ground roll: 630 feet
Weights
    Gross: 3400 pounds
    Empty: 1846 pounds
Seats: Seven
Dimensions
    Length: 27 feet 9 inches
    Height: 7 feet 11 inches
    Span: 32 feet 9 inches

Make: Piper   Model: PA-32/301 Saratoga
Year: 1979 – 90
Engine
    Make: Lycoming
    Model: IO-540-K1G5D (Turbocharging is optional)
    Horsepower: 300
    TBO: 2000 hours

Fig. 10-13. Piper PA-32/301 Saratoga.

Speeds
    Maximum: 175 mph
    Cruise: 172 mph
    Stall: 67 mph
Fuel capacity: 102 gallons
Rate of climb: 990 fpm
Transitions
    Takeoff over 50-foot obstacle: 1759 feet
    Ground run: 1183 feet
    Landing over 50-foot obstacle: 1612 feet
    Ground roll: 732 feet
Weights
    Gross: 3600 pounds
    Empty: 1940 pounds
Seats: Seven
Dimensions
    Length: 27 feet 8 inches
    Height: 8 feet 2 inches
    Span: 36 feet 2 inches

11

Affordable twins

TWIN-ENGINE AIRPLANES OFFER the most in safety, speed, and comfort. The twin is well respected, is the ultimate in IFR operations, and makes positive impressions in the flying community: snob appeal. (Well, at least that's what the manufacturers infer.)

Although it does make sense that when there is duplicity you will have increased safety, if only by sheer numbers. Unfortunately, when examining small twin-engine airplanes, the safety margins do not always exist.

Flying a twin-engine airplane requires pilot expertise and an FAA multi-engine rating to attest to that expertise. Sadly, many pilots obtain the multi-rating and fly twins, yet don't maintain the high levels of proficiency required for emergency procedures. This lulls the pilot into a sense of false security until the eventual engine-out and the panic that follows.

A twin-engine airplane is always expensive to own and operate. When purchasing a used twin, you must realize that they are very complex airplanes with retractable landing gear, constant-speed propellers, complicated fuel systems, and more. Of course there is two of just about everything that could ever require maintenance—all adding up to high maintenance costs.

AERO COMMANDER

Aero Commander twin-engine airplanes have a high wing, giving them a unique appearance and making them the easiest of all twins to board. They are excellent air taxis and have seen service all over the world as the mainstay for many small airlines.

An Aero Commander twin once flew single-engine from Oklahoma to Washington, D.C., non-stop, and at maximum gross weight. This trip would be difficult for any small twin, but the Aero Commander took off and landed on one engine. The inoperative engine's propeller was carried as baggage, inside the airplane.

Aero Commanders may be found in used airplane listings under Aero Commander, Gulfstream, or Rockwell (Fig. 11-1).

Fig. 11-1. Aero Commander 500.

Make: Aero Commander   Model: 500
Year: 1958 – 59
Engines
    Make: Lycoming
    Model: O-540-A2B
    Horsepower: 250
    TBO: 2000 hours
Speeds
    Maximum: 218 mph
    Cruise: 205 mph
    Stall: 63 mph
Fuel capacity: 156 gallons
Rate of climb: 1400 fpm (290 single)
Transitions
    Takeoff over 50-foot obstacle: 1250 feet
    Ground run: 1000 feet
    Landing over 50-foot obstacle: 1350 feet
    Ground roll: 950 feet
Weights
    Gross: 6000 pounds
    Empty: 3850 pounds
Seats: Seven
Dimensions
    Length: 35 feet 1 inch
    Height: 14 feet 5 inches
    Span: 49 feet

Make: Aero Commander   Model: 500A
Year: 1960 – 63

Engines
  Make: Continental
  Model: IO-470-M
  Horsepower: 260
  TBO: 1500 hours
Speeds
  Maximum: 228 mph
  Cruise: 218 mph
  Stall: 62 mph
Fuel capacity: 156 gallons
Rate of climb: 1400 fpm (320 single)
Transitions
  Takeoff over 50-foot obstacle: 1210 feet
  Ground run: 970 feet
  Landing over 50-foot obstacle: 1150 feet
  Ground roll: 865 feet
Weights
  Gross: 6250 pounds
  Empty: 4255 pounds
Seats: Seven
Dimensions
  Length: 35 feet 1 inch
  Height: 14 feet 5 inches
  Span: 49 feet 5 inches

BEECHCRAFT

The oldest Beechcraft twin normally encountered is the Beech 18. It has radial engines, making the "right sounds", and is a small airliner that for many years was flown by regional air carriers and corporations. Unfortunately, they now are old and very expensive to maintain.

The Twin Bonanza Model 50 was built for nearly 10 years. First production units had 260-hp engines. Later versions included 295- and 340-hp engines. The "T-Bone" went out of production in 1963.

In 1958, the Travelair 95 was introduced. It was powered with two 180-hp engines with seats for four, which was eventually increased to six. Approximately 700 Travelairs were built before the end of the line in 1968.

The first Beech Baron 55s were seen in 1961, seated six, and were powered by 260- to 340-hp engines. More than 5,700 were built.

The last Beechcraft entry into the small-twin field was the Duchess Model 76, a T-tailed craft with counter-rotating engines. Counter-rotating propellers take some danger out of engine-out operations by eliminating most of the critical-engine factor.

Beechcraft airplanes are always tough and strong, and their twins, like their singles, are expensive to maintain. They are, however, the roomiest of the small twins (Figs. 11-2 through 11-6).

Fig. 11-2. Beechcraft E18S.

Beechcraft

Make: Beechcraft   Model: D-18S
Year: 1946 – 69
Engines
    Make: Pratt & Whitney
    Model: R-985
    Horsepower: 450
    TBO: 1600 hours

Speeds
    Maximum: 230 mph
    Cruise: 214 mph
    Stall: 84 mph
Fuel capacity: 198 gallons
Rate of climb: 1410 fpm (255 single)
Transitions
    Takeoff over 50-foot obstacle: 1980 feet
    Ground run: 1445 feet
    Landing over 50-foot obstacle: 1850 feet
    Ground roll: 1036 feet
Weights
    Gross: 9700 pounds
    Empty: 5910 pounds
Seats: seven to nine (and crew)
Dimensions
    Length: 35 feet 2 inches
    Height: 10 feet 5 inches
    Span: 49 feet 8 inches

Make: Beechcraft   Model: 50 and B/C-50
Year: 1952 – 62
Engines
    Make: Lycoming
    Model: GO-435
    Horsepower: 260 (275 on C model)
    TBO: 1200 hours
Speeds
    Maximum: 203 mph
    Cruise: 183 mph
    Stall: 69 mph
Fuel capacity: 134 gallons
Rate of climb: 1450 fpm (300 single)
Transitions
    Takeoff over 50-foot obstacle: 1344 feet
    Ground run: 1080 feet
    Landing over 50-foot obstacle: 1215 feet
    Ground roll: 975 feet
Weights
    Gross: 6000 pounds
    Empty: 3940 pounds
Seats: Six
Dimensions
    Length: 31 feet 5 inches
    Height: 11 feet 5 inches
    Span: 45 feet 2 inches

Fig. 11-3. Beechcraft D50 Twin Bonanza.

Make: Beechcraft   Model: D-50
Year: 1956 – 61
Engines
    Make: Lycoming
    Model: GO-480
    Horsepower: 295
    TBO: 1400 hours
Speeds
    Maximum: 214 mph
    Cruise: 203 mph
    Stall: 71 mph
Fuel capacity: 134 gallons
Rate of climb: 1450 fpm (300 single)
Transitions
    Takeoff over 50-foot obstacle: 1260 feet
    Ground run: 1000 feet
    Landing over 50-foot obstacle: 1455 feet
    Ground roll: 1010 feet
Weights
    Gross: 6300 pounds
    Empty: 4100 pounds
Seats: Seven
Dimensions
    Length: 31 feet 5 inches
    Height: 11 feet 5 inches
    Span: 45 feet 9 inches

Make: Beechcraft   Model: E/F-50
Year: 1957 – 58

Engines
    Make: Lycoming
    Model: GSO-480
    Horsepower: 340
    TBO: 1400 hours
Speeds
    Maximum: 240 mph
    Cruise: 212 mph
    Stall: 83 mph
Fuel capacity: 180 gallons
Rate of climb: 1320 fpm (325 single)
Transitions
    Takeoff over 50-foot obstacle: 1250 feet
    Ground run: 975 feet
    Landing over 50-foot obstacle: 1840 feet
    Ground roll: 1250 feet
Weights
    Gross: 7000 pounds
    Empty: 4460 pounds
Seats: Seven
Dimensions
    Length: 31 feet 5 inches
    Height: 11 feet 5 inches
    Span: 45 feet 9 inches

Fig. 11-4. Beechcraft Travel Air 95.

Make: Beechcraft   Model: 95 Travelair
Year: 1958 – 68
Engines
    Make: Lycoming
    Model: O-360-A1A (fuel inj. after 1960)

Horsepower: 180
TBO: 2000 hours
Speeds
    Maximum: 210 mph
    Cruise: 200 mph
    Stall: 70 mph
Fuel capacity: 80 gallons
Rate of climb: 1250 fpm (205 single)
Transitions
    Takeoff over 50-foot obstacle: 1280 feet
    Ground run: 1000 feet
    Landing over 50-foot obstacle: 1850 feet
    Ground roll: 1015 feet
Weights
    Gross: 4200 pounds
    Empty: 2635 pounds
Seats: Four (six after 1960)
Dimensions
    Length: 25 feet 3 inches
    Height: 9 feet 6 inches
    Span: 37 feet 9 inches

Fig. 11-5. Beechcraft B55.

Make: Beechcraft   Model: 55 (all)
Year: 1961–82
Engines
    Make: Continental
    Model: IO-470
    Horsepower: 260
    TBO: 1500 hours
Speeds
    Maximum: 236 mph
    Cruise: 225 mph

Stall: 78 mph
Fuel capacity: 112 gallons
Rate of climb: 1670 fpm (320 single)
Transitions
    Takeoff over 50-foot obstacle: 1664 feet
    Ground run: 1339 feet
    Landing over 50-foot obstacle: 1853 feet
    Ground roll: 945 feet
Weights
    Gross: 5100 pounds
    Empty: 3070 pounds
Seats: Six
Dimensions
    Length: 27 feet
    Height: 9 feet 7 inches
    Span: 37 feet 10 inches

Beechcraft

Fig. 11-6. Beechcraft Dutchess 76.

Make: Beechcraft   Model: 76 Duchess
Year: 1978 – 82
Engines
    Make: Lycoming
    Model: O-360-A1G6D
    Horsepower: 180
    TBO: 2000 hp
Speeds
    Maximum: 197 mph
    Cruise: 182 mph
    Stall: 69 mph

Fuel capacity: 100 gallons
Rate of climb: 1248 fpm (235 single)
Transitions
    Takeoff over 50-foot obstacle: 2119 feet
    Ground run: 1017 feet
    Landing over 50-foot obstacle: 1880 feet
    Ground roll: 1000 feet
Weights
    Gross: 3900 pounds
    Empty: 2460 pounds
Seats: Four
Dimensions
    Length: 29 feet
    Height: 9 feet 6 inches
    Span: 38 feet

CESSNA

Modern Cessna light twins have always been marked by their graceful lines, speed, and reliability. Two basic versions of the conventional Cessna twin are the original models 310 and sister ship 320.

The 310 was introduced in 1954 with two 240-hp engines. Since that date numerous changes have been made:

- 1956, additional window space
- 1959, 260-hp engines
- 1960, swept tail
- 1963, six seats
- 1969, 285-hp engines

The model 320 was turbocharged engines (260-hp each) entered production in 1962. In 1966, the engine size was increased to 285-hp and a sixth seat was added.

The second twin from Cessna was the model 336. It has centerline thrust with one engine in front of the cabin and one in the rear. It was built to be a simple twin to fly with very easy engine-out procedures; it even had fixed landing gear. Cessna thought easy handling would make it a great seller. It wasn't! The next year, 1965, Cessna introduced the 337 with better cooling, quieter operation, and retractable landing gear.

The 337s are officially called the Skymaster while in hangar-ese they are known as "mixmasters". Either way, they saw heavy use with military forces in Vietnam as the O-2.

Cessna twins are plentiful and, as twins go, maintenance is reasonable. The high-wing 337s make excellent workhorses, while the 310 and 320 series make long trips fast (Figs. 11-7 through 11-10).

Make: Cessna   Model: 310 and A-B
Year: 1955 – 58
Engines
    Make: Continental
    Model: O-470-B
    Horsepower: 240 hp
    TBO: 1500 hours
Speeds
    Maximum: 232 mph
    Cruise: 213 mph
    Stall: 74 mph
Fuel capacity: 102 gallons
Rate of climb: 1660 fpm (450 single)
Transitions
    Takeoff over 50-foot obstacle: 1410 feet
    Ground run: 810 feet

Fig. 11-7. Cessna 310 early.

    Landing over 50-foot obstacle: 1720 feet
    Ground roll: 620 feet
Weights
    Gross: 4700 pounds
    Empty: 2900 pounds
Seats: Five
Dimensions
    Length: 26 feet
    Height: 10 feet 6 inches
    Span: 35 feet 9 inches

Make: Cessna   Model: 310 C-Q
Year: 1959–74
Engines
    Make: Continental
    Model: IO-470
    Horsepower: 260
    TBO: 1500 hours
Speeds
    Maximum: 240 mph
    Cruise: 223 mph
    Stall: 76 mph
Fuel capacity: 102 gallons
Rate of climb: 1690 fpm (380 single)
Transitions
    Takeoff over 50-foot obstacle: 1545 feet

Ground run: 920 feet
Landing over 50-foot obstacle: 1900 feet
Ground roll: 690 feet
Weights
Gross: 5100 pounds
Empty: 3063 pounds
Seats: Six
Dimensions
Length: 29 feet 5 inches
Height: 9 feet 11 inches
Span: 36 feet 11 inches

Fig. 11-8. Cessna 310 late.

Make: Cessna   Model: 310 P-R
Year: 1969 – 81
Engines
Make: Continental
Model: IO-520-M (turbocharger opt.)
Horsepower: 285
TBO: 1700 hours
Speeds
Maximum: 238 mph
Cruise: 223 mph
Stall: 81 mph
Fuel capacity: 102 gallons
Rate of climb: 1662 fpm (370 single)
Transitions
Takeoff over 50-foot obstacle: 1700 feet
Ground run: 1335 feet
Landing over 50-foot obstacle: 1790 feet
Ground roll: 640

Weights
    Gross: 5500 pounds
    Empty: 3603 pounds
Seats: Six
Dimensions
    Length: 31 feet 11 inches
    Height: 10 feet 8 inches
    Span: 36 feet 11 inches

Fig. 11-9. Cessna 320.

Make: Cessna   Model: 320 (through C)
Year: 1962 – 65
Engines
    Make: Continental
    Model: TSIO-470
    Horsepower: 260
    TBO: 1400 hours
Speeds
    Maximum: 265 mph
    Cruise: 235 mph
    Stall: 78 mph
Fuel capacity: 102 gallons
Rate of climb: 1820 fpm (400 single)
Transitions
    Takeoff over 50-foot obstacle: 1890 feet
    Ground run: 870 feet
    Landing over 50-foot obstacle: 2056 feet
    Ground roll: 640 feet

Weights
    Gross: 4990 pounds
    Empty: 3190 pounds
Seats: Six
Dimensions
    Length: 29 feet 5 inches
    Height: 10 feet 3 inches
    Span: 36 feet 9 inches

Make: Cessna   Model: 320 D-F
Year: 1966 – 68
Engines
    Make: Continental
    Model: TSIO-520
    Horsepower: 285
    TBO: 1400 hours
Speeds
    Maximum: 275 mph
    Cruise: 260 mph
    Stall: 74 mph
Fuel capacity: 102 gallons
Rate of climb: 1924 fpm (475 single)
Transitions
    Takeoff over 50-foot obstacle: 1515 feet
    Ground run: 1190 feet
    Landing over 50-foot obstacle: 1736 feet
    Ground roll: 614 feet
Weights
    Gross: 5300 pounds
    Empty: 3273 pounds
Seats: Six
Dimensions
    Length: 29 feet 5 inches
    Height: 10 feet 3 inches
    Span: 36 feet 9 inches

Make: Cessna   Model: 336
Year: 1964
Engines
    Make: Continental
    Model: IO-360-C
    Horsepower: 210
    TBO: 1500 hours
Speeds
    Maximum: 183 mph
    Cruise: 173 mph

Stall: 60 mph
Fuel capacity: 93 gallons
Rate of climb: 1340 fpm (355 single)
Transitions
    Takeoff over 50-foot obstacle: 1145 feet
    Ground run: 625 feet
    Landing over 50-foot obstacle: 1395 feet
    Ground roll: 655 feet
Weights
    Gross: 3900 pounds
    Empty: 2340 pounds
Seats: Four (six optional)
Dimensions
    Length: 29 feet 7 inches
    Height: 9 feet 4 inches
    Span: 38 feet

Fig. 11-10. Cessna 337.

Make: Cessna   Model: 337 (all)
Year: 1965 – 80
Engines
    Make: Continental
    Model: IO-360-C
    Horsepower: 210
    TBO: 1500 hours
Speeds
    Maximum: 199 mph
    Cruise: 190 mph
    Stall: 70 mph

Fuel capacity: 93 gallons
Rate of climb: 1100 fpm (235 single)
Transitions
    Takeoff over 50-foot obstacle: 1675 feet
    Ground run: 1000 feet
    Landing over 50-foot obstacle: 1650 feet
    Ground roll: 700 feet
Weights
    Gross: 4360 pounds
    Empty: 2695 pounds
Seats: Six
Dimensions
    Length: 29 feet 9 inches
    Height: 9 feet 4 inches
    Span: 38 feet 2 inches

GULFSTREAM

The Gulfstream Cougar GA-7 was introduced in 1978 and went out of production the next year, as did its single engine cousins (see Chapters 7 and 8).

Although somewhat underpowered by most twin standards, with a pair of 160-hp Lycomings, the Cougar carried four with reasonable comfort and speed for a period in excess of five hours between fuel stops.

A total of only 110 Cougars were produced, therefore they are somewhat scarce on the market. Being scarce can mean parts and service problems, especially as the Cougar is an orphan airplane. On the other hand, the Cougar represents a lot of airplane for the money, generally being priced well below older Piper Twin Comanches (Fig. 11-11).

Fig. 11-11. Gulfstream GA-7.

Make: Gulfstream   Model: GA-7 Cougar
Year: 1978 – 79
Engines
    Make: Lycoming
    Model: O-320-D1D
    Horsepower: 160
    TBO: 2000 hours
Speeds
    Maximum: 193 mph
    Cruise: 184 mph
    Stall: 82 mph
Fuel capacity: 118 gallons
Rate of climb: 1160 fpm (200 single)
Transitions
    Takeoff over 50-foot obstacle: 1850 feet
    Ground run: 1000 feet

Landing over 50-foot obstacle: 1330 feet
Ground roll: 710 feet
Weights
Gross: 3800 pounds
Empty: 2569 pounds
Seats: Four
Dimensions
Length: 29 feet 7 inches
Height: 10 feet 4 inches
Span: 36 feet 9 inches

PIPER

Piper entered the light twin market in 1954 with the PA-23 Apache, an unusually poor performer with ungainly looks (some called it the flying potato). When operating single-engine, the Apache's pilot had to look for a place to land because landing would soon come. Although the specifications indicate single-engine climb numbers, it does not climb on one engine.

Several major changes improved the Apache's power problems and increased seating:

- 1958, 160-hp engines
- 1960, five seats
- 1963, 235-hp engines

Apaches can be acquired cheap and while the low-powered models have poor performance, they do represent a lot of plane for the money. The last year of production was 1963.

Piper introduced the Aztec in 1960 as a PA-23 (same model number as the Apache). It was a sleeker looking plane than the Apache and had a swept tail. Originally powered with 250-hp engines and seating five, it was soon updated to seat six. The Aztec is an excellent instrument plane and some are even equipped with de-ice equipment.

The Twin Comanche PA-30 was introduced in 1963. It was similar in appearance to the Cessna 310, powered by 160-hp engines and sat low to the ground. Unlike the 310, it was docile in flight. The Twin Comanche became the PA-39 in 1970 with the addition of counter-rotating propellers. Twin Comanche production ceased in 1972.

The Seneca was introduced in 1970 (a Cherokee Six with two engines) as the PA-34. The PA-34 Seminole was built from 1979 to 1982 as an entry-level twin, similar to the Beech Duchess.

Piper twins can appear to be a lot of airplane for the money; however, be warned that the older models require continuing and expensive maintenance. The new models are somewhat more wallet-friendly (see Figs. 11-11 through 11-16).

Make: Piper   Model: PA-23 Apache
Year: 1954–57
Engines
    Make: Lycoming
    Model: O-320-A1A
    Horsepower: 150
    TBO: 2000 hours
Speeds
    Maximum: 180 mph
    Cruise: 170 mph
    Stall: 59 mph
Fuel capacity: 72 gallons

Fig. 11-12. Piper PA-23 Apache.

Rate of climb: 1250 fpm (240 single)
Transitions
    Takeoff over 50-foot obstacle: 1600 feet
    Ground run: 900 feet
    Landing over 50-foot obstacle: 1360 feet
    Ground roll: 670 feet
Weights
    Gross: 3500 pounds
    Empty: 2180 pounds
Seats: Five
Dimensions
    Length: 27 feet 4 inches
    Height: 9 feet 6 inches
    Span: 37 feet 1 inch

Make: Piper   Model: PA-23 D/E/F Apache
Year: 1957–61
Engines
    Make: Lycoming
    Model: O-320-B3B
    Horsepower: 160
    TBO: 2000 hours
Speeds
    Maximum: 183 mph
    Cruise: 173 mph
    Stall: 61 mph
Fuel capacity: 72 gallons
Rate of climb: 1260 fpm (240 single)
Transitions
    Takeoff over 50-foot obstacle: 1550 feet
    Ground run: 1190 feet

Landing over 50-foot obstacle: 1360 feet
Ground roll: 750 feet
Weights
Gross: 3800 pounds
Empty: 2230 pounds
Seats: Five
Dimensions
Length: 27 feet 4 inches
Height: 9 feet 6 inches
Span: 37 feet 1 inch

Make: Piper   Model: PA-23 235 Apache
Year: 1962–65
Engines
Make: Lycoming
Model: O-540-B1A5
Horsepower: 235
TBO: 2000 hours
Speeds
Maximum: 202 mph
Cruise: 191 mph
Stall: 62 mph
Fuel capacity: 144 gallons
Rate of climb: 1450 fpm (220 single)
Transitions
Takeoff over 50-foot obstacle: 1280 feet
Ground run: 830 feet
Landing over 50-foot obstacle: 1360 feet
Ground roll: 880 feet
Weights
Gross: 4800 pounds
Empty: 2735 pounds
Seats: Five
Dimensions
Length: 27 feet 7 inches
Height: 10 feet 3 inches
Span: 37 feet 1 inch

Make: Piper   Model: PA-23 Aztec
Year: 1960–81
Engines
Make: Lycoming
Model: IO-540-C4B5 (turbocharger opt.)
Horsepower: 250
TBO: 2000 hours (1800 if turbocharged)

Fig. 11-13. Piper PA-23 Aztec early.

Fig. 11-14. Piper PA-23 Aztec late.

Speeds
    Maximum: 215 mph
    Cruise: 205 mph
    Stall: 62 mph

Fuel capacity: 144 gallons
Rate of climb: 1650 fpm (365 single)
Transitions
    Takeoff over 50-foot obstacle: 1100 feet
    Ground run: 750 feet
    Landing over 50-foot obstacle: 1260 feet
    Ground roll: 900 feet
Weights
    Gross: 4800 pounds
    Empty: 2900 pounds
Seats: Six
Dimensions
    Length: 27 feet 7 inches
    Height: 10 feet 3 inches
    Span: 37 feet 1 inch

Fig. 11-15. Piper PA-39 Twin Comanche.

Make: Piper   Model: PA-30/39 Twin Comanche
Year: 1963 – 72
Engines
    Make: Lycoming
    Model: IO-320-B1A (turbocharger opt.)
    Horsepower: 160
    TBO: 2000 hours (1800 if turbocharged)
Speeds
    Maximum: 205 mph
    Cruise: 198 mph
    Stall: 70 mph
Fuel capacity: 90 gallons
Rate of climb: 1460 fpm (260 single)
Transitions
    Takeoff over 50-foot obstacle: 1530 feet
    Ground run: 940 feet

Landing over 50-foot obstacle: 1870 feet
Ground roll: 700 feet
Weights
Gross: 3600 pounds
Empty: 2270 pounds
Seats: Four (six after 1965)
Dimensions
Length: 25 feet 2 inches
Height: 8 feet 3 inches
Span: 36 feet

Make: Piper   Model: PA-34 200 Seneca
Year: 1972–74
Engines
Make: Lycoming
Model: IO-360-C1E6
Horsepower: 200
TBO: 1800 hours
Speeds
Maximum: 196 mph
Cruise: 187 mph
Stall: 67 mph
Fuel capacity: 100 gallons
Rate of climb: 1460 fpm (190 single)
Transitions
Takeoff over 50-foot obstacle: 1140 feet
Ground run: 750 feet
Landing over 50-foot obstacle: 1335 feet
Ground roll: 705 feet
Weights
Gross: 4000 pounds
Empty: 2586 pounds
Seats: Six
Dimensions
Length: 28 feet 6 inches
Height: 9 feet 10 inches
Span: 38 feet 10 inches

Make: Piper   Model: PA-34 200T Seneca
Year: 1975–81
Engines
Make: Lycoming
Model: TSIO-360-E
Horsepower: 220
TBO: 1800 hours

Fig. 11-16. Piper 1984 PA-34 Seneca.

Speeds
    Maximum: 225 mph
    Cruise: 205 mph
    Stall: 74 mph
Fuel capacity: 93 gallons
Rate of climb: 1400 fpm (240 single)
Transitions
    Takeoff over 50-foot obstacle: 1210 feet
    Ground run: 920 feet
    Landing over 50-foot obstacle: 2160 feet
    Ground roll: 1400 feet
Weights
    Gross: 4750 pounds
    Empty: 2852 pounds
Seats: Seven
Dimensions
    Length: 28 feet 7 inches
    Height: 9 feet 11 inches
    Span: 38 feet 11 inches

Make: Piper   Model: PA-44 Seminole
Year: 1979 – 82
Engines
    Make: Lycoming
    Model: IO-360-E1A6D (turbocharger opt.)
    Horsepower: 180
    TBO: 2000 hours

Speeds
    Maximum: 193 mph
    Cruise: 185 mph
    Stall: 63 mph
Fuel capacity: 108 gallons
Rate of climb: 1340 fpm (217 single)
Transitions
    Takeoff over 50-foot obstacle: 1400 feet
    Ground run: 880 feet
    Landing over 50-foot obstacle: 1400 feet
    Ground roll: 595 feet
Weights
    Gross: 3800 pounds
    Empty: 2406 pounds
Seats: Four
Dimensions
    Length: 27 feet 7 inches
    Height: 8 feet 6 inches
    Span: 38 feet 7 inches

Part III

Tall tales, tidbits, and hot information

12

Hangar flying used airplanes

THE FOLLOWING PAGES are devoted to comments, statements, rumors, and facts that are often heard about used airplanes (attribution in parentheses).

BEECHCRAFT

"Beechcraft 19, 23, Sport, and Musketeer airplanes have speed-to-horsepower ratios that are low when compared to other planes in their class. The 150-hp versions take off and climb marginally on hot days, and at high altitudes. Stalls are abrupt and complete, unlike the Cessna and Piper stalls. Resale prices are poor on these planes and there is little demand for them. Additionally, Beech parts are notoriously expensive." (Broker)

"My Bonanza Vee-tail has never worried me. I know there was a speed limit, but I never worried. When I had the AD modification done, cracks were found. Next time some problem indicates a need to slow down, you can bet I'll do what I am told." (Owner)

"I prefer the three-piece tail over the Vee. It seems more stable laterally." (Owner)

"Resale on lower models of Beech, such as the 19 and 23 series, are poor." (Dealer)

"The Musketeers have wonderfully large cabins. Much bigger than Piper or Cessna." (Spouse)

"My Musketeer has two doors, many don't." (Owner)

"Many model 33, 35, and 36 planes are not equipped with dual controls." (Broker)

"The Skipper has two doors, Piper should have done the same on their Tomahawk." (Tomahawk owner)

"Those Vee-tails are the classiest planes out there." (Sunday driver)

"If you need AD work on D-18 wings you might as well junk it." (Mechanic)

"The gear on the Model 23 is about the stoutest in the industry." (Mechanic)

"No such thing as a cheap Beech part." (Mechanic)

CESSNA

"The Cessna 150 is the best two-place airplane for the money in today's market. The 172 is the same for four-placers. Either will take care of you, as long as you take care of it." (Author)

"The Lycoming O-320-H2AD engine is the worst thing that ever happened to general aviation. It is found only in 1977 through 1980 Cessna 172s. It is an engine capable of self-destruction and has been the subject of many very expensive ADs." (Mechanic)

"The Cessna 172 is so good that one even got past the Russian Air Defense system in May 1987 when a 19-year-old German pilot flew hundreds of miles over the USSR and landed in Red Square." (History)

"Before purchasing a used 182, check the firewall for damage from hard landings. The nosegear can cause the firewall to buckle if the airplane is landed wheelbarrow fashion." (Broker)

"My 175 has an O-360 engine. Common sense told me that the GO-300 engine running at 3,000 rpms will wear out faster than one operating at 2,400 rpms and the gear box needed regular maintenance." (Owner)

"The 182 is a true four-place plane. It will carry four people and all their luggage." (Owner)

"Insuring the Cessna 172 is easy, with no real secrets to them. They are reliable, easy to fly, and replacement parts are available." (Underwriter)

"Cessna gives very poor support to small airplane owners." (Owner)

"I just paid over $600 for a set of seat tracks for my Cessna 182. I feel ripped off, they couldn't possibly be worth more than $20 or $30." (Owner)

"The 150-hp Cardinal is an underpowered dog!" (Instructor)

"I see all kinds of planes, and some are real expensive, but I really like to see an old 172 that has been all fixed up. The pilot is usually the guy who fixed it, and he's real proud of it." (Line boy)

"I could afford to buy a retractable if I wanted it, but why pay for all the extra maintenance for a little extra speed? Slow down and enjoy life." (Owner)

"The 172 flies like a 150, just bigger." (Owner)

"I just had a 180-hp engine installed in my 172. Wow! What get-up and-go! This really helps, as the ranch strip is kinda bad in the spring." (Rancher)

"The visibility in a busy traffic pattern is poor, but that's the same for all high-wingers." (Instructor)

"Love the barn door flaps because they can really save a high approach." (Rancher)

"I have a '63 model with manual flaps, and plan to keep it. I don't like the electric flaps because there's too much that can break on them." (Owner)

"I have Deemers wing tips on the plane, and they allow me to make it into my farm strip easier. The strip is only 990 feet long, but clear on both ends." (Farmer)

"I use mogas in my '64 Hawk. Seems okay, and it saves me money. I wish the FBO would pump it because the gas in the trunk of the car scares me." (Owner)

"172s sell themselves. They are roomy, look good, and are reasonable in price. They're just real good value; something you don't often see these days." (Broker)

"I have rarely seen a bargain 172; generally, you get what you pay for." (Mechanic)

ERCOUPE

"Cute, but glides like a piano." (Instructor)

"Watch for corrosion in the wingroot." (Mechanic)

"My legs got messed up in the war. If it weren't for the 'Coupe I'd be sitting on the ground instead of flying!" (Owner)

"Our A model was cheap to buy, but loads of work has gone into it. I don't think I would recommend them as cheap airplanes." (Owner)

"Some of the 'Coupes are fast nearing the half century mark and require real tender loving care." (Mechanic)

"I like to fly with the window open." (Owner)

"Sure am glad Univair is around to supply parts." (Owner)

GULFSTREAM

"The nosewheel is a swivel affair. You have no control of it except by differential brake steering. It is very good in close quarters." (Owner)

"Watch for delamination of the control and wing surfaces. There is an AD about this problem." (Mechanic)

"The laminated fiberglass landing gear will save most botched landings. They are great mistake absorbers." (Instructor)

"You need miles for takeoff on a real hot day." (Instructor)

"Glad to see them back in production." (Owner)

HELIO

"Just because it is slow and STOL, don't forget that it's a tail dragger and just waiting to eat your lunch." (Former owner)

"The crosswind gears work great." (Owner)

"The geared engines are expensive to rebuild, but it's a low price to pay for the STOL work I can do." (Patrol pilot)

LUSCOMBE

"A pilot's airplane. Keeps you in shape on crosswind landings." (Instructor)

"Luscombes have a poor reputation for ground loops." (FBO)

"Too bad they didn't keep going. The Sedan was way ahead of everyone else." (Owner)

"Wax and polish is all I ever do, but it looks good." (Owner)

MAULE

"Most pilots will tell you they are good performers for the market they are built for. That is, utility use. They are noisy and drafty." (Patrol Pilot)

"The specification numbers given for Maule airplanes are somewhat higher than what I see." (Owner)

PIPER

"The PA-22 Tri-Pacer is probably the last of the four-place affordable airplanes. Just remember it is fabric covered. Like a Maule, the PA-22 is noisy and drafty." (FBO)

"Some PA-28s are not true four-place planes; a two-place with the rear seat added." (Instructor)

"The warrior is very stable for instrument work." (Owner)

"Any Cub is an investment, if you take care of it." (FBO)

"Watch the lift struts on all older Pipers. They tend to rust and crack. There is an AD out about this problem." (Mechanic)

"The PA-28 180 is a true four-place airplane." (Owner)

"That great big throttle quadrant and only 112 horses." (Tomahawk owner)

"The first Apaches flew like a rock on one engine." (FBO)

"I bought a Super Cub that had been a sprayer. Had to rebuild most of the airframe. Those chemicals ate it all up. Think what they do to people." (Owner)

"It is very easy to overload the Seneca. It's just so big!" (Rancher)

"The tail shakes like it will fall off when a stall breaks." (Tomahawk student)

"The Tee-tailed Lance doesn't fly as well as the straight-tailed version. It lacks authority on takeoff and requires a faster and longer roll." (Owner)

"Wish Piper had put two doors on [the Tomahawk] like the Skipper." (Instructor)

"I had a bug get caught in the gear sensor and couldn't get the gear up on my Arrow." (Owner)

"The automatically operated gear on the Arrow leads to complacency in retractable pilots." (Insurance carrier)

"I have had nothing but trouble with my cabin door. It never wants to stay closed." (Owner)

STINSON

"The barn door fin on the Stinson will become a weathercock in heavy winds." (Owner)

"My wagon is metalized. Nice, but I wonder what's going on under there." (Owner)

"On my next major I'm going to get an STC for a 200-hp Lycoming or Continental to replace the Franklin. It'll give better performance and be cheaper to maintain in the long run." (Owner)

"Thank the Lord for Univair and all the Stinson stuff they sell." (Owner)

"The Old Franks [Franklin engines] are getting mighty expensive to fix." (Mechanic)

SWIFT

"There is only room for two people in my Swift. The luggage compartment is a joke. You can take your toothbrush if you pack it carefully." (Owner)

"The landing felt super smooth as I flared, then I realized the gear wasn't down." (Past owner)

TAYLORCRAFT

"T-Crafts are good performers, just remember they are fabric covered." (FBO)

"Kind of light in heavy winds, but enough control to handle it though." (Owner)

"The O-200 engine is very reliable." (Patrol pilot)

"I bought mine for $2,500 from a fellow not wanting to finish rebuilding it. It was all in boxes except for the airframe." (Owner)

"Not sophisticated, but cheap!" (Owner)

13

Alternative aircraft

EVERYONE IS NOT THE TYPICAL AIRPLANE BUYER. In fact, most are very individual, with different flying interests, varied financial backgrounds, and assorted pilot skills. Fortunately, there is considerable flexibility in flying, allowing for specialized pursuits.

FLOATPLANES

Ever wish you could go someplace and really get away from it all? Perhaps the answer to your dream is a floatplane. Water-based airplanes offer a means of transportation to otherwise inaccessible locations (Fig. 13-1).

To fly a water-based plane, you will need a Seaplane Rating which is relatively easy to obtain. Many flying schools around the country offer seaplane training (see *Trade-A-Plane*). Training for a Seaplane Rating is practical in nature, involving only flight training. There is no written test. Often the price for training is fixed and the rating guaranteed.

Insurance rates for water-flight planes are high, unless you have extensive floatplane experience with no accident history. Even then, the rates will be higher for a float-equipped airplane than a comparable land-only plane. The reasoning behind the higher rates is the higher loss ratio with floatplanes compared to land planes.

For example, a typical ground loop in a land-based aircraft can result in several hundred dollars damage. The damaged aircraft can often be taxied to a repair facility. The same type of mishap on the water could mean a sunken airplane, resulting in difficult or impossible recovery, and thousands of dollars in damages.

More maintenance is required on floatplanes, mainly corrosion control and hull repair for struck objects, than on land-only planes.

Areas of floatplane activity

Floatplane flying is found in every state of the union, although some states have more activity than others. The following states offer excellent float flying:

Fig. 13-1. Float equipped planes open new vistas of enjoyment and utility.

Alaska, California, Florida, Louisiana, Maine, Massachusetts, Minnesota, Washington, and Wisconsin.

Canada offers some of the finest floatplane flying in the world, as many locations are accessible only by air.

For more information

AOPA sponsors the Seaplane Pilots Association (SPA). The group was formed in 1972 and now claims several thousand members. SPA's objective is to assist seaplane pilots with technical problems, provide a national lobbying effort, and more. Membership includes the quarterly magazine *Water Flying, Water Flying Annual*, and other written communications that include timely tips and safety measures. SPA sponsors numerous fly-ins.

Seaplane Pilots Association
412 Aviation Way
Frederick, MD 21701
(301) 695-2000

HOMEBUILTS

Airplane homebuilding has been with us since the Wright brothers. It is really the grassroots of general aviation. Today, the homebuilt airplane field accounts for a large percentage of all newly registered airplanes (Figs. 13-2 through 13-4).

Homebuilders construct an airplane most suitable to their needs and tastes: utility, speed, maneuverability, or individuality. Airplanes built by their owners may be constructed of tube-and-fabric, metal, or composite methods and materials. The latter is a method of construction using materials similar to those found in fiberglass powerboats. Generally the builder is building to make the plane his and his alone. If there was a motive to save money, he would most likely have purchased a factory-built airplane.

Fig. 13-2. Homebuilt tube and fabric aircraft.

Fig. 13-3. Homebuilt composite airplane, the Lancair.

Homebuilding is not cheap, but rewards are plentiful. No one is prouder than the builder pointing to an airplane and saying, "I built that." This will make up for the years spent constructing the plane (Fig. 13-5). Contact:

Experimental Aircraft Association
P.O. Box 3086
Oshkosh, WI 54903-3086
(414) 426-4800

Fig. 13-4. The Avid Flyer comes as a complete kit, all parts included. No welding is needed either!

Fig. 13-5. Thousands come to see the homebuilt airplanes each year at Oshkosh.

GLIDERS

Most pilots have heard at one time or another that obtaining a glider rating makes a better pilot. No doubt there is some truth to that statement. After all, the glider pilot gets only one shot at a landing; the powered airplane pilot can always go around and do it again (Figs. 13-6 and 13-7).

We "power pilots" tend to only think of getting there in a hurry. Glider flying is more back to the basics, more attuned to the surroundings. Yet—make no mistake—gliders are very sophisticated aircraft. For information about gliding contact:

Soaring Society of America
P.O. Box E
Hobbs, MN 88241

Fig. 13-6. This entry level glider offers loads of performance.

Fig. 13-7. Hi-performance gliders set world class records.

POWERED GLIDERS

The powered glider, first brought to popularity in Europe, is perhaps one of the most intriguing types of aircraft ever built. It offers good glider flight characteristics, yet can be flown under power over long distances. They are new to the United States and costs, as in all of aviation, are quite high (Fig. 13-8).

Fig. 13-8. This powered glider offers interest from both worlds of sport aviation.

WAR BIRDS

World War II saw the greatest use of air power the world has ever seen. Many fine examples of the war's historic aircraft have been restored to like-new condition.

The fighters, bombers, and patrol airplanes can be seen at many air shows around the country. Some of the planes are small, the Army L-3 (Aeronca) and L-4 (Piper), which are also known as Aeronca 7AC and Piper J3. Others are big and powerful like the famous Mustang, Bearcat, and B17 (Fig. 13-9).

Some modern small airplanes, the Cessna T-41 (C-172) and O-2 (C-337), can also be claimed as war birds. They were used for training, logistical, and forward fire control duties.

Unfortunately, most war birds are not for the average pilot. They drink fuel at a rate only OPEC could appreciate, although the direct operating costs are quite nominal when compared to the very costly maintenance required. This is to say

Fig. 13-9. P-51.

nothing of purchase and insurance costs. The larger fighters and bombers require pilot skills few general aviation pilots possess.

Many ex-military planes are owned by the CAF (Confederate Air Force) and Warbirds of America (a division of the EAA). For more information contact:

Warbirds of America, Inc.
P.O. Box 3086
Oshkosh, WI 54903-3086
(414) 426-4800

Appendix A

Airworthiness directives

WARNING: This listing of ADs is incomplete and should not be used for maintenance or inspection purposes. It is intended to serve as a guide for the prospective purchaser, as an aid in determining values and choices. Some ADs might not apply to every airplane of a particular model and some are excluded from this list. Serial number checks must be made for specific aircraft. Consult with an A&P mechanic for additional information.

Note that some manufacturers appear to have many ADs listed: the more airplanes built the more ADs issued. The list is formatted to include aircraft make, AD number, AD procedure, and aircraft model(s) affected.

Aero Commander

61-14-1, reinforce the engine mounts: 500s
65-6-1, reinforce the front spar cap: 500s
(Check Gulfstream and Rockwell for additional information)

Aeronca

61-16-1, periodic inspection of the lift strut fittings: 15-series
(Check Bellanca for additional Aeronca and Champion information)

Beechcraft

47-33-5, reinforce the horizontal spar: 35 (1-378)
57-18-1, inspect the fuselage bulkhead for cracks: 35 (D1-D1500)
68-13-2, 400 hours inspect Hartzell prop: S35/V35/V35A/C33A/E33A
68-17-6, modify the master brake cylinder: 23 series
70-12-2, modify the seat tracks: 36/36A (E1-201)
73-20-7, inspect the wing brackets: 23/23 series
73-23-3, replace the carb induction system: 23/24 series
73-23-6, inspect/replace the throttle assembly: 23 series

76-4-5, each 1,000 hours inspect the stabilizer: 35 series
76-25-5, install strap in the wing trailing edge: 23/24 series
77-3-5, dye inspect the main landing gear housing: 23/24 series
77-11-3, dye check/replace the prop pitch control: 35H/J/K/L/N/P
78-4-1, replace the flap control weld assembly: 23/24 series
79-23-5, inspect the wing attach bolts: 77 series
80-7-7, replace the aileron bearings: 77 series
80-21-10, rework the engine mount and bolts: 77 series
83-23-3, reinforce the rudder balance weight bracket: 77 series
87-2-8, inspect the stabilator hinge: most 23/24 series
87-18-6, replace seat handle: F33A, V35B, A36
87-20-2, install placard for speed limit on all V-tail models
88-20-1, remove sound deadener material from firewall: F33A & A36
88-21-2, fill holes in seat track: F33, V35, 36, 55, & 58 series
89-5-2, inspect/replace elevator: 33, T34, 35, 36, 55, 55 series
89-24-9, install inspection openings in wings: most 23 & 24 series
89-26-8, inspect/modify propeller: most 33, 35, 36 series
90-8-14, inspect wing structure: 55 & 95 series
90-11-4, inspect rudder forward spar: 33, 35, 36 series

Bellanca

63-6-2, each 100 hours inspect/replace rudder bellcrank: 14 series
68-23-8, modify the elevator trim tab system: 14-19-3A/17-30
69-12-4, each 25 hours inspect/replace rear strut clevises: 14-19-3A/17-30
72-20-6, replace control cables: 7ECA/GCAA/GCBS/KCAB
73-5-2, replace the rudder shaft assemblies: 17-30/31
74-23-4, inspect the wing ribs for cracks: 8KCAB (4-159)
75-17-16, replace the carb air valves: 7/8 series
75-20-6, inspect the fuselage tubes for cracks: 14-19-3A/17-30/31
76-8-4, annual check for deterioration in wood wing: 14/17 series
76-20-7, inspect the wood wing spar for moisture/decay: 14 series
76-23-3, each 100 hours inspect the exhaust system: 17 series
77-22-5, replace the wing front lift struts: 7 series
79-19-5, inspect the aileron rigging: 14 series
79-22-1, inspect the exhaust system for cracks: 7ECA/8KCAB
86-25-6, install a fuel drain valve: 17-30/31
89-18-6, inspect lower seat fram weld & hinge: 7 & 8 series
90-2-17, inspect/replace drag strut landing gear assy: 14 & 17 series
90-2-23, inspect/replace prop hub: 8 & 17 series
90-15-15, magnetic particle inspection of front spar fittings: 8KCAB

Cessna

47-50-2, reinforce the fuselage bulkhead: 120/140
50-31-1, reinforce the fin spar: 120/140

51-11-2, reinforce the elevator spar: 190/195
68-7-9, modify the flap system: 177
71-1-3, inspect/rework the stabilator attach points: 177
71-22-2, each 1,000 hours inspect/replace nosegear fork: most tri-gear
72-3-3, each 100 hours inspect flap screw jack: many 100/200 series
72-7-9, check for cracks & loose bolts on fin and rudder: 182
73-23-7, replace the wing attach fitting: 100 series
74-4-1, inspect for cracks in aft bulkhead: 172
76-14-7, each 1,000 hours replace the landing gear saddle: 210
77-2-9, replace flap actuator ball nut assembly: 150/172/182/207/207
78-1-13, inspect the rear prop hub: T-337
78-7-1, replace the turbocharger housing: T206/207/210
78-25-7, replace the vertical fin brackets: A150/A152
79-2-6, inspect/replace the heater muffler: 152/A152
79-3-3, inspect/replace turbocharger housing: TU206G/T207A/T210M
79-8-3, remove the cigarette lighter wiring: most models
79-25-7, modify the alternator installation: many from 180 up
80-1-6, modify the flap actuator assembly: 152/A152/172RG
80-11-4, replace the nut plates in the tail assembly: 150/152
81-14-6, replace the rudder trim/nosegear bungees: 172RG (1-769)
82-27-2, dye check the prop blade: most from 172RG up
83-22-6, modify/replace the aileron hinges: 152-185 series
83-24-11, dye check the prop blades: 180/206/210 series
84-10-1, install quick fuel drains/inspect tanks: 180 and up
85-11-7, replace the turbo oil reservoir, 210 series
85-17-7, inspect/install doubler in rear wing spar: 206/207 series
86-19-11, modify the fuel quick drain system: 172 and up
86-24-7, modify engine control rod ends: most single engines
87-20-3, inspect and replace the seat rails on nearly all planes
87-20-3, inspect and repair seat rails: all high wing planes
87-20-4, install quick fuel tank drains: some 185s
87-21-5, install placard for no spins: most 150 & 152 airplanes
88-12-12, install control on fuel quick drain: 177RG
88-15-6, secure battery/battery box: most 150 series
90-5-1, inspect flap bellcrank: 208 series
90-5-4, inspect engine mount: 208 series
90-6-3, test exhaust heater: 172 series
90-21-8, modify/install fuel bladder or placard: older 180s

Ercoupe

46-49-1, replace the nosewheel: 415
47-20-5, reinforce the belly skin: 415
47-20-6, reinforce the aileron skin: 415
47-42-20, inspect and replace control column shaft: 415
59-5-4, reinforce the rear spar: 415

59-25-5, reinforce the rudder: 415
60-9-2, replace the nosegear bolts: all
67-6-3, modify the rudder control: 415

Gulfstream

70-25-5, replace the bungee mounting plate: AA-1
75-9-7, replace the mixture control wires: AA-1/A/B
76-1-2, replace the engine cowl hinge: AA-5 series
76-17-3, rework some bonded skins: AA-1/AA-5 series
76-22-9, replace the oil cooler: AA-5 series
77-7-4, replace the carb heat valve: AA-5/AA-5A
78-13-4, replace the fuel gauge floats: AA-1
79-22-4, rework the aileron control system: AA-5 series
88-5-6, inspect/replace vertical stabilizer attach: 112 & 114 series
89-15-8, inspect fuel tanks and fuel pump: AA-5 series
90-4-7, inspect for cracks in landing gear: 112 & 114 series

Lake

65-15-3, rework the nosegear drag strut bolt: LA-4
74-26-2, each 100 hours replace the rudder bellcrank: LA-4/200
76-24-2, replace the oil cooler: LA-4-200
78-14-5, inspect and replace the wing beam fittings: LA-4-200
79-6-1, replace the engine mount straps: LA-4-200

Luscombe

48-49-1, reinforce the vertical stabilizer spar: 8 series
79-25-5, each 100 hours inspect stabilizer attachments: 8 series

Maule

65-18-1, reinforce the fuselage fabric: M-4 series
69-20-2, replace the aileron control pulley: M-4 series
71-6-6, rework the seat tracks: M-4 180C/220C
79-12-1, modify the tail and fuselage attachment: M-4/5
81-14-2, modify the rudder bar: M-4/5
84-9-7, replace the fuel drain fittings: M-4/5 series

Mooney

63-10-5, replace the empennage brackets: M20/A
67-11-5, replace the tail truss: M20/M20A
73-21-1, rework flight controls & landing gear: M20/A/B/C/D/E/F/G
75-9-8, inspect the engine mount for cracks: M20C/D/E/F/G

77-17-4, each 100 hours inspect control wheel shaft: M20/A/B/C/D/E/F/G
77-18-1, check and replace the oil cooler: M20E/F/J
78-15-2, replace the landing gear brace bolts: M20F/J
80-13-3, inspect the fuel tanks: M20/22 series
85-24-3, each 12 months perform load test on wooden wings: M20/A
88-25-11, modify baggage dr & install placard: M20J & K

Navion

64-4-5, each 100 hours inspect/replace outer wing panel: all through G

Piper

59-13-2, reinforce the aileron balance weight: PA-24
62-26-5, rework the exhaust system: PA-24
62-26-6, rework the exhaust system: PA-28 150-/160-hp
64-6-6, dye check and replace the control wheel: PA-28
64-21-5, replace Hartzell propeller governor relief valve: PA-23/30
66-20-5, modify the propeller spinner: PA-28
67-20-4, replace the torque links: PA-28/32
68-12-4, rework the gear retraction system: PA-28R
69-22-2, inspect the control wheel: PA-28/32
70-18-5, replace the landing gear bolts: PA-28/32
70-26-4, dye inspect and replace the stabilator tube: PA-28/32
74-6-1, rework the turbochargers: PA-23
74-16-8, rework to prevent cracking in aft bulkhead: PA-30/39
74-24-12, rebuild the aileron centering assembly: PA-28
75-2-3, heat treat and replace the nosewheel fork: PA-28/32
75-12-6, each 100 hours magnify inspect fin spar attach point: PA-24
75-16-4, rework the carburetor air box: PA-28-151
76-18-5, inspect the forward fin channel for cracks: PA-30/39
76-19-7, replace the stabilator weight tube assembly: PA-24
77-1-3, modify the air filter box: PA-28-151
77-3-8, inspect the lift struts: most tube and fabric series
77-13-21, each 500 hours inspect landing gear (bungee cords): PA-24s
78-2-3, each 100 hours inspect the stabilator system: PA-23-250
78-8-3, dye and magnify inspect the rudder hinges: PA-23-150/160
78-22-1, install rudder kit: PA-28
78-22-7, replace the control column stop sleeve: PA-32RT
78-23-1, each 100 hours inspect the fuel drain: PA-28-235/PA-32
78-23-4, modify the rear wing spar attachment fittings: PA-38
78-23-9, modify and replace the control wheels: PA-38
78-26-6, dye check and replace the fin spar plate: PA-38
79-3-2, install rudder hinge kit: PA-38
79-8-2, dye inspect the stabilizer fittings: PA-38
79-11-6, replace the gear selector lever: PA-23

79-13-4, install a steel fuel line: PA-32RT
80-19-1, inspect & repair muffler leaks: PA-28R-180/200/201/RT201
80-22-13, replace the rudder hinge brackets: PA-38
81-12-4, modify the rudder system: PA-28RT/201T
81-23-7, modify and replace the engine mount: PA-38
81-24-7, modify the nosegear: PA-32R series
81-25-5, replace the strut forks: J3/PA-11/12/14/16/18/20/22
82-2-1, install an aileron balance reinforcement kit: PA-38
82-19-1, dye check the wing spar caps and plates: PA-24
82-27-8, dye check and replace the fin spar: PA-38
83-5-4, replace the landing gear bolts: PA-38
83-14-8, install kit and replace airspeed indicator: PA-38
83-19-1, each 100 hours inspect and modify the fin spars: PA-38
83-19-3, inspect the spar cap: PA-24 series
85-11-6, modify the control wheel shaft: PA-38
86-17-1, replace the ammeter: PA-28/32 series
87-8-8, inspect the lower spar caps and upper skin: PA-28/32s
88-21-7, inspect fuel/vent lines and cell caps: PA-23
90-2-23, inspect/replace prop hub: PA-32 series
90-23-18, modify fuel system—new preflight: most PA-32s
91-7-8, IFR flight restrictions: Malibu only

Rockwell

68-12-5, modify the rudder control arms: 100/100A
68-21-2, inspect/replace the aileron cable assembly: 100 series
73-1-1, inspect and repair the exhaust system: 100 series

Stinson

51-15-2, inspect for cracked crankcase: 6A4-165-B3 Franklin engines

Taylorcraft

75-18-5, 100 hours inspect/replace the engine mount bolts: F-19
79-4-4, rewire the starter solenoid to switch: F-19 (1-132)
87-3-8, inspect/replace oil gauge assy: F-19, 21, 21A

Varga

80-2-8, check for bolts in rudder balance weight: 2150/A
80-13-8, install a throttle stop: 2150/A
82-8-4, replace the elevator balance arm: 2150A/2180

All small airplanes

84-26-2, each 500 hours replace paper air-filter element

Airborne-brand Equipment

86-1-6, replace dry vacuum pumps: many aircraft

Bendix-brand Equipment

82-11-5, comply with service bulletin: many engines
82-20-1, inspect impulse couplers: many engines

Brackett-brand Equipment

81-15-3, replace inlet air filter: most small aircraft

Slick-brand Equipment

80-6-5, test the magneto impulse coupling: many engines
81-16-5, inspect the magneto coil: many engines

Continental engines

60-12-1, replace the piston pins: E-185/E-225/O-470
63-15-1, replace the exhaust valves: E-165/E-185/E-225/O-470
72-20-2, inspect/replace the cylinders: O-470 engines
77-13-22, inspect the crankcase for cracks: O-520 series
81-7-6, inspect/replace the fuel pump: A-65/75/C-75/85/90/C-125/O-200
81-13-10, rework the oil pump drive: IO-360 series
85-8-2, replace the exhaust valves: O-470 series

Lycoming Engines

71-11-2, replace the tappet plungers: IO-360 A/C series
75-8-9, replace the oil pump shaft and impeller: O-235/320/360/540
77-7-7, modify the oil filter: O-320-H series
77-20-7, replace the tappets: O-320-H series
78-12-8, replace the oil pump impeller: O-320-H series
78-12-9, replace the crankshaft: O-320-H series
78-25-1, replace the Slick magneto: PA-38
80-4-3, replace valve springs, seats, and lifters: O-320
80-14-7, inspect exhaust valve springs and seats: O-320-H/O-360-E
80-25-2, inspect the valve pushrods: O-235 series
81-18-4, replace the oil pump impeller & shaft: most engines
83-22-4, replace the fuel diaphram: IO-540 series
87-10-6, inspect and replace the rocker arm assembly: many engines

Appendix B

NTSB accident ranking of small airplanes

The National Transportation Safety Board (NTSB) and FAA investigates all airplane accidents. Based upon thousands of investigations, the board has amassed a tremendous amount of numerical data. This information has been reduced to chart form by comparing specific types of aircraft accidents with makes/models of small airplanes.

The placement of an aircraft make/model on NTSB charts is determined by the frequency of accidents compared to other aircraft listed on the same chart; aircraft with poor accident records at the top, aircraft with better records at the bottom.

Note: Some makes/models do not appear on a chart due to the limited numbers of records available for analysis and that all data is based upon rate per 100,000 flying hours.

Fatal Accident by Manufacturer	Rate per 100,000 hours
Bellanca	4.84
Grumman	4.13
Beechcraft	2.54
Mooney	2.50
Piper	2.48
Cessna	1.65

Accidents Caused by Engine Failure	Rate per 100,000 hours
Globe GC-1	12.36
Stinson 108	10.65
Ercoupe	9.50
Grumman AA-1	8.71
Navion	7.84
Piper J-3	7.61
Luscombe 8	7.58
Cessna 120/140	6.73
Piper PA-12	6.54
Bellanca 14-19	5.98
Piper PA-22	5.67
Cessna 195	4.69
Piper PA-32	4.39
Cessna 210/205	4.25
Aeronca 7	4.23
Aeronca 11	4.10
Taylorcraft	3.81
Piper PA-24	3.61
Beech 23	3.58
Cessna 175	3.48
Mooney M-20	3.42

	Rate per 100,000 hours
Piper PA-18	3.37
Cessna 177	3.33
Cessna 206	3.30
Cessna 180	3.24
Cessna 170	2.88
Cessna 185	2.73
Cessna 150	2.48
Piper PA-28	2.37
Beech 33/35/36	2.22
Grumman AA-5	2.20
Cessna 182	2.08
Cessna 172	1.41

Accidents Caused by In-flight Airframe Failure

	Rate per 100,000 hours
Bellanca 14-19	1.49
Globe GC-1	1.03
Ercoupe	0.97
Cessna 195	0.94
Navion	0.90
Aeronca 11	0.59
Beech 33/35/36	0.58
Luscombe 8	0.54
Piper PA-24	0.42
Cessna 170	0.36
Cessna 210/205	0.34
Cessna 180	0.31
Piper PA-22	0.30
Aeronca 7	0.27
Beech 23	0.27
Cessna 120/140	0.27
Piper PA-32	0.24
Taylorcraft	0.24
Piper J-3	0.23
Mooney M-20	0.18
Piper PA-28	0.16
Cessna 177	0.16
Cessna 182	0.12
Cessna 206	0.11
Grumman AA-1	0.09
Cessna 172	0.03
Cessna 150	0.02

Accidents Resulting from a Stall

	Rate per 100,000 hours
Aeronca 7	22.47
Aeronca 1	18.21
Taylorcraft	6.44
Piper J-3	5.88
Luscombe 8	5.78
Pipe PA-18	5.49
Globe GC-1	5.15
Cessna 170	4.38
Grumman AA-1	4.23
Piper PA-12	3.27
Cessna 120/140	2.51
Stinson 108	2.09
Navion	1.81
Piper PA-22	1.78
Cessna 177	1.77
Grumman AA-5	1.76
Cessna 185	1.47
Cessna 150	1.42
Beech 23	1.41
Ercoupe	1.29
Cessna 180	1.08
Piper PA-24	0.98
Beech 33/35/36	0.94
Cessna 175	0.83
Piper PA-28	0.80
Mooney M-20	0.80
Cessna 172	0.77
Cessna 210/205	0.71
Bellanca 14-19	0.60
Piper PA-32	0.57
Cessna 206	0.54
Cessna 195	0.47
Cessna 182	0.36

Accidents Caused by Hard Landings

	Rate per 100,000 hours
Beech 23	3.50
Grumman AA-1	3.02
Ercoupe	2.90
Cessna 177	2.60
Globe GC-1	2.58

Luscombe 8	2.35
Cessna 182	2.17
Cessna 170	1.89
Beech 33/35/36	1.45
Cessna 150	1.37
Cessna 120/140	1.35
Cessna 206	1.30
Piper PA-24	1.29
Aeronca 7	1.20
Piper J-3	1.04
Grumman AA-5	1.03
Cessna 175	1.00
Cessna 180	0.93
Cessna 210/205	0.82
Piper PA-28	0.81
Cessna 172	0.71
Piper PA-22	0.69
Taylorcraft BC	0.48
Cessna 195	0.47
Piper PA-18	0.43
Piper PA-32	0.42
Cessna 185	0.42
Navion	0.36
Mooney M-20	0.31
Piper PA-12	0.23
Stinson 108	0.19

Beech 23	2.33
Bellanca 14-19	2.10
Piper J-3	2.07
Cessna 206	1.73
Cessna 177	1.61
Grumman AA-5	1.47
Piper PA-32	1.42
Cessna 150	1.37
Piper PA-28	1.36
Piper PA-24	1.29
Cessna 210/205	1.08
Cessna 182	1.06
Cessna 172	1.00
Mooney M-20	0.65
Beech 33/35/36	0.55
Navion	0.36
Cessna 175	0.17

Accidents Resulting from a Ground Loop

	Rate per 100,000 hours
Cessna 195	22.06
Stinson 108	13.50
Luscombe 8	13.00
Cessna 170	9.91
Cessna 120/140	8.99
Aeronca 11	7.86
Aeronca 7	7.48
Cessna 180	6.49
Cessna 185	4.72
Piper PA-12	4.67
Piper PA-18	3.90
Taylorcraft BC	3.58
Globe GC-1	3.09
Grumman AA-1	2.85
Piper PA-22	2.76
Ercoupe	2.74

Accidents Caused by Undershot Landings

	Rate per 100,000 hours
Ercoupe	2.41
Luscombe 8	1.62
Piper PA-12	1.40
Globe GC-1	1.03
Cessna 175	0.99
Grumman AA-1	0.95
Taylorcraft BC	0.95
Piper PA-22	0.83
Piper PA-32	0.70
Bellanca 14-19	0.60
Aeronca 11	0.59
Piper PA-28	0.59
Aeronca 7	0.59
Piper PA-24	0.57
Piper J-3	0.57
Stinson 108	0.57
Cessna 120/140	0.53
Cessna 195	0.47
Grumman AA-5	0.44
Piper PA-18	0.43
Beech 23	0.43
Cessna 185	0.41
Mooney M-20	0.37
Cessna 170	0.36
Navion	0.36

	Rate per 100,000 hours
Cessna 150	0.35
Cessna 210/205	0.33
Cessna 206	0.32
Cessna 172	0.26
Cessna 182	0.24
Beech 33/35/36	0.21
Cessna 180	0.15
Cessna 177	0.10

Accidents Resulting
from Landing Overshoot

	Rate per 100,000 hours
Grumman AA-5	2.35
Cessna 195	2.34
Beech 23	1.95
Piper PA-24	1.61
Piper PA-22	1.33
Cessna 175	1.33
Stinson 108	1.33
Cessna 182	1.21
Aeronca 11	1.17
Luscombe 8	1.08
Piper PA-32	1.03
Globe GC-1	1.03
Mooney M-20	1.01
Cessna 172	1.00
Cessna 170	0.99
Grumman AA-1	0.95
Piper PA-12	0.93
Cessna 210/205	0.89
Cessna 177	0.88
Piper PA-18	0.81
Cessna 206	0.81
Piper PA-28	0.80
Cessna 120/140	0.71
Ercoupe	0.64
Bellanca 14-19	0.60
Cessna 180	0.56
Navion	0.54
Aeronca 7	0.48
Cessna 150	0.35
Piper J-3	0.34
Cessna 185	0.31
Beech 33/35/36	0.23

Appendix C

FAA FSDO locations

Whenever you need a question about general aviation answered, or you have a question about aviation aircraft, you can always turn to the Federal Aviation Administration. They have many offices spread around the country with experts to serve the public.

In the many years that I have been associated with general aviation I have never been disappointed with help I received from the FAA. When a problem arises, contact them.

ALABAMA

FSDO 09
6500 43rd Avenue North
Birmingham, AL 35206
(205) 731-1393

ALASKA

FSDO 01
6348 Old Airport Way
Fairbanks, AK 99701
(907) 474-0276

FSDO 03
4510 West Int'l Airport Road, Suite 216
Anchorage, AK 99502
(907) 243-1902

FSDO 05
1910 Alex Holden Way, Suite A
Juneau, AK 99701
(907) 789-0231

ARIZONA

FSDO
15041 North Airport Drive
Scottsdale, AZ 85260
(602) 640-2561

ARKANSAS

FSDO 65
1701 Bond Street
Little Rock, AR 72202
(501) 378-5565

CALIFORNIA

FSDO
5885 West Imperial Way
Los Angeles, CA 90045
(213) 215-2150

FSDO
831 Mitten Rd., Rm 105
Burlingame, CA 94010
(415) 876-2771

FSDO
16501 Sherman Way, Suite 330
Van Nuys, CA 91406
(818) 904-6291

FSDO
1250 Aviation Ave., Suite 295
San Jose, CA 95110-1119
(408) 291-7681

FSDO
8525 Gibbs Drive, Suite 120
San Diego, CA 92123
(619) 557-5281

FSDO
Fresno Air Terminal
4955 East Anderson, Suite 110
Fresno, CA 93727-1521
(209) 487-5306

FSDO
Riverside Municipal Airport
6961 Flight Road
Riverside, CA 92504
(714) 351-6701

FSDO
Executive Airport
Sacramento, CA 95822
(916) 551-1721

FSDO
P.O. Box 2397
Airport Station
Oakland, CA 94614
(415) 273-7155

FSDO
2815 East Spring Street
Long Beach, CA 90806
(213) 426-7134

COLORADO

FSDO
5440 Roslyn St., Suite 201, Rm 202
Denver, CO 80216
(303) 286-5400

CONNECTICUT

FSDO 03
Building 85-214
Bradley International Airport
Windsor Locks, CT 06096
(203) 654-1000

DISTRICT OF COLUMBIA

FSDO 27
GT Bldg., Suite 112
Box 17325
Dulles International Airport
Washington, D.C. 20041
(202) 557-5360

FLORIDA

FSDO
FAA Building
Craig Municipal Airport
855 Saint John's Bluff Road
Jacksonville, FL 32225
(904) 641-7311

FSDO 15
Saint Petersburg/Clearwater Airport
Clearwater, FL 34622
(813) 531-1434

FSDO 15
9677 Tradport Dr., Suite 101
Orlando, FL 32827
(407) 648-6840

FSDO 17
286 South West 34th St.
Ft. Lauderdale, FL 33315
(305) 463-4841

FSDO 19
P.O. Box 592015
Miami, FL 33159
(305) 526-2572

GEORGIA

FSDO 11
1680 Phoenix Pkwy., Suite 403
College Park, GA 30349
(404) 994-5276

HAWAII

FSDO
90 Nakolo Place, Rm 215
Honolulu, HI 96819
(808) 836-0615

ILLINOIS

FSDO 03
Post Office Box H
DuPage County Airport
West Chicago, IL 60185
(312) 377-4500

FSDO 19
Capitol Airport
#3 North Airport Dr.
Springfield, IL 62707
(217) 492-4238

FSDO 31
9950 West Lawrence Ave., Suite 400
Schiller Park, IL 60176
(312) 353-7787

INDIANA

FSDO 11
Indianapolis International Airport
6801 Pierson Drive
Indianapolis, IN 46241
(317) 247-2491

FSDO 17
1843 Commerce Drive
South Bend, IN 46628
(219) 236-8480

IOWA

FSDO 61
3021 Army Post Road
Des Moines, IA 50321
(515) 285-9895

KANSAS

FSDO 64
Mid-Continent Airport
1801 Airport Rd., Rm 103
Wichita, KS 67209
(316) 946-4462

KENTUCKY

FSDO
Kaden Building, 5th Flr
6100 Dutchmans Lane
Louisville, KY 40205
(502) 582-5941

LOUISIANA

FSDO
Ryan Airport
9191 Plan1 Rd.
Baton Rouge, LA 70811
(504) 356-5701

MAINE

FSDO 05
L2 A1 McKay Ave.
Portland, ME 04102
(207) 780-3263

MARYLAND

FSDO 07
890 Airport Park Rd., Suite 101
Glen Burnie, MD 21061
(301) 859-5780

MASSACHUSETTS

FSDO 01
Civil Air Terminal Bldg., 2nd Flr.
Hanscom Field
Bedford, MA 01730
(617) 274-7130

MICHIGAN

FSDO 09
Kent County International Airport
5500 44th Street SE
Grand Rapids, MI 49508
(616) 456-2427

FSDO 23
Willow Run Airport
8800 Beck Road
Belleville, MI 48111
(313) 485-2550

MINNESOTA

FSDO 15
6201 34th Avenue South, Rm 201
Minneapolis, MN 55450
(612) 725-4211

MISSISSIPPI

FSDO 07
120 North Hangar Drive, Suite C
Jackson Municipal Airport
Jackson, MS 39208
(601) 960-4633

MISSOURI

FSDO 62
FAA Bldg
10801 Pear Tree Ln., Suite 200
St. Ann, MO 63074
(314) 429-1006

FSDO 63
Kansas City International Airport
525 Mexico City Ave.
Kansas City, MO 64153
(816) 243-3800

MONTANA

FSDO
FAA Building, Rm 3
Helena Airport
Helena, MT 59601
(406) 499-5270

NEBRASKA

FSDO 65
General Aviation Building
Lincoln Municipal Airport
Lincoln, NE 68524
(402) 437-5485

NEVADA

FSDO
601 South Rock Blvd., Suite 102
Reno, NV 89502
(702) 784-5321

FSDO
241 East Reno Avenue, Suite 200
Las Vegas, NV 89119
(702) 388-6482

NEW JERSEY

FSDO 25
150 Fred Wehran Drive, Rm 5
Teterboro Airport
Teterboro, NJ 07608
(201) 288-1745

NEW MEXICO

FSDO
1601 Randolph Road, SE Suite 200N
Albuquerque, NM 87106
(505) 247-0156

NEW YORK

FSDO 01
Albany County Airport
Albany, NY 12211
(518) 869-8482

FSDO 11
Administration Building
Republic Airport
Farmingdale, NY 11735
(516) 694-5530

FSDO 15
181 South Franklin Ave., 4th Flr
Valley Stream, NY 11581
(718) 917-1848

FSDO 23
1 Airport Way, Suite 110
Rochester, NY 14624
(716) 263-5880

NORTH CAROLINA

FSDO 05
8025 North Point Blvd., Suite 250
Winston-Salem, NC 27106
(919) 631-5147

FSDO 06
2000 Aerial Center Pkwy., Suite 120
Morrisville, NC 27263
(919) 840-5510

FSDO 08
FAA Building
5318 Morris Field Drive
Charlotte, NC 28208
(704) 392-3214

NORTH DAKOTA

FSDO 21
1801 23rd Ave. North
Fargo, ND 58105
(701) 232-8949

OHIO

FSDO 05
4242 Airport Road
Lunken Executive Building
Cincinnati, OH 45226
(513) 533-8110

FSDO 07
3939 International Gateway, 2nd Flr.
Port Columbus International Airport
Columbus, OH 43219
(614) 469-7476

FSDO 25
Federal Facilities Building
Cleveland Hopkins International Airport
Cleveland, OH 44135
(216) 267-0220

OKLAHOMA

FSDO
1300 South Meridian, Suite 601
Bethany, OK 73008
(405) 231-4196

OREGON

FSDO
Portland/Hillsboro Airport
3355 NE Cornell Road
Hillsboro, OR 97124
(503) 221-2104

PENNSYLVANIA

FSDO 03
Allegheny County Airport
Terminal Bldg., Rm 213
West Mifflin, PA 15122
(412) 462-5507

FSDO 05
Allentown-Bethlehem-Easton Airport
Allentown, PA 18103
(215)264-2888

FSDO 13
Administration Building, Rm 201
Capitol City Airport
New Cumberland, PA 17070
(717) 782-4528

FSDO 17
Scott Plaza 2, 2nd Flr.
Philadelphia, PA 19113
(215) 596-0673

FSDO 19
One Thorn Center, Suite 200
1187 Thorn Run Ext.
Corapolis, PA 15108
(412) 644-5406

SOUTH CAROLINA

FSDO 13
Columbia Metropolitan Airport
2819 Aviation Way
West Columbia, SC 29169
(803) 765-5931

SOUTH DAKOTA

FSDO 66
Rapid City Regional Airport
P.O. Box 4750
Rapid City, SD 57701
(605) 393-1359

TENNESSEE

FSDO 03
2 International Plaza Dr., Suite 700
Nashville, TN 37217
(615) 736-5539

FSDO 03
3385 Airways Blvd., Suite 115
Memphis, TN 38116
(901) 521-3820

TEXAS

FSDO
7701 North Stemmons Fwy
Dallas, TX 75247
(214) 767-5850

FSDO
Dallas/Fort Worth Regional Airport
P.O. Box 619020
Dallas/Fort Worth Airport, TX 75261
(214) 575-3111

FSDO
8800 Paul B Koonce Drive
Rm 152
Houston, TX 77061
(713) 522-6610

FSDO
Route 3, Box 51
Lubbock, TX 79401
(806) 762-0335

FSDO
10100 Reunion Place, Suite 200
San Antonio, TX 78216
(512) 314-4371

UTAH

FSDO
116 North 2400 West
Salt Lake City, UT 84116
(801) 524-4247

VIRGINIA

FSDO 21
Byrd International Airport
Terminal Bldg., 2nd Flr.
Sandstone, VA 23150-2594
(804) 222-7494

FSDO 27
GT Building, Suite 112
Box 17325
Dulles International Airport
Washington, DC 20041
(703) 557-5360

WASHINGTON

FSDO
1601 Lind Ave., SW
Renton, WA 98055-4046
(206) 227-2810

WEST VIRGINIA

FSDO 09
Yeager Airport
301 Eagle Mountain Road, Rm 144
Kanawha Airport
Charleston, WV 25311
(304) 343-4689

WISCONSIN

FSDO 13
4915 South Howell Avenue, 4th Flr.
Milwaukee, WI 53207
(414) 747-5531

Appendix D

State aviation agencies

When it comes to daily living it seems that everyone wants to make a regulation. Aviation is no exception, just look at the FARs. And if the Feds are not enough, most states have an aviation agency of one type or another that has additional regulations for you to follow.

Some state aviation agencies offer assistance and up-to-date news and information to their pilots. Unfortunately, a few states use their aviation agencies as taxing houses.

Contact your state's aviation agency and see what is offered and/or required.

ALABAMA

Department of Aeronautics
555 South Perry St., Suite 308
Montgomery, AL 36130-0101
(205) 242-4480

ALASKA

Department of Transportation
P.O. Box 196900
Anchorage, AK 99519-6900
(907) 266-1460

ARIZONA

Division of Aeronautics
Arizona Department of Transportation
2612 South 46th St.
Phoenix, AZ 85034
(602) 255-7691

ARKANSAS

Department of Aeronautics
Regional Airport Terminal
1 Airport Drive, 3rd Flr.
Little Rock, AR 72202
(501) 376-6781

CALIFORNIA

Division of Aeronautics
California Department of Transportation
P.O. Box 942873
Sacramento, CA 94273-0001
(916) 322-3090

COLORADO

Division of Aviation
Colorado Department of Military Affairs
6848 South Revere Pkwy, Suite 101
Englewood, CO 80112-6703
(303) 397-3039

CONNECTICUT

Bureau of Aeronautics
Connecticut Department of Transportation
P.O. Drawer A
24 Wolcott Hill Rd.
Wethersfield, CT 06109
(203) 566-4417

DELAWARE

Aeronautics Administration
Delaware Transportation Authority
Department of Transportation
P.O. Box 778
Dover, DE 19903
(302) 739-3244

FLORIDA

Aviation Office
Florida Department of Transportation
605 Swannee St., M.S. 46
Tallahassee, FL 32399-0450
(904) 488-8444

GEORGIA

Bureau of Aeronautics
Georgia Department of Transportation
2017 Flightway Drive
Chamblee, GA 30341
(404) 986-1350

HAWAII

Airports Division
Hawaii Department of Transportation
Honolulu International Airport
Honolulu, HI 96819-1898
(808) 836-6432

IDAHO

Bureau of Aeronautics
Idaho Transportation Department
3483 Rickenbacker St.
Boise, ID 83705
(208) 334-8775

ILLINOIS

Division of Aeronautics
Illinois Department of Transportation
Capital Airport
1 Langhorne Bond Dr.
Springfield, IL 62707-8415
(217) 785-8500

INDIANA

Division of Aeronautics
Indiana Department of Transportation
143 West Market St., Suite 300
Indianapolis, IN 46204
(317) 232-1470

IOWA

Air and Transit Division
Iowa Department of Transportation
International Airport
Des Moines, IA 50321
(515) 287-2802

KANSAS

Division of Aviation
Kansas Department of Transportation
Docking State Office Building
Topeka, KS 66612-1568
(913) 296-2553

KENTUCKY

Office of Aeronautics
Kentucky Transportation Cabinet
421 Ann St.
Frankfort, KY 40622
(502) 564-4480

LOUISANA

Aviation Division
Department of Transportation
   and Development
P.O. Box 94245
Baton Rouge, LA 70804-9245
(504) 379-1242

MAINE

Air Transport Division
Maine Department of Transportation
State House Station #16
Augusta, ME 04333
(207) 289-3185

MARYLAND

Maryland Aviation Administration
Maryland Department of Transportation
P.O. Box 8766
Baltimore, MD 21240
(301) 859-7100

MASSACHUSETTS

Aeronautics Commission
10 Park Plaza, Rm 6620
Boston, MA 02116-3966
(617) 973-7350

MICHIGAN

Bureau of Aeronautics
Department of Transportation
2nd Flr., Terminal Building
Capital City Airport
Lansing, MI 48906
(517) 373-1834

MINNESOTA

Aeronautics Office
Minnesota Department of Transportation
State Transportation Building
Rm 417
John Ireland Blvd.
St. Paul, MN 55155
(612) 296-8202

MISSISSIPPI

Mississippi Aeronautics Bureau
1701 Walter Sillers State Office Bldg.
P.O. Box 5
Jackson, MS 39205
(601) 354-6970

MISSOURI

Department of Highways & Transportation
Aviation Section
P.O. Box 270
Jefferson City, MO 65102
(314) 751-2589

MONTANA

Aeronautics Division
Department of Commerce
P.O. Box 5178
Helena, MT 59604
(406) 444-2506

NEBRASKA

Department of Aeronautics
P.O. Box 82088
Lincoln, NE 68501
(402) 471-2371

NEVADA

Department of Transportation
1263 S. Stewart St.
Carson City, NV 89712
(702) 687-5440

NEW HAMPSHIRE

Division of Aeronautics
New Hampshire
  Department of Transportation
Municipal Airport
65 Airport Rd.
Concord, NH 03301-5298
(603) 271-2551

NEW JERSEY

Office of Aviation
New Jersey Department of Transportation
1035 Parkway Ave., CN 600
Trenton, NJ 08625
(609) 530-2900

NEW MEXICO

Aviation Division
P.O. Box 1149
Sante Fe, NM 87504-1149
(505) 827-0332

NEW YORK

Aviation Division
New York State Department of Transportation
1220 Washington Ave.
Albany, NY 12232
(518) 457-2820

NORTH CAROLINA

Division of Aviation
North Carolina Department of Transportation
P.O. Box 25201
Raleigh, NC 27611
(919) 787-9618

NORTH DAKOTA

North Dakota Aeronautics Commission
Bismark Airport
P.O. Box 5020
Bismark, ND 58502
(701) 224-2748

OHIO

Ohio Department of Transportation
Division of Aviation
2829 West Dublin-Granville Rd.
Columbus, OH 43235
(614) 466-7120

OKLAHOMA

Oklahoma Aeronautics Commission
Department of Transportation Bldg.
200 NE 21st St., Rm B-7 (1st flr)
Oklahoma City, OK 73105
(405) 521-2377

OREGON

Division of Aeronautics
Oregon Department of Transportation
3040 25th St. SE
Salem, OR 97310
(503) 378-4880

PENNSYLVANIA

Bureau of Aviation
Pennsylvania Department of Transportation
Transportation & Safety Bldg., Rm 506
Harrisburg, PA 17120
(717) 783-2280

RHODE ISLAND

Division of Airports
Theodore Francis Green State Airport
Warwick, RI 02886
(401) 737-4000

SOUTH CAROLINA

South Carolina Aeronautics Commission
P.O. Box 280068
Columbia, SC 29228-0068
(803) 822-5401

SOUTH DAKOTA

Office of Aeronautics
700 Broadway Ave. E
Pierre, SD 57501-2586
(605) 773-3574

TENNESSEE

Office of Aeronautics
Tennessee Department of Transportation
P.O. Box 17326
Nashville, TN 37217
(615) 741-3208

TEXAS

Texas Department of Aviation
P.O. Box 12607
Austin, TX 78711
(512) 476-9262

UTAH

Aeronautical Operations Division
Utah Department of Transportation
135 North 2400 West
Salt Lake City, UT 84116
(801) 328-2066

VERMONT

Agency of Transportation
133 State St.
Montpelier, VT 05633
(802) 828-2093

VIRGINIA

Department of Aviation
4508 South Laburnum Ave.
Richmond, VA 23231-2422
(804) 786-1364

WASHINGTON

Division of Aeronautics
Washington Department of Transportation
8600 Perimeter Rd., Boeing Field
Seattle, WA 98108-3885
(206) 764-4131

WEST VIRGINIA

Department of Transportation
Building 5, Rm A-109
West Virginia State Capitol
Charleston, WV 25305
(304) 348-0444

WISCONSIN

Bureau of Aeronautics
Division of Transportation Assistance
Wisconsin Department of Transportation
P.O. Box 7914
Madison, WI 53707-7194
(608) 266-3351

WYOMING

Aeronautics Division
5300 Bishop Blvd.
P.O. Box 1708
Cheyenne, WY 82002-9019
(307) 777-7481

Appendix E

Resources for the small airplane owner

The small-airplane owner often must have resources to turn to for assistance in the ownership, operation, and maintenance of his airplane. In most instances, he can contact his airplane's manufacturer or an airplane type club for support.

Manufacturers

Some manufacturers are excellent sources of information, parts, and service for all planes built under their name while others only support modern (current) planes of their manufacture. Unfortunately, many of the airplanes available on today's used market are without manufacturer-provided owner support. Why you ask? Because the manufacturers, for one reason or another, are no longer in business.

Type clubs

Most of the popular makes and models of small planes, such as those seen in this book, have a type club representing them. A type club is an association of persons interested in a particular make/model of airplane.

These organizations generally publish a newsletter, host national or regional gatherings, and can answer questions about their particular type of airplanes. I strongly recommend that you join and support the club that applies to your airplane.

The following list of manufacturers and type clubs was compiled with the assistance of Julia Downie. Current manufacturers, if any, are placed at the top of each group.

AERO COMMANDER

Commander Aircraft Co.
7200 N.W. 63rd St.
Bethany, OK 73008
(405) 495-8080

Aero Newsletter
5630 S. Washington Rd.
Lansing, MI 48911-4999
(800) 594-4634
(517) 882-8433

Commander Alliance
P.O. Box 3103
Antioch, CA 94531
(415) 754-6033

Commander Flying Association
899 West Foothill Blvd #E
Monrovia, CA 91016-1938
(818) 359-1040

AERONCA (also see CHAMPION)

Aeronca Aviators Club
511 Terrace Lake Road
Columbus, IN 47201
(812) 324-6878

Aeronca Sedan Club
115 Wendy Court
Union City, CA 94587
(510) 487-3070

International Aeronca Association
401 1st St. East
Clark, SD 57225
(605) 532-3862

National Aeronca Association
806 Lockport Rd.
P.O. Box 2219
Terre Haute, IN 47802
(812)232-1491

BEECHCRAFT

Beech Aircraft Corp.
P.O. Box 85
Wichita, KS 67201-0085
(316) 681-7111

American Bonanza Society
Mid-Continent Airport
P.O. Box 12888
Wichita, KS 67277
(316) 945-6913

Baron Newsletter
5630 S. Washington Rd.
Lansing, MI 48911-4999
(800) 594-4634
(517) 882-8433

Musketeer Newsletter
5630 S. Washington Rd.
Lansing, MI 48911-4999
(800) 594-4634
(517) 882-8433

Skipper Newsletter
5630 S. Washington Rd.
Lansing, MI 48911-4999
(800) 594-4634
(517) 882-8433

Staggerwing Club
1885 Millsboro Road
Mansfield, OH 44906
(419) 755-1011

Twin Beech Association, Inc.
P.O. Box 8186
Fountain Valley, CA 92728-8186
(714) 964-4864

Twin Bonanza Association
19684 Lakeshore Dr.
Three Rivers, MI 49093
(616) 279-2540

World Beechcraft Society
1436 Muirlands Dr.
La Jolla, CA 92037
(619) 459-5901

BELLANCA

Bellanca, Inc.
Municipal Airport
P.O. Box 964
Alexandria, MN 56308
(612) 762-1501

Bellanca-Champion Club
P.O. Box 708
Brookfield, WI 53008-0708
(414) 784-4544

CESSNA

Cessna Aircraft Company
P.O. Box 1521
Wichita, KS 67201
(316) 685-9111

Cardinal Club
1701 St. Andrew's Dr.
Lawrence, KS 66044
(913) 842-7016

Cessna 150/152 Club
P.O. Box 15388
Durham, NC 27704
(919) 471-9492

Cessna Owners Organization, Inc.
P.O. Box 337
Iola, WI 54945
(800) 331-0038

Cessna Pilots Association
P.O. Box 12948
Wichita, KS 67277
(316) 946-4777

Eastern Cessna 190/195 Association
25575 Butternut Ridge Rd.
North Olmsted, OH 44070
(216) 777-4025

International Cessna 120/140 Association
P.O. Box 830092
Richardson, TX 75083-0092
(817) 497-4757

International 170 Association
P.O. Box 1667
Lebanon, MO 65536
(417) 532-4847

International 180/185 Club
P.O. Box 222
Georgetown, TX 78627
(512) 863-7284

International 195 Club
P.O. Box 737
Merced, CA 95341
(209) 722-6283

National 210 Owners Association
P.O. Box 1065
La Canada, CA 91011
(818) 952-6212

Skymaster Club
P.O. Box 1950
Liberal, KS 67905
(316) 624-2281

Straight Tail Cessnas
2 Forest Lane
Gales Ferry, CT 06335

West Coast Cessna 120/140 Club
Post Office Box 727
Rosebud, OR 97470
(503) 459-5103

310 Owners of America
8531 Wealthwood
New Haven, IN 46774
(219) 749-2520
(800) 825-5310
FAX (219) 749-6140

310/310 Newsletter
5630 S. Washington Rd.
Lansing, MI 48911-4999
(800) 594-4634
(517) 882-8433

336/337 Newsletter
5630 S. Washington Rd.
Lansing, MI 48911-4999
(800) 594-4634
(517) 882-8433

CHAMPION (also see AERONCA)

American Champion Aircraft
P.O. Box 37
Rochester, WI 55167
(414) 534-6315

Bellanca-Champion Club
P.O. Box 708
Brookfield, WI 53008-0708
(414) 784-4544

CHRISTEN

Aviat, Inc.
P.O. Box 1149
South Washington St.
Afton, WY 83110
(307) 886-3151

ERCOUPE

Univair (parts manufacturer)
2500 Himalaya Rd.
Aurora, CO 80011
(303) 375-8882

Ercoupe Owners Club
P.O. Box 15388
Durham, NC 27704
(919) 471-9492

GULFSTREAM

American General Aircraft
P.O. Box 5757
Greenville, MS 38703
(601) 332-2422

Fletchair Inc.
7786 Braniff St.
Houston, TX 77061
(713) 641-2023

American Yankee Association
P.O. Box 1531
Cameron Park, CA 95682
(916) 676-4292

AA-1 Newsletter
5630 S. Washington Rd.
Lansing, MI 48911-4999
(800) 594-4634
(517) 882-8433

AA-5 Newsletter
5630 S. Washington Rd.
Lansing, MI 48911-4999
(800) 594-4634
(517) 882-8433

HELIO

Helio Newsletter
5630 S. Washington Rd.
Lansing, MI 48911-4999
(800) 594-4634
(517) 882-8433

LAKE

Lake Aircraft
Laconia Airport
Laconia, NH 03246
(603) 524-5868

Lake Amphibian Flyers Club
815 North Lake Reedy Blvd.
Frostproof, FL 33843
(813) 635-3381

LUSCOMBE

Univair (parts manufacturer)
2500 Himalaya Rd.
Aurora, CO 80011
(303) 375-8882

Continental Luscombe Association
5736 Esmar Road
Ceres, CA 95307
(209) 537-9934

Luscombe Association
6438 W. Millbrook
Remus, MI 49340
(517) 561-2393

MAULE

Maule Air, Inc.
Lake Maule - Rt # 5
Moultrie, GA 31768
(912) 985-2045

Maule Newsletter
5630 S. Washington Rd.
Lansing, MI 48910-4999
(800) 594-4634
(517) 882-8433

MEYERS

Meyers Aircraft Owners Association
26 Rt. 17K
Newburgh, NY 12550
(914) 565-8005

MOONEY

Mooney Aircraft
P.O. Box 72
Kerrville, TX 78028
(512) 896-6000

Mooney Aircraft Pilots Association
314 Stardust Dr.
San Antonio, TX 78228
(512) 434-5959

NAVION

American Navion Society
P.O. Box 1810
Lodi, CA 95241-1810
(209) 339-4213

PIPER

Piper Aircraft
2926 Piper Dr.
Vero Beach, FL 32960
(407) 567-4361

Arrow Newsletter
5630 S. Washington Rd.
Lansing, MI 48910-4999
(800) 594-4634
(517) 882-8433

Aztec Newsletter
5630 S. Washington Rd.
Lansing, MI 48910-4999
(800) 594-4634
(517) 882-8433

Cherokee Pilots Association
P.O. Box 7927
Tampa, FL 33673
(813) 935-7492

Cub Club
6438 W. Milbrook
Remus, MI 49340
(517) 561-2393

Flying Apache Association
6778 Skyline Dr.
Delray Beach, FL 33446
(407) 499-1115

International Comanche Society Inc.
P.O. Box 400
Grant, NE 69140
(308) 352-4275

Malibu Newsletter
5630 S. Washington Rd.
Lansing, MI 48910-4999
(800) 594-4634
(517) 882-8433

PA-32 Newsletter
5630 S. Washington Rd.
Lansing, MI 48910-4999
(800) 594-4634
(517) 882-8433

PA-34 Newsletter
5630 S. Washington Rd.
Lansing, MI 48910-4999
(800) 594-4634
(517) 882-8433

PA-38 Newsletter
5630 S. Washington Rd.
Lansing, MI 48910-4999
(800) 594-4634
(517) 882-8433

Piper Owner Society
P.O. Box 337
Iola, WI 54945
(715) 445-5000

Short Wing Piper Club, Inc.
1412 10th St.
Aurora, NE 68818
(402) 694-2218

Super Cub Pilot's Association
P.O. Box 9823
Yakima, WA 98909
(509) 248-9491

Tomahawk Society
Mountaintop Airstrip, 4RWY32
Wolfeboro Falls, OH 03896

SEABEE

Seabee Club International
6761 N.W. 32nd Avenue
Ft. Lauderdale, FL 33309
(305) 979-5470

STINSON

Univair (parts manufacturer)
2500 Himalaya Rd.
Aurora, CO 80011
(303) 375-8882

National Stinson Club
115 Heinley Rd.
Lake Placid, FL 33852
(813) 465-6101

Northeast Stinson Flying Club
8 Grimes Brook Rd.
Simsbury, CT 06070
(203) 658-1566

Southwest Stinson Club
812 Shady Glen
Martinez, CA 94553
(510) 228-4176

SWIFT

International Swift Association
P.O. Box 644
Athens, TN 37303
(615) 745-9547

TAYLORCRAFT

International Taylorcraft Owners Club
12809 Greenbower Rd.
Alliance, OH 44601
(216) 823-9748

VARGA

Varga Newsletter
5630 S. Washington Rd.
Lansing, MI 48910-4999
(800) 594-4634
(517) 882-8433

Appendix F

Used airplane prices

Prices fluctuate depending upon market demands. Newer planes will see yearly drops, until a plateau is reached, generally at about 15 years. Drastic price reductions will be noted on planes experiencing expensive maintenance problems or costly ADs. Many late-model aircraft actually increase in value due to the increased costs of new airplanes and the general lack of availability of good quality used airplanes. Remember, in most cases they aren't making them anymore!

Average airplane asking prices might vary as much as 30 percent from those contained in this list. Variations can be caused by the geographical location of the aircraft, condition of the airplane, or how badly the owner wishes to sell the airplane.

In practice, the selling price can be defined as the sum mutually agreed upon by the seller and the buyer, with regard to the need to sell, and the need to buy, and the value of the airplane. The latter is often the least significant figure.

AERO COMMANDER

Darter	$9,000
Lark	$14,000
112	$30,000
112TC	$40,000
114	$50,000
Meyers 200	$38,000
500/500A	$40,000

AERONCA

7AC	$9,500
11AC	$8,500
Champ 7ACA	$9,000
Traveler 7EC	$8,500
Tri-Traveler 7FC	$9,500
Citabria 7ECA	$12–21,000
Citabria 7KCAB	$19–27,000
Champ 7GC	$10–22,000
Scout 8GCBC	$25–40,000
Decathlon 8KCAB	$30–50,000

BEECHCRAFT

Staggerwing 17	$100,000 and up
Twin Beech 18	$20–48,000
Sport 19	$14,000
Musketeer 23	$10–16,000
Musketeer 24–23	$15,000
Sundowner 23 73–79	$17–26,000
Sundowner 23 80–83	$30–45,000
Sierra 24 70–75	$23,000
Sierra 24 76–79	$33,500
Sierra 24 80–83	$38–55,000
Debonair 33	$33–53,000
Bonanza 33 68–74	$50–71,000

Bonanza 33 75–81	$75–110,000
Mentor T34	$100,000 and up
Bonanza 35 47–56	$18–25,000
Bonanza 35 57–65	$25–44,000
Bonanza 35 66–74	$50–70,000
Bonanza 36 68–69	$62,000
Bonanza A36 70–77	$65–95,000
Twin Bonanza 50	$20–50,000
Baron B55 61–68	$35–55,000
Baron B55 69–73	$60–75,000
Duchess 76	$56–74,000
Skipper 77	$16,000
Travelair 95 58–65	$36,000
Travelair 95 66–68	$46,000

BELLANCA

14-13	$10,000
14-19	$13,000
Viking 17-30/31 67-71	$23,000
Viking 17-30/31 72-80	$33,000

CESSNA

120/140	$9–16,000
150 59-72	$11,000
150 73-77	$13,000
152 78-82	$20–30,000
170	$16,000
172 56-68	$18,000
172 69-76	$17–28,000
172 77-80	$25–36,000
172 81-86	$36–70,000
172-RG 80-85	$42–60,000
175	$14,000
177 68-75	$25,000
177 76-78	$34,000
177-RG	$32,000
180 53-65	$25,000
180 66-70	$30,000
180 71-75	$36,000
180 76-81	$40–60,000
182 56-66	$18–25,000
182 67-75	$25–42,000
182 76-82	$40–80,000
182-RG 78-83	$51–99,000
185 61-70	$30–40,000
185 70-82	$40–70,000

195	$30–60,000
205	$28,000
P206	$32–45,000
U206 64-70	$36–48,000
U206 71-75	$44–64,000
U206 76-81	$61–100,000
207 69-75	$43–60,000
207 76-82	$59–100,000
210 60-70	$23–38,000
210 71-75	$43–60,000
210 76-82	$62–100,000
310 55-65	$18–32,000
310 66-74	$35–65,000
310 75-79	$70–100,000
320	$30–53,000
336	$15,500
337 65-74	$21–36,000
337 75-77	$42,500

CHRISTEN

Husky	$50–70,000

ERCOUPE

415	$8,000
Alon A2	$10,500
Mooney Cadet	$10,000

GULFSTREAM

AA1 series	$11–14,000
AA5 150 hp	$18–26,000
AA5 180 hp	$28,000
GA7	$44,000

HELIO

H-295	NA
H-395	NA

LAKE

LA-4 60-70	$25,000
LA-4 200 hp 70-80	$38–62,000
LA-250	$160,000 and up

LUSCOMBE

8A	$8,000
8E	$10,000
8F	$10–15,000
Sedan	$15,000

MAULE

M4 145 hp	$10,000
M4 180 hp	$11,500
M4 210 hp	$14,000
M4 220 hp	$15,000
M5 210 hp	$23,000
M5 235 hp	$28,000
M6 235 hp	$38,000
M7 180 hp	$34,000
M7 235 hp	$40 – 70,000

MOONEY

M20	$17,000
M20C	$22 – 30,000
M20E	$26 – 35,000
M20F	$27 – 41,000
201	$47 – 90,000
231	$58 – 110,000
M22	$42,000

PIPER

J3	$13,000
J4	$12,000
J5	$14,000
PA-11	$12,000
PA-12	$13,500
PA-15/17	$9,500
PA-16	$9,500
PA-18	$12 – 70,000
PA-20	$10,000
PA-22 Colt	$8,000
PA-22 Tri-Pacer	$11,500
PA-23 150 hp	$16,000
PA-23 160 hp	$20,000
PA-23 235 hp	$27,000
PA-23 Aztec 60-65	$26 – 35,000
PA-23 66-72	$35 – 55,000
PA-23 73-81	$50 – 90,000
PA-24 180	$20 – 23,000
PA-24 250 hp	$23 – 29,000
PA-24 260 hp	$36 – 52,000
PA-28 140 Cherokee	$13 – 18,000
PA-28 140 Cruiser	$18 – 21,000
PA-28 150/160 Cherokee	$14,000
PA-28 180 Archer	$18 – 29,000

PA-28 235 Pathfinder	$25 – 40,000
PA-28 151 Warrior	$25,000
PA-28 161 Warrior II 77-81	$27 – 35,000
PA-28 161 Warrior II 82-88	$40 – 74,000
PA-28 181 Archer II 76-84	$35 – 65,000
PA-28 236 Dakota 79-81	$58,000
PA-28R Arrow 69-78	$26 – 44,000
PA-30 Twin Comanche	$35 – 50,000
PA-32 Cherokee Six	$29 – 55,000
PA-32R-300 Lance 76-79	$53,000
PA-32-301 Saratoga 80-83	$75 – 110,000
PA-34 Seneca 72-74	$35,000
PA-34 Seneca 75-79	$51 – 75,000
PA-38 Tomahawk 78-82	$12,000
PA-39 Twin Comanche	$55,000

REPUBLIC

SeaBee	$15 – 35,000

STINSON

108 series	$10 – 16,000

SWIFT

GC-1B	$20 – 40,000

TAYLORCRAFT

BC-12	$10,000
F19	$11 – 15,000
F21	$14 – 35,000

VARGA

150 hp	$20,000
180 hp	$24,000

Index

insurance (*cont.*)

  hull insurance, 63

  liability insurance, 63   theft, theft prevention, 80-82

L

Lake

  airworthiness directives, 304

  clubs, 326

  complex airplanes, 212-214

  LA-250 Renegade, 213-214

  LA-4 200/200EP Buccaneer, 213

  LA-4, 212-213

  price guide, 332

landing gear

  modifications, 25

  two-place airplanes, conventional vs. tricycle, 85

liability insurance, 63

liens, release of lien, AC Form 8050-41, 58

limitations/exclusions, insurance policies, 63-64

loans (*see* financing airplane purchases)

localizer/glide slope (LOC/GS), 27

logbooks, 56

  inspection procedure, 51-52

  maintenance, 70

Loran-C, 27, 28

Luscombe

  accident rankings, 308-311

  airworthiness directives, 304

  clubs, 326

  commentary/assessments, 292

  four-place easy fliers, Model 11 Sedan, 162-163

  Luscombe 8A, 118

  Luscombe 8E, 118-119

  Luscombe 8F, 119-120

  price guide, 332

  two-place airplanes, 117-120

Lycoming engines, airworthiness directives, 307

M

magazines and periodicals, 30-33

magnaflux/magnaglow engine inspection, 21

maintenance, 13-15, 67-82

  airworthiness directives, 14-15

  cleaning the exterior, 79-80

  fixed base operators (FBO), 67

general aviation airworthiness alerts, 14-15

general-maintenance fund, 5

logbooks, 70

malfunction or defect reports (MDRs), 14-15

preventive maintenance, 41

preventive maintenance, owner-allowable, 68-70

repairs and alterations, 41

storage (*see* storage)

tools, 70-71

malfunction or defect reports (MDRs), 14-15

manufacturers' literature, information, 323

marker beacon receiver (MBR), 27

market availability, price guidelines, 18-19

Maule

  airworthiness directives, 304

  clubs, 326-327

  commentary/assessments, 292

  four-place easy fliers, 164-166

  heavy-haulers, 248-255

  M-4 Jeteson, 164-165

  M-4/180 Astro Rocket, 248-249

  M-4/210 Rocket, 249

  M-4/220 Strata Rocket, 249-250

  M-5/180 C, 250-251

  M-5/210 Lunar Rocket, 251-252

  M-5/235, 252

  M-6/235 Super Rocket, 252-253

  M-7/180, 253-254

  M-7/180D, 165-166

  M-7/235, 254-255

  price guide, 332

mechanic's inspection, pre-purchase inspection, 52-53

Meyers (*see also* Aero Commander), 327

military aircraft (*see* war birds)

modifications, 23-26, 41

  auto-fuel use modifications, 25-26

  fuel tanks, auxiliary, 25

  gap seals, 25

  landing gear, 25

  power-increase modifications, 24

  short takeoff and landing (STOL) gear, 23

  wing tips, 24

mogas (*see* automotive fuel use; fuel)

Other Bestsellers of Related Interest

AIM/FAR 1992: Airman's Information Manual/
Federal Aviation Regulations—TAB/AERO Staff

With this single, easy-to-use volume, pilots can have fingertip access to information and rules that would otherwise take hours, days, or even weeks of research to find. Some of the topics covered include pilot certificate requirements; inspection requirements, waivers, certifications, operating rules, and restrictions; DUAT procedures for obtaining weather information and filing flight plans, plus a list of weather codes for DUAT translations; Aviation Safety Reporting System form; extensive indexing that includes cross-referencing between AIM and FAR; and commercial pilot practical test standards. 592 pages, Illustrated. Book No. 24393, $12.95 paperback only

THE PILOT'S HANDBOOK OF AERONAUTICAL
KNOWLEDGE: Revised and Expanded Edition
—Paul E. Illman

The federal government last published *The Pilot's Handbook of Aeronautical Knowledge* in 1980. Now, after a decade of growth and change in the world of aviation, that classic volume has been updated for the 1990's. Enhanced with the latest technical data, flying tips, and general aviation guidance, you'll get up-to-the-minute facts on everything from navigation technologies and flight planning through radio communications and dealing with air traffic control. 432 pages, 227 illustrations. Book No. 3517, $18.95 paperback, $27.95 hardcover

VAN SICKLE'S MODERN AIRMANSHIP
—6th Edition—Edited by John F. Welch
Reviews of previous editions:
". . . *useful to pilots of all skill levels.*"
—*Colorado CAP Flyer*
". . . *an excellent volume for those new to flying, as well as 'experienced' pilots who need to brush up.*"
—*HAC Techline*

This one-volume library of flying facts, charts, and illustrations has long been considered one of the most useful "instruments" in aviation. Now, revised and expanded for the 1990s, it continues to be the most comprehensive aviation guidebook available. 864 pages, 539 illustrations. Book No. 2451, $39.95 hardcover only

VECTORS: The Author's Favorite Columns from
FLYING—Len Morgan

The third, and perhaps best, collection of witty and thought-provoking articles takes a warm and personal look at the people, places, and machines that have influenced Morgan during a career that spanned the days from propeller-driven airplanes to intercontinental jumbo jets. Each article presents a brief, but fascinating look into Morgan's personal experiences, and demonstrates why Morgan has become one of the most respected and widely read writers in aviation today. 240 pages, 60 illustrations. Book No. 3741, $14.95 paperback, $22.95 hardcover

COMMERCIAL AVIATION SAFETY
—Alexander Wells, Ed.D.

This ideal on-the-job reference provides aviation professionals with much-needed analysis of current aviation safety policies and programs as they have developed since the Airline Deregulation Act of 1978. It takes a comprehensive look at how existing regulations, procedures, and technologies work to insure safety in commercial aviation, as well as what both government and industry can do to ease the strain on the nation's increasingly overcrowded airspace. 352 pages, 41 illustrations. Book No. 3754, $32.95 hardcover only

STANDARD AIRCRAFT HANDBOOK—5th Edition
—Edited by Larry Reithmaier, originally compiled and edited by Stuart Leavell and Stanley Bungay

Now updated to cover the latest in aircraft parts, equipment, and construction techniques, this classic reference provides practical information on FAA-approved metal airplane hardware. Techniques are presented in step-by-step fashion and explained in shop terms without unnecessary theory and background. All data on materials and procedures is derived from current reports by the nations's largest aircraft manufacturers. 240 pages, 213 illustrations. Book No. 3634 V, $11.95 V

AIRPORT PLANNING AND MANAGEMENT
—Alexander T. Wells, Ed.D.

Covering all aspects of modern airport design, planning, and management, this book bridges the gap between highly technical government publications and hands-on specialty manuals. It's a well-illustrated, example-filled reference for anyone involved in airport planning or management—or anticipating a career in these fields. 432 pages, 80 illustrations. Book No. 2389, $29.95 hardcover only

ABCs OF SAFE FLYING—3rd Edition—David Frazier

This book gives you a wealth of flight safety information in a fun to read, easily digestible format. The author's anecdotal episodes as well as NTSB accident reports lend both humor and sobering reality to the text. Detailed photographs, maps, and illustrations ensure that you'll understand key concepts and techniques. If you want to make sure you have the right skills each time you fly, this book is your one-stop source. 192 pages, Illustrated. Book No. 3757, $14.95 paperback, $22.95 hardcover only

GENERAL AVIATION LAW—Jerry A. Eichenberger

Although the regulatory burden that is part of flying sometimes seems overwhelming, it need not take the pleasure out of your flight time. Eichenberger provides an up-to-date survey of many aviation regulations, and gives you a solid understanding of FAA procedures and functions, airman ratings and maintenance certificates, the implications of aircraft ownership, and more. This book allows you to recognize legal problems before they result in FAA investigations and the potentially serious consequences. 240 pages. Book No. 3431, $16.95 paperback only

THE PILOT'S GUIDE TO WEATHER REPORTS, FORECASTS & FLIGHT PLANNING
—Terry T. Lankford

This comprehensive guide to aviation weather for all pilots offers clear explanations, real-life examples, and effective illustrations. It shows you how to access weather services efficiently, translate briefings correctly, and apply reports and forecasts to specific preflight and in-flight situations to expand your margin of safety. 397 pages, 123 illustrations. Book No. 3582, $19.95 paperback only

REFLECTIONS OF A PILOT—Len Morgan

No Len Morgan fan will want to miss this one-time opportunity to have this collection of nearly five years of Len Morgan's most popular feature articles from *Flying* Magazine—55 in all! Here in a single, action-packed volume are all those Morgan columns you wish you had clipped and saved. Here, as only Morgan can tell them, are the stories and observations of what it was like to be a transport pilot in World War II, a co-pilot of an airline DC-3, and the captain of an intercontinental 747. 224 pages. Book No. 2398, $12.95 paperback only

The classic you've been searching for . . .
STICK AND RUDDER: An Explanation of the Art of Flying—Wolfgang Langewiesche

Students, certificated pilots, and instructors alike have praised this book as *"the most useful guide to flying ever written."* The book explains the important phases of the art of flying, in a way the learner can use. It shows precisely what the pilot does when he flies, just how he does it, and why. 395 pages, Illustrated. Book No. 3820, $19.95 hardcover only